# TEN DAYS IN HARLEM

*by the same author*

1956: THE WORLD IN REVOLT

# SIMON HALL

# ★ TEN DAYS IN HARLEM

## FIDEL CASTRO AND THE MAKING OF THE 1960s

faber

First published in the UK and the USA in 2020
by Faber & Faber Limited
74–77 Great Russell Street
London WC1B 3DA

Typeset by Faber & Faber Ltd
Printed in the UK by CPI Group (UK) Ltd, Croydon, CR0 4YY

*Every effort has been made to trace or contact all copyright holders. The publishers would be
pleased to rectify at the earliest opportunity any omissions or errors brought to their notice.*

A CIP record for this book
is available from the British Library

ISBN 978–0–571–35306–4

2 4 6 8 10 9 7 5 3 1

For János

# CONTENTS

# PROLOGUE

The voice of our leader will be heard in every corner of the
UN hall and in every corner of the world . . . More than
the voice of Cuba, Fidel will be the valiant voice of all the
oppressed . . .

CUBAN RADIO, 15 SEPTEMBER 1960

It was, to say the least, idiosyncratic behaviour for a prime minister. But, for Fidel Castro – a man who liked to hold cabinet
meetings at midnight, and who had a habit of turning up at hotel
kitchens unannounced in the hopes of rustling up a quick meal
– it was entirely in character. One afternoon in early September
1960, the leader of Cuba's revolutionary government was strolling
along Calle Doce y Veintitrés, one of the chicest parts of Havana,
famous for its art galleries, cinemas and cafes, while snacking on
some spicy Creole oysters. It was a pastime that he had enjoyed
many times while a student in the late 1940s. Suddenly, the Cuban
prime minister made a beeline for a shoeshine boy, who was well
known as the best source of gossip in the capital. 'What do you say
I go up to New York,' Fidel asked, smiling, 'and speak at the UN?'
'*Caballo*,'* replied the boy, enthusiastically, 'get on up there and
put it to those damn Yankees.'[1]

Soon, all of Havana was buzzing with speculation that Fidel
would be attending the Fifteenth Session of the UN General

* During the early years of the revolution Fidel was known as El Caballo,
'The Horse' – which was the pictorial representation of the number one in
the lottery. The origin of the nickname is ascribed to the popular Cuban
entertainer Beny Moré, who is said to have exclaimed, 'Here comes the Horse,'
after hearing Castro pass by one night – see Richard Gott, *Cuba: A New
History* (New Haven: Yale University Press, 2004), 175.

Assembly. Due to open on 20 September, the gathering would afford Fidel the chance to defend the Cuban Revolution on the world stage, and from inside the very heart of the United States at a time of deepening acrimony between the two countries. His presence in New York, then, would be guaranteed to make waves. Early on the morning of Tuesday 6 September, America's 'man in Havana', Philip W. Bonsal, cabled the Secretary of State to report on the growing rumours that Fidel was planning to attend the UN. Bonsal, a fifty-seven-year-old Yale alumnus and career diplomat, who had been in post for eighteen months, judged that the Cuban leader's attendance 'appears probable'.[2] Then, on the evening of Saturday 10 September, came another tantalizing hint. During a television newscast, Mario Kuchilan – editor of *Prensa Libre* (*Free Press*) – teased viewers by confessing that he knew of a head of government who was planning to attend the General Assembly, before going on to explain that 'for the moment I cannot divulge this news'. Three days later, a statement from the presidential palace made it official: Fidel Castro was going to New York.[3]

# THE STAGE IS SET

Cuba certainly is going to remain hot . . .
LIVINGSTON T. MERCHANT, US UNDER SECRETARY OF
STATE FOR POLITICAL AFFAIRS, 8 APRIL 1960

The opportunity [for] antagonistic foreign leaders to come
right on our doorstep and abuse us is one of the evils that
goes with being host to the U.N.
SENATOR GORDON ALLOTT — REPUBLICAN, COLORADO,
9 SEPTEMBER 1960

Fidel Castro – champion of the oppressed, scourge of colonialism, critic of racial segregation, and beatnik revolutionary – had certainly picked his moment to face down the 'Yankee imperialists' in their own backyard. In the autumn of 1960, the US government was beset by a series of deepening crises. On the domestic front, Washington was confronted with intensifying demands from African Americans for equal rights, as a new generation of students launched a wave of direct-action protests that rocked the South and exposed President Eisenhower's gradualist approach to the race problem as hopelessly out of touch. Meanwhile, on the international stage, America's leaders were scrambling frantically to counter a newly belligerent Soviet Union, which saw, in the rapid (and often chaotic) end of European empire, the chance to steal a march on her Cold War rivals.

For Fidel, the opportunity to add to America's discomfort was far too good to pass up. During his stay in New York, which lasted from 18 to 28 September, the Cuban leader would receive a rapturous reception from the city's black community, hold court with a succession of political, intellectual and cultural luminaries –

including Malcolm X, Nikita Khrushchev, Gamal Abdel Nasser, C. Wright Mills and Allen Ginsberg – and promote the politics of anti-imperialism, racial equality and leftist revolution with a fervour and an audacity that was to make him an icon of the 1960s counterculture, and his country a centre of the global anti-imperialist movement. Fidel's sojourn in New York helped to place the Global South – including his own Latin America – at the very centre of the Cold War, while his new-found and very public closeness with Khrushchev, whom he met for the first time there, all but guaranteed a decisive and fateful rupture in US–Cuban relations. Meanwhile, his valorizing of black freedom fighters, celebration of 'Third World' revolutionaries and association with 'radical chic' offered an early glimpse of the cultural politics – the fêting of Black Power activists, open support for the Viet Cong and an instinctive condemnation of American 'empire' – that would soon become *de rigueur* for a generation of young leftists across the United States and Western Europe. Although no one knew it at the time, then, this brief trip proved to be both a turning point in the history of the Cold War and a foundational moment in the creation of what we think of as 'the Sixties'.

The opening session of the Fifteenth General Assembly brought together an unprecedented galaxy of international statesmen, the like of which the United Nations – and its predecessor, the League of Nations – had seldom seen. Among the ten heads of state, thirteen prime ministers and seventy or more foreign ministers and other senior government ministers in attendance were some of the biggest global political stars of all: Dwight David Eisenhower, the thirty-fourth president of the United States and a Second World War hero; Nikita Khrushchev, the pugnacious leader of the world's other superpower, the Union of Soviet Socialist Republics; the prime ministers of Great Britain, Canada and Australia; and major players from the Global South, including Jawaharlal

Nehru (India), Sukarno (Indonesia), Kwame Nkrumah (Ghana) and Gamal Abdel Nasser (United Arab Republic).[1]

Rising out of the ashes of the Second World War, the United Nations symbolized the post-war hopes for a new international order. In the words of its founding charter, the organization's purpose was to 'save succeeding generations from the scourge of war', to affirm and protect fundamental human rights, and to advance the cause of social and economic progress.[2] Formally established in San Francisco on 24 October 1945, the UN was rooted in a universal appeal to freedom, equality and rights. At the same time, though, the decision to grant permanent membership of the Security Council – and the accompanying veto power – to the USA, Britain, France and the USSR (along with China) preserved the influence of the traditional Western powers. The advent of the Cold War in 1947–8 rendered the Security Council – the only body with the power to authorize the use of force – more or less impotent when it came to the major issues of war and peace. And with the Security Council stymied, the General Assembly, in which every nation had an equal voice, came to take centre stage.[3]

Founded by its 'great power architects' as an 'institution tolerant of empire' (otherwise Britain and France, who had no intention of giving up their colonies without a fight, would never have supported it), the United Nations, according to the historian Mark Mazower, 'turned astonishingly quickly into a key forum for anti-colonialism'.[4] An early sign of this had come in 1946 when, under the leadership of Jawaharlal Nehru, India – one of only four founding members that were not independent at the time of admission – had protested the second-class treatment afforded to Indians living and working in South Africa. The government in Pretoria was, Nehru argued, in breach of its Charter obligations.[5] In the course of the following decade, the European powers – economically ravaged by the Second World War, overstretched militarily, and under intense and growing pressure from indigenous nationalist movements – saw their empires collapse on a scale, and at a pace, that had been scarcely imaginable in 1945. Among those joining India in the UN were Pakistan (1947), Burma (1948), Indonesia (1950), Cambodia, Ceylon, Laos (1955), Morocco, Sudan, Tunisia (1956), Ghana and Malaya (1957) and Guinea (1958). Then, in 1960, the so-called Year of Africa, sixteen of the seventeen new nations admitted to the United Nations were newly independent African states.* The original founding membership of fifty-one, of which Cuba was one, had virtually doubled in just fifteen years, and the so-called Afro-Asian bloc now made up forty-six out of ninety-nine votes.[6]

Although the General Assembly lacked teeth and a two-thirds majority was needed to pass resolutions dealing with peace, security and other major issues, it came to serve as a major forum for debate and the shaping, and reshaping, of international opinion. As Mazower puts it, 'even though the UN had been established by the great powers, Third World nationalists took its universalism at face value, exploited its mechanisms, and fostered international public opposition to continued colonial rule.'[7] They also – as the historian Adom Getachew has highlighted – worked tirelessly to promote the idea of 'self-determination as a human right', refashioning it 'as a prerequisite to other human rights' and insisting that it required an 'immediate end to colonial rule'. This stood in stark contrast to the position held by the UN's founders, who subordinated the right to self-determination 'to the larger aim of securing "peaceful and friendly relations among nations"' (the concept did not appear at all in the Universal Declaration of Human Rights).[8] A mere fifteen years after its founding, anticolonial nationalists had successfully captured the UN and transformed the General

---

* Cameroon, Central African Republic, Chad, Congo (Brazzaville), Congo (Léopoldville), Dahomey, Gabon, Ivory Coast, Malagasy Republic, Mali, Niger, Nigeria, Senegal, Somalia, Togo, Upper Volta.

Assembly into a platform for the international politics of decolonization.[9]

As well as taking place at a key moment in the history of decolonization, the Fifteenth Session of the General Assembly was also opening against a wider backdrop of international tension. Despite a brief thaw in the Cold War, which had seen Khrushchev meet with Eisenhower at Camp David, Maryland, in September 1959, hopes for a meaningful rapprochement had quickly soured. In the bitter aftermath of the U-2 incident, in which an American spy plane had been shot down over Russia on 1 May 1960, Khrushchev lashed out at the perfidy of the United States. Storming out of disarmament talks in Paris later that month, the Soviet leader retaliated by ratcheting up the tension over Berlin. Deep in communist East Germany, the divided city – which, fifteen years after the end of the Second World War, remained occupied by Britain, France, the United States and the Soviet Union – was viewed by Khrushchev as a 'fishbone in his throat'. The exodus of thousands of East Germans – many of them young and well educated – to the West via Berlin constituted an existential threat to the German Democratic Republic. Travelling back from Paris, Khrushchev had stopped off in East Berlin where, before an audience of 10,000 communists, he had denounced Eisenhower's 'treachery' and, not for the first time, threatened to sign a separate peace treaty with the GDR – a move that would bring an end to Western rights of occupation in the city. On 7 September, Allen Dulles, the CIA director, told President Eisenhower's National Security Council that Khrushchev appeared to be 'deliberately stirring up the Berlin situation in order to have it at boiling point' by the opening of the General Assembly.[10] The West German government of Chancellor Konrad Adenauer, meanwhile, fretted that Khrushchev's impending appearance at the UN General Assembly 'might be the beginning of new and more dramatic moves by the Soviets'.[11]

[ 5 ]

While diplomats were keeping a nervous eye on Berlin, an even greater crisis was underway in the Congo. Occupying a vast swathe of central Africa, the Belgian Congo boasted huge mineral wealth, notably in copper, tin, cobalt, uranium and diamonds. The personal possession of King Leopold II from 1885, the territory had been organized as a formal colony of Belgium in 1908. The colonial masters brutalized, impoverished and exploited its people, and left its infrastructure criminally underdeveloped. On the eve of its independence on 30 June 1960, the Congo had no real road system, no locally born doctors, high school teachers or military officers, and only sixteen university graduates in a population of more than twelve million. In pre-independence elections, held in May, the Mouvement National Congolais emerged as the biggest party, and its leader, Patrice Lumumba – a former postal clerk, and left-wing nationalist – became prime minister. The Belgians, who, to put it mildly, had little time for Lumumba, were further incensed when, in an independence-day speech delivered before an audience that included Baudouin, King of the Belgians, he excoriated the 'injustice, oppression, and exploitation' of the former colonial regime and celebrated the 'end to the humiliating bondage which was imposed upon us by force'. 'We shall show the world', Lumumba declared, 'what the black man can do when working in liberty, and we shall make the Congo the pride of Africa.'[12]

It was not to be. Almost immediately, the country began to fragment; in July, with the active encouragement of Belgian mining interests and government officials, the mineral-rich province of Katanga, headed by staunch anti-communist and one-time accountant Moïse Tshombe, attempted to secede.[13] As the country slipped into chaos, and Belgium sent in troops to protect its citizens, in violation of the Congo's newly established sovereignty, Lumumba appealed to the United Nations for help. On 13 July, the Security Council voted to send thousands of peacekeepers to oversee a Belgian withdrawal and ensure the country's stability. But, dismayed that the UN forces would not be immediately sent into Katanga (the UN had little appetite for placing its troops in the middle of a civil war), Lumumba turned to Moscow for assistance.[14]

During the early years of the Cold War, Stalin had viewed non-communist movements for national liberation in Africa and Asia as 'class enemies'.[15] His successor, though, took a very different approach. Khrushchev was, in fact, keen to build anti-imperialist alliances across the rapidly decolonizing Third World, and argued that the Soviet Union offered the newly independent nations a clear alternative to the capitalist West's model of economic modernization; one that was free from the stain of colonial exploitation. 'Today,' Khrushchev explained, the former colonies 'need not go begging for up-to-date equipment to their former oppressors. They can get it in the socialist countries, without assuming any political or military commitments.'[16] Confident that the future belonged to socialism, Khrushchev declared: 'Let us verify in practice whose system is better. We say to the leaders of the capitalist states: Let us compete without war.'[17] Alongside long-term credit, technical assistance, trade agreements, scientific cooperation and arms came a charm offensive: in the autumn of 1955, for instance, Khrushchev spent almost two months in Asia, travelling thousands of miles, visiting cultural and historic sites, and greeting crowds that turned out in their hundreds of thousands.[18] During his decade in power, the Soviet Union sponsored some 6,000 projects across the Third World, often at enormous expense.[19] High-profile recipients of largesse from Moscow and her Eastern bloc allies during the 1950s and 1960s included India, Ghana, Egypt, Cuba – and, briefly, the Congo.

In early August 1960, Khrushchev promised Lumumba the 'friendly and disinterested help of the Soviet government'. Arms – including weapons, ammunition and IL-14 transport planes – as well as humanitarian aid, soon followed. US officials were now convinced that the Congolese prime minister was 'a Castro or worse'. Fearing the prospect of a 'second Cuba', Washington began covertly to seek Lumumba's removal: the CIA hatched an assassination plot, and the Eisenhower administration encouraged the Congolese military to take over. On 14 September, with the opening of the UN General Assembly now just days away, Joseph-Désiré Mobutu, a Lumumba confidant and newly appointed army chief of staff, staged what was, for now at least, a bloodless coup. Lumumba, holed up in his official residence, was now reliant on UN troops to prevent his arrest.[20]

While these extraordinary international dramas were unfolding, the UN's host country, the United States, was itself on the cusp of seismic political and social change.

Back on 1 February, a bold new front in the struggle for African American civil rights had opened up, when four students at North Carolina's Agricultural and Technical College, in Greensboro, had sat at a segregated Woolworth's lunch counter and demanded service. One of the idiosyncrasies of the South's entrenched system of white supremacy – known colloquially as 'Jim Crow' – was that, while African Americans could shop in the store, they could not eat at the store's lunch counter. After being refused service, the young men remained seated for an hour – politely rebuffing requests to leave – until the store closed. The experience was personally, as well as politically, transformative; one of the four, nineteen-year-old Franklin McCain, explained:

> . . . if it's possible to know what it means to have your soul cleansed – I felt pretty clean at that time. I probably felt better on that day than I've ever felt in my life . . . a lot of feelings of guilt or what-have-you suddenly left me, and I felt as though I had gained my manhood, so to speak.

The following morning, McCain and his three friends were joined by more than a dozen others. Within a month, more than thirty towns had been affected by sit-ins; by the end of April, some 50,000 students had taken part in protests across more than seventy southern towns and cities, with 2,000 arrested.[21] There were sympathy boycotts, too, in northern cities, and even overseas. In Cuba, where a common history of struggle against slavery, racism and oppression, as well as shared connections across the Caribbean diaspora, had long served to foster deep and meaningful connections between black Cubans and African Americans, students picketed the American-owned Woolworth store in downtown Havana. Their placards read: 'Woolworth Denies Democratic Rights to Black People'.*[22]

The African American students' audacious challenge to segregation grabbed headlines, and was sustained by local organizations that included chapters of the National Association for the Advancement of Colored People (NAACP; founded in 1909, it was America's largest and oldest civil rights organization) and the Baptist church. Aided by continued media interest, the emerging movement also benefited from the uncompromising stance of their opponents. The contrast was unmissable between the well-dressed, polite and disciplined nonviolent activists, on the one hand, and the implacable defenders of Jim Crow, who often resorted to intimidation, taunts and violence (students were splattered with eggs and coffee, had cigarette butts stuffed down their collars, and some were beaten up), on the other.[23] An editorial in the conservative *News Leader*, written during the height of the sit-in protests in Richmond, Virginia, noted that:

* During the fight for independence from Spain, African Americans rallied behind the Cuban cause, and drew particular pride from the role played by prominent Cubans of African descent. In the twentieth century, meanwhile, many Cubans were inspired by – and offered support to – African Americans' efforts to secure first-class citizenship.

Here were the colored students, in coats, white shirts, ties, and one of them was reading Goethe and one was taking notes from a biology text. And here, on the sidewalk outside, was a gang of white boys come to heckle, a ragtail rabble, slack-jawed, black-jacketed, grinning fit to kill, and some of them, God save the mark, were waving the proud and honored flag of the Southern States in the last war fought by gentlemen. Eheu! It gives one pause.[24]

Capturing, with perfect moral clarity, the iniquities of racial segregation and the righteousness of the crusade that was now being waged against it, the sit-ins launched a new era of mass protests that would, within just a few years, transform the face of the Jim Crow South.

Meanwhile, the first stirrings of the wider student revolt that would dominate the 1960s were being felt in San Francisco. There, during the second week of May, college students from across the Bay Area gathered at City Hall to protest hearings that were being convened by the House Committee on Un-American Activities (HUAC) – the congressional body that had played a leading role in the 1950s 'red scare' by investigating the communist infiltration (both real and imagined) of labour unions, the teaching profession, civil rights organizations and the Hollywood film industry, ruining numerous lives in the process.

On Friday 13 May, faced with hundreds of peaceful protesters singing 'The Star-Spangled Banner' and 'We Shall Not Be Moved', the police turned firehoses on the demonstrators, blasting them down the building's imposing marble staircase, and dragging others away. The attempt to crush the protest was, though, wholly counterproductive: 5,000 people turned out to denounce HUAC the following day, and in a subsequent court hearing all the charges were dismissed, with the judge describing the protesters as 'clean-cut American students'. *Operation Abolition*, a propaganda film that portrayed the demonstrations as the work of highly trained communist agents, also backfired, inspiring many thousands of young people to enrol at the University of California-Berkeley, which quickly found itself at the centre of the 1960s student movement.[25]

If racial and social tumult was not enough, the United States was also in the midst of a gripping political contest. With President Dwight Eisenhower just about to turn seventy and in his final year of office, the forty-seven-year-old Republican Richard Nixon was battling John F. Kennedy, his forty-three-year-old Democratic rival for the presidency. In this close-fought race, one thing was certain: power would shortly pass to a new generation of leaders, the first to be born in the twentieth century. As vice president for eight years, Nixon was the candidate of experience; a figure who had been at the very heart of the Eisenhower administration (after Ike suffered a massive heart attack in September 1955, Nixon had effectively served as 'acting president' for several weeks, presiding over regular meetings of both the cabinet and the National Security Council).[26] Pointing with pride to what he characterized as the 'best eight-year record of any Administration' in American history, Nixon promised to build on this 'great record' in order to forge 'a better America' and to realize the dreams of millions of people, in the United States and throughout the world, 'for a fuller, freer, richer life than men have ever known in the history of mankind'.[27]

Meanwhile, the senator from Massachusetts who, like Nixon, had enjoyed a meteoric political rise, sought to harness the spirit of a new era to propel his bid for the White House. Decrying the Republicans as the 'party of the past', and a vote for Nixon as a 'vote for the status quo', Kennedy proclaimed that 'we stand today on the edge of a New Frontier – the frontier of the 1960s – a frontier of unknown opportunities and perils – a frontier of unfulfilled hopes and threats'. Calling on his fellow Americans to rise to the challenge posed by 'uncharted areas of science and space, unsolved problems of peace and war, unconquered pockets of ignorance and prejudice, unanswered questions of poverty and surplus', he declared that 'the times demand new invention, innovation, imagination, decision'.[28]

In some respects, Fidel Castro and John F. Kennedy were not dissimilar. Fidel, like Kennedy, was born into privilege: the Castro family home was a rambling, plantation-style mansion that sat on a 25,000-acre sugar cane farm in Oriente province. Like Kennedy, he grew up in the shadow of a domineering patriarch – his father, Ángel Castro y Argiz, a self-made immigrant from Galicia, northwest Spain, was famously stern.[29] And, like Kennedy, Fidel was a devout patriot with a gift for oratory, who would come to personify the idealism of a new generation.

Kennedy's rise to power was gilded. In 1940 he graduated *cum laude* from Harvard, where he had majored in government and international relations. After wartime service in the US navy, where he saw action in the Pacific and was decorated for heroism, he was elected to the House of Representatives in the mid-term elections of 1946; elevation to the Senate came just six years later. In 1957, he won the Pulitzer Prize for biography for his – largely ghost-written – book, *Profiles in Courage*. Fidel's path to the top, though, would be quite different.

Fidel, the only pupil in his elementary school class who owned shoes, later claimed that his passion for social justice had been forged during his childhood. Mayarí, the region where he grew up, was dominated by the all-powerful, American-owned fruit and sugar companies, such as United Fruit and Cuban-American Sugar. And with these companies came stark inequalities of wealth and opportunity. Cuban cane cutters – including the fathers of Fidel's childhood friends – lived in squalid shacks, earning just a dollar a day, sometimes less, during the four months of the sugar harvest and eking out a hand-to-mouth existence during the so-called dead time. Meanwhile, the companies' American employees and their families enjoyed a sumptuous lifestyle, in gated communities that boasted luxury stores, swimming pools and access to private beach resorts.[30]

Fidel, whose rebelliousness, stubbornness, lack of discipline, and recklessness had earned him the nickname 'El Loco' (the crazy one), enrolled at the University of Havana in the autumn of 1945 to study law. He later set up a legal practice with two of his classmates, in a slightly shabby neighbourhood, to defend the rights of the poor. His first love, though, had always been politics: aged just thirteen, he had attempted to organize a strike among the workers on his father's own sugar plantation and, at university, he had immersed himself in the cut-and-thrust of student politics. A keen debater, Fidel had overcome an early fear of public speaking, and his great hero and role model was José Martí. Born in January 1853 in Havana, this poet, philosopher, journalist and revolutionary spent most of the 1880s and early 1890s in exile in New York, where he developed a powerful critique of American imperialism and corporate capitalism.* Then, in April 1895, Martí returned to his native Cuba to help lead the nationalist uprising. His death at the hands of the Spanish, on 19 May, during the Battle of Boca de Dos Rios, made him a martyr.[31]

Like Martí, Fidel was committed to eliminating the vested interests, the inequality and the corruption that marred his homeland. During late 1951 through early 1952, he had been preparing to run for Cuba's National Assembly, as a member of the left-wing

---

* This was an era when, having pushed the boundaries of the United States to the Pacific (the frontier officially closed in 1890), some leading US politicians began calling for overseas expansion, citing America's 'civilizing mission' to the world. At the same time, vast amounts of wealth, as well as economic and political power, became concentrated in the hands of a few 'captains of industry' (or, less charitably, 'robber barons'), such as Andrew Carnegie (steel), J. P. Morgan (finance), John D. Rockefeller (oil) and Cornelius Vanderbilt (railroads).

Partido Ortodoxo. But then, on 10 March 1952, Fulgencio Batista, Cuba's leader from 1934 to 1944, returned to power in a coup, and immediately suspended the constitution and cancelled the elections. Whereas Batista's first period of rule had been relatively progressive, his new government soon descended into a corrupt and brutal dictatorship. With the democratic route closed off, Fidel turned to the politics of revolution. On 26 July 1953, he led an assault on the Moncada Barracks, in Santiago in the south of the country, in a doomed attempt to spark a popular uprising. While many of his fellow rebels were killed, or subsequently hunted down, Fidel was captured alive and, three years into a fifteen-year jail term, was granted an amnesty. He headed to exile in Mexico with a promise to return 'with the beheaded tyranny at one's feet'.

Fidel was as good as his word. In November 1956 he arrived back in Cuba aboard the *Granma*, a rickety leisure yacht that had been purchased from an ex-pat American dentist. After a disastrous landing, and the death or capture of most of the eighty or so rebels, Fidel, his younger brother Raúl, the young Argentine doctor Ernesto 'Che' Guevara and a dozen other survivors regrouped in the Sierra Maestra mountains. It was from here that Fidel and his 26 July Movement launched a remarkable military campaign that culminated in the Maximum Leader's triumphant march into Havana on 8 January 1959. Batista had fled into exile nine days earlier.[32]

Having stunned the world by overthrowing El Hombre ('the Man') and then establishing a genuinely revolutionary government right on America's doorstep, it did not take very long for Fidel to turn his attention to the international arena. In the spring of 1959, he travelled across the Americas – visiting Canada, the United States, Brazil, Uruguay and Argentina – in an attempt to win public and political support for his revolution, and to champion the cause of Latin American solidarity. On 22 April, after touring the UN Building in New York and conferring for thirty minutes with Secretary General Dag Hammarskjöld, Fidel told waiting reporters that Cuba – hitherto a rock-solid ally of Washington – would now be pursuing a more independent course at the United Nations. He also declared that, while it might provide a helpful example to his sister republics in the hemisphere, the Cuban Revolution was 'not for export'. In São Paulo, a few weeks later, Fidel proclaimed that 'our aspirations are the same as those of all Latin America' and, at an economic conference in Buenos Aires, he called for a Marshall Aid-style programme of economic development for the continent.*[33] Now, in the Fifteenth General Assembly of the United Nations – which was bringing together leading international statesmen against a backdrop of major geopolitical and social change – he saw an unparalleled opportunity to burnish his credentials on the world stage.

An insight into Fidel's motivations in attending the General Assembly can be found in the pages of *Revolución* – the official newspaper of the 26 July Movement, and the *de facto* mouthpiece of the government. According to his biographer, Tad Szulc, from the beginning Fidel acted as the newspaper's 'supereditor, visiting its offices, conferring almost daily with Carlos Franqui, who was the editor and chief propagandist, and seeing to it that the revolutionary line was phrased precisely the way he wanted it to be every time'.[34] On 15 September, *Revolución's* Juan Arcocha reported that the official announcement that the Maximum Leader would be attending the Fifteenth General Assembly had 'provoked enthusiasm in the streets . . . The citizenry, overjoyed, commented that Fidel was going to New York "to throw the Americans out".' This was, Arcocha claimed, 'evidence that popular wisdom has dutifully

* Between 1948 and 1951, under the direction of Secretary of State George C. Marshall, the United States provided some $13 billion (*c*.$100 billion in 2018 prices) in economic assistance to sixteen European countries to help them to rebuild after the devastation of the Second World War.

grasped one of the important aspects of the trip, one of its advantages: the fact that the Prime Minister will thereby have a global platform . . . from which he will be able to launch to all corners of the world the revolutionary message of Cuba'. But, Arcocha continued, the Cuban people 'appear to have given very little thought to another aspect of Fidel's trip, less apparent and perhaps infinitely more important. Fidel at the UN will be a historic event of the highest magnitude. It will be, possibly, the first knock at the door marking the end of imperialism.'

At the end of the Second World War, Arcocha explained, Winston Churchill had worried that, in creating the United Nations, the great powers risked 'giving life to a small Frankenstein'. In the years that had followed, 'the subjugated peoples began to wake up. The colonial countries of Asia and Africa were liberating themselves one after another . . . from the colonial yoke.' In April 1955, in a striking display of their new-found power, representatives of twenty-nine newly independent countries from across Africa, Asia and the Middle East convened in the Indonesian city of Bandung with the aims of fostering cooperation among Third World nations, coordinating the ongoing fight against colonialism and white supremacy, affirming the right of all nations to self-determination, and promoting world peace. With the formation of the Afro-Asian bloc, Arcocha explained, 'winds of change began to blow in the General Assembly of the United Nations' and 'imperialism began to beat a hasty retreat'. 'And then', Arcocha continued, 'Fidel came down from the *Sierra*.' Now, 'the podium is ready . . . the little Frankenstein is stirring, and Fidel is going to New York to rouse him.'[35]

## 2

# INTO THE BELLY OF THE BEAST

Welcome Fidel, Give Them Hell
PRO-CASTRO PLACARD AT IDLEWILD AIRPORT

On the morning of Sunday 18 September, Fidel's mother, Lina Ruz, and his sister, Juanita, as well as thousands of supporters, gathered at Rancho-Boyeros airport, south-west of Havana, to cheer the Cuban leader's departure. As his mother, concerned for his safety, began 'fussing' over her son, Fidel exclaimed, 'Ay! Don't worry, old woman. I've taken worse trips than this, and nothing's happened to me yet. Remember the *Granma* . . .' As Lina Ruz began to sob, her son 'consoled her with a look'. Then he turned and strode purposefully towards the waiting aircraft, accompanied by senior government figures, including his brother Raúl and the Cuban president, Osvaldo Dorticós ('dressed democratically in a fresh loose white shirt', Dorticós had, it was reported, even driven his own car to the airport).

Wearing his trademark drab-olive fatigues and, according to reports, carrying an army knapsack and a hammock (the same one, it was said, that he had used while fighting in the Sierra Maestra), Fidel paused briefly at the aircraft steps to exchange a few words with his brother, who would be acting premier during the leader's absence, and to present him symbolically with his ammunition belt and pistol. Fidel then boarded the plane, along with more than fifty of his fellow revolutionaries. 'From the wide terrace', reported the leading pro-government weekly, *Bohemia*, 'thousands of people witnessed the departure. Voices, slogans, enthusiasm rained down on the Head of the revolution, beneath the generous sun of Cuba.' As the Britannia Jet-Prop airliner soared into the bright, blue sky, and headed north, the compañeros settled back into their seats and relaxed.[1]

But, despite his earlier display of bravado, Fidel was clearly rattled. As his anxiety increased, the Maximum Leader turned to his security chief, Ramiro Valdés, to ask whether an escort plane had been arranged. When Valdés 'stuttered out a no', Fidel responded, 'We're in danger. If I were running the CIA, I'd shoot down the plane at sea and report the whole thing as an accident.' According to Carlos Franqui, editor of *Revolución* and part of the entourage, everyone now 'started to look around' apprehensively. The mood on board was not improved when, amid a 'huge roar', a squadron of American fighter jets suddenly appeared alongside. 'Everybody panicked', Franqui recalled, 'except me.' Having consumed several travel sickness pills and downed a couple of daiquiris, he was able to sit back and observe 'the warriors turn pale'. But when Fidel realized that they were approaching the US mainland, he quickly recovered his poise: after all, he reasoned, the Americans would not dare risk shooting the plane down over their own territory. Soon enough, the aircraft was descending through the grey clouds above Manhattan, headed for the airport in the easternmost borough of Queens.[2]

New York was a city that Fidel knew reasonably well. Back in the autumn of 1948 he had spent the best part of three months there, honeymooning with his new bride, Mirta Díaz-Balart (the daughter of a provincial mayor). Having rented an apartment in the Bronx, the future revolutionary had enrolled in English language classes, dipped into Karl Marx's *Das Kapital* (a copy of which he had purchased from a local bookstore) and driven around the city in a fancy Lincoln convertible. He even briefly considered applying to study at Columbia University, before deciding to return to Havana to resume both his legal studies and his political activism.[3] Then, in April 1959, just months after overthrowing the dictatorship of Fulgencio Batista, Castro made a second trip to New York, this time as part of a wider tour of North America under the auspices of the American Society of Newspaper Editors. For Castro, this was an ideal opportunity to launch a charm offensive that, he hoped, would win the support of the American people. During four jam-packed days in the Big Apple, Fidel visited the floor of the New York Stock Exchange, climbed the Empire State Building, spoke about agrarian reform at Columbia, met with baseball star Jackie Robinson, addressed a rally of 35,000 Cuban Americans in Central Park (where he announced that the goal of the Cuban Revolution was 'Bread with Liberty'), and took a tour of the Bronx Zoo – where he won over the press, and much of the American public, by eating hot dogs and ice cream, hugging children, patting a tiger and feeding peanuts to the elephants. He was even presented with the keys to the city. Although Washington was lukewarm about his trip (Eisenhower preferred to play golf at Augusta, and left it to Vice President Richard Nixon to meet with Castro), for Fidel it had been a public relations triumph.[4]

By the autumn of 1960, though, relations between Cuba and the United States were at breaking point. Washington was particularly alarmed by the new government's economic policies, which, while welcomed by many ordinary Cubans, proved less popular among those who had done well under the old regime. The agrarian reform programme, for instance, which was launched in May 1959, restricted holdings to 1,000 acres, with a 3,333-acre exemption for land used for rice, sugar and livestock. Many of the larger estates – including those owned by US citizens and companies – were expropriated and transformed into cooperatives. American-owned sugar mills, it was estimated, stood to lose 1,800,000 acres of the 1,864,000 acres that they had accumulated over the years. Worse still – at least from the point of view of the proprietors – was that compensation was to be paid in long-term government bonds, with a maturation of twenty years, and the value of the land being determined by the amount that the former owners had previously (under)declared for tax purposes.[5] Havana also launched an aggressive programme of economic intervention and nationalization – opening up formerly private beaches to the public, taking hotels (including the Havana Hilton) and private clubs (such as the Biltmore Yacht and Country Club) into public ownership, and moving against large financial, corporate and industrial interests.[6] With some $1 billion (roughly $8.5 billion in 2018 prices) invested on the island – in banking, utilities, tourism, mining and agriculture – American business owners had plenty to lose, and were understandably unnerved by the new, more hostile climate.[7] In January 1960, for instance, senior managers of the United Fruit company informed the State Department that trade union officials had begun to attend meetings with management 'armed with Tommy guns'. A month later, the owners of a bakery in Georgia, which imported some 200,000 pounds of glazed pineapple from Cuba annually, sought government advice about 'whether it is your feeling that we will be able to secure shipments out of Cuba during the next ninety days'.[8] By the early summer, the State Department was complaining that:

> property has been confiscated, expropriated or intervened,
> frequently without receipt, and the owners, many of
> whom have made substantial contributions to Cuban
> national development, have physically been expelled from
> their lands. Individually owned properties as well as large
> corporations with thousands of small stockholders, both
> Cuban and American, have been subjected to arbitrary
> intervention and control by the Government of Cuba,
> which has resulted in a tremendous loss in capital values and
> the destruction of vital credit ratings.

They also pointed out that 'payments due to American export-
ers for goods shipped in good faith over the past year have accumulated to over $100 million'.[9] Many ordinary Americans were
appalled. One outraged Texan wrote to the White House to
demand that the United States take 'immediate action to avenge
the barbaric thievery practiced by Fidel Castro'. If the Cuban
leader refused to 'return' all of the 'stolen American property'
then 'we must go immediately and take it back'. 'Our dignity', he
declared, 'has been invaded by a gangster, and you must not rest
until he is punished.'[10]

If the direct challenge to its own economic interests (and the
political influence that came with it) was not bad enough, the
Cuban government's 'authoritarian turn' also set alarm bells ringing in Washington. Throughout 1960, for instance, Fidel's government bore down on the free press and media, taking control
– either directly or indirectly – of newspapers, radio stations and
television companies. In February, the numerous radio and television stations that had been appropriated by the government
were reorganized into the FIEL (Independent Federation of Free
Radios) network, whose stated purpose was to 'consolidate the
revolution and orient the people' (tellingly, the acronym spelled
out the Spanish word for loyal). Meanwhile, what one British
diplomat characterized as a 'spring-cleaning' of the press elimi-
nated the last remaining independent Spanish-language dailies.
Strong-arm methods were sometimes deployed. On 10 May, for
instance, an 'armed band, with police acquiescence' invaded the
offices of the highly respected independent newspaper *Diario
de la Marina*, where they proceeded to smash up equipment,
force the paper's director into hiding and seize control of the
newspaper. A few days later, *Prensa Libre* suffered a similar fate.[11]
In August, the University of Havana was purged – 120 faculty
members were dismissed from their posts – and the independence of the judiciary was compromised.[12] Cuba was, President

Eisenhower was warned, 'rapidly being taken to the point of no return'.[13]

As Fidel and his fellow revolutionaries strengthened their hold on Cuba, they turned increasingly to Moscow and the wider communist world for support – signing trade deals, instigating cultural links, welcoming technical experts and advisers to the island, sending high-profile delegations abroad, and purchasing sizeable quantities of arms.[14] On 17 June, for instance, the American embassy in Havana reported that:

> The first two weeks of June have seen an unprecedented number of Communist commercial and cultural missions arriving in Cuba. The parade began on June 1 with the arrival of the Peking Opera Company from Red China. On June 2 a Bulgarian mission reached Havana. On June 6 the Minister of Foreign Commerce of Czechoslovakia arrived to put the final touches on several agreements negotiated by a Czech commercial mission that had been in Havana for some time.

During this same period 'it was announced that a Polish Commercial mission was on its way to Cuba as well as an 80-man ballet group from the Soviet Union'. Meanwhile, Antonio Núñez Jiménez, the head of the powerful National Agrarian Reform Institute (INRA) was in Moscow, leading a Cuban trade mission (they had also visited Warsaw, Prague and East Berlin), and Major William Gálvez, Inspector General of the Cuban Armed Forces, was in the People's Republic of China, being 'wined and dined' by Chairman Mao and Prime Minister Zhou Enlai.[15]

This flurry of overseas diplomacy did yield concrete results. Back in February 1960, Cuba signed a landmark trade deal with Moscow, under which the Soviet Union would provide oil, manufactured goods and technical assistance in return for 425,000 tons of sugar (in year one), and one million tons in each of the following four years.[16] But in June, when the Cubans ordered Standard Oil and Texaco to process the first supplies of Soviet crude, they refused (the pressure applied by the US government proved critical); their refineries were promptly nationalized. Shortly thereafter, President Eisenhower signed a law cutting the Cuban sugar quota – under which the US government guaranteed to purchase an annual amount of the sugar crop each year, at a price artificially inflated so as to benefit the American-owned sugar producers. Fidel responded with fury, telling a mass meeting of metalworkers that Cuba was the victim of foreign 'henchmen', and pledging that they would never 'bow down under the yoke' or 'sell our independence'.[17] The Soviets quickly came to the rescue by agreeing to purchase the shortfall – albeit at world prices, and in kind rather than in cash.[18] The following month, while speaking at the First Latin American Youth Congress, at Havana's Cerro Stadium, Fidel announced – to wild, raucous cheers – that, in the face of continuing US economic aggression, the government would be nationalizing a further twenty-six American-owned enterprises, including the telephone and electricity companies; the Texaco, Esso and Sinclair oil companies; United Fruit; and all of the Cuban sugar mills that were owned by US firms.[19]

The economic tit-for-tat between Cuba and the United States was accompanied by an increasingly bitter war of words. US foreign policy, for instance, was described as the work of 'political mafias and gangsters', while a leading Cuban newspaper pictured Uncle Sam as a long-fanged vampire. In attacking 'Yankee imperialism', the revolutionary government in Havana drew on long-suppressed resentment at Washington's oversized role in the island. Although Cuba had achieved nominal independence in 1898, following the US victory in the Spanish-American war, under the terms of the Platt Amendment the Americans had retained the legal right to interfere in the republic's domestic affairs in order to protect property rights and uphold law and order. They had restricted Cuba's ability to forge an independent foreign policy, and maintained a large naval presence at Guantánamo Bay. Even after Franklin Roosevelt abrogated the Platt Amendment in 1934, the United States continued to exert a decisive influence over Cuba's economy and political culture. And, of course, Washington had provided crucial support, over many years, to the hated dictatorship of Fulgencio Batista.[20] When Fidel accused the United States of having robbed and exploited Cuba, then, his remarks resonated with many millions of his fellow countrymen who, having experienced first-hand the reality of American imperialism, had welcomed the 1959 revolution enthusiastically.[21]

During early 1960, as the island swirled with rumours of counter-revolutionary plots and conspiracies – fuelled by the mysterious torching of sugar cane fields – both the government in Havana and the government-controlled radio warned that the United States was preparing to launch a 'criminal attack' on Cuba.[22] Such alarm was well founded: in June 1954, for instance, the Eisenhower administration – convinced that 'the Reds' were now firmly in charge – had sponsored a coup in Guatemala, overthrowing the democratically elected government of Jacobo Árbenz. His government had outraged executives of United Fruit, and other powerful American interests, by having the temerity to expropriate land and then redistribute it to tens of thousands of impoverished peasants.[23]

When it came to Cuba, despite a brief 'cooling-off' period at the start of 1960, which was designed to try and improve relations, things took a turn for the worse in the immediate aftermath of the *La Coubre* incident.[24] On the morning of 4 March, *La Coubre* – a French ship containing a significant cargo of rifles, rifle-grenades and ammunition – arrived in Havana harbour. Although standard procedure would have been to anchor the vessel offshore and use barges to bring the arms ashore, *La Coubre* was dockside, close to a number of buildings. An official cable from the British Embassy described what happened next:

> At about 3.00pm, when all the cases containing
> ammunition and some of those containing grenades had
> been unloaded, there occurred the first explosion which
> killed all the stevedores at work in the hold. The second
> explosion followed about three quarters of an hour later,
> killing or wounding many of those engaged in rescue,
> including a number of soldiers. Estimates of the casualties
> have differed widely, but the latest figures indicate that
> about sixty persons may have been killed (there are still a
> number of persons missing) and two hundred and seventy
> injured. Considerable damage was done to the dock and to
> buildings in the neighbourhood.

The final death toll might have been as high as one hundred.

The following day – a national day of mourning – a state
funeral took place for many of the victims at Havana's Colón
cemetery. Perhaps as many as half a million Cubans turned out to
pay their respects that afternoon. They waited in tense silence as
Fidel prepared to speak. In electrifying remarks that were broadcast on television and radio, he claimed that the explosion must
have been a result of sabotage and pointed the finger firmly at the
Americans, who had after all refused to sell weapons to Cuba and
then pressured other countries into doing the same. Their aim,
he stated, was to 'keep us defenceless in order to suppress us'. He
declared, 'We have the right to believe that those who tried to
prevent us by diplomatic means from receiving these arms might
also have tried by other means. We do not affirm that they did so,
because we do not have convincing proof, and if we had we would
present it to the people of the world [. . .] But', he continued, 'I
say we definitely have the right to believe that those who sought
to achieve their ends one way, and in several ways, later turned
to different procedures . . .'[25] The Americans responded with outrage: Secretary of State Christian Herter hauled in the Cuban

*chargé d'affaires* to inform him that the accusations were 'baseless, erroneous, and misleading', and would serve only to further worsen relations between the two countries.* [26]

The attacks on the 'Yankee imperialists', though, would continue. Speaking on Cuban television, Foreign Minister Raúl Roa described his US counterpart, Christian Herter, as a 'blown-up pigskin with no capacity for ideas'.[27] President Eisenhower fared even worse. A Cuban radio broadcast of 26 March characterized him as decrepit, bottle-fed and senile, with a nurse on hand to wipe the drool from his mouth and feed him his malted milk, while lamenting the fact that 'world progress' was dependent on a 'man so likeable and so foolish, so smiling and so stupid'.[28]

By the summer, the bad feeling between Havana and Washington even spilled over into baseball – which, in Cuba, was something of a secular religion. On 7 July, under pressure from the Eisenhower administration, Frank Shaughnessy, president of the International Baseball League (one of the most prestigious minor leagues), announced that the Havana Sugar Kings would be forcibly relocated to Jersey City, in order to secure the players' safety. The loss of the team – which had won the Little World Series the previous year and seemed poised to gain a berth in the major leagues – was a bitter blow. Fidel, who was a keen baseball fan, even offered to pay the team's debts to keep them in Havana. It was to no avail. Just a week later, the Sugar Kings (hastily renamed the 'Jerseys') were taking on the Columbus Jets in their new home, leaving Fidel to fume about this violation of 'all codes of sportsmanship'. One of the most important cultural and psychological ties between Cuba and the United States had now been ripped away, leading the influential columnist Walter Lippmann to warn

* Officially the cause of the explosion remains a mystery, although in her 2012 book, *Visions of Power in Cuba: Revolution, Redemption and Resistance, 1959–1971*, the historian Lillian Guerra was, on the basis of her research, prepared to describe the ship's destruction as 'deliberate' (p. 108).

that 'the thing we should never do in dealing with revolutionary countries, in which the world abounds, is to push them behind an iron curtain raised by ourselves'. 'On the contrary', he argued, 'the right thing to do is to keep the way open for their return.'[29]

Alarmed by the Cuban Revolution's drift to the left, Havana's growing closeness to Moscow, and what the State Department characterized as a 'campaign of slander against the United States' that was 'among the most vicious ever encountered from any source', Washington eventually turned to the regional body, the Organization of American States, for support.[30] Founded in 1948, at the urging of US Secretary of State George C. Marshall, the organization was designed to provide collective security for the hemisphere, facilitate the peaceful resolution of disputes, promote social, cultural and economic cooperation and, crucially, act as a bulwark against communism.[31] At a meeting of OAS foreign ministers held in San José, Costa Rica, at the end of August, Christian Herter managed to persuade his Latin American counterparts to pass a resolution that condemned 'emphatically the intervention or the threat of intervention . . . by an extracontinental power in the affairs of the American republics' and reaffirmed that 'the inter-American system is incompatible with any form of totalitarianism'. But his attempt to single Cuba out for criticism (which had prompted Foreign Minister Raúl Roa to walk out of the meeting) ended in failure. Indeed, Mexico insisted on issuing a separate statement making clear that the resolution was 'general in character' and 'in no way is it a condemnation or a threat against Cuba, whose aspirations for economic improvement and social justice have deepest sympathy of the Government and the people of Mexico.'[32]

On the afternoon of 2 September, before a sea of 400,000 people, who had gathered in Havana's Civic Plaza for what was termed a 'General National Assembly of the People', Fidel – accompanied by the roars of the crowd – ripped up the mutual aid treaty that had been signed by the Cuban and US governments in 1952, before proclaiming the 'Declaration of Havana' – his fiery response to the 'Declaration of San José'. Denouncing America's 'criminal' history of imperialism in the region, the Cuban leader called for hemispheric revolution, expressing the hope that 'Latin America will soon be marching, united and triumphant, free from the control that turns its economy over to North American imperialism and prevents its true voice from being heard'. He also asserted the right of every nation to show solidarity with the oppressed, the downtrodden and the exploited, on any continent: 'all the peoples of the world', he declared, 'are brothers.'[33]

It was dynamite stuff, guaranteed to rile the Yankees. Bob Taber, an American journalist and supporter of the Cuban Revolution, warned that 'when he descends from the plane at the international airport in New York . . . Fidel will enter an atmosphere more poisonous than that which the Cubans breathed in the hellish Havana of the days of Batista.'[34] As the Havana Airways jet began its final approach into Idlewild (modern-day JFK), the Maximum Leader must have wondered just what kind of reception lay in wait.

Mae Mallory, the Harlem-based black activist and supporter of the Cuban Revolution, described Sunday 18 September as 'wet and dreary. It was one of those mornings that makes you decide to stay in bed all day.' And that, she confessed, was 'where I certainly would have been' had she not noticed, on the way home from work the previous evening, a leaflet calling for people to join a 'motorcade to welcome Fidel Castro'. 'It was', she declared, 'wonderful to see the way the people responded, to welcome the true leader of the Latin American countries.' Buses were lined up for five blocks, and more than a hundred cars – 'of every description and model, and from as far away as Texas' – joined 'this vast motorcade'. Despite the grey clouds and persistent rain, an exuberant crowd of some 3,000 – most of them Cuban and Cuban-American supporters of the revolution, together with Puerto Ricans, Venezuelans, Dominicans and others who took huge pride in Fidel's historic achievements – gathered at the main terminal in eager anticipation (meanwhile, some enterprising supporters managed to hang a giant 'Welcome, Fidel' banner from the top of the Empire State Building). Several hundred police officers were on hand to keep a watchful eye over the demonstrators, who shouted '*Viva Castro!*' and waved placards that declared 'Welcome Fidel, Give Them Hell' as they strained for a glimpse of their hero. Unfortunately for them, the authorities decreed that for security reasons Fidel's plane – which finally touched down at 4:32 p.m., two hours late – should be directed to Hangar 17, in a remote corner of the airport some two miles away.[35] They did, though, allow several hundred of his supporters to gather there, where they were fenced in by what one described as 'a strong chicken wired stockade'. Even this could not dampen their enthusiasm, and as the Cuban plane taxied to the hangar, 'a deafening roar of "Welcome Fidel" and "Venceremos" ("We Shall Win") thundered through the air'.[36]

A few minutes later, after cursory checks by immigration and health officials, the Cuban prime minister emerged from the aeroplane, accompanied by his foreign minister, Raúl Roa; Antonio Núñez Jiménez – head of INRA; and Celia Sánchez, his personal assistant, gatekeeper and confidante. After waving to the crowd, and clasping his hands above his head, Fidel was greeted at the foot of the aircraft steps by Jehan de Noue, the UN Chief of Protocol, who was representing the Secretary General. According to one journalist, the Cuban leader 'had to be coaxed into smiling for the photographers' and appeared 'ill at ease'. After conferring briefly with his aides, he then stepped to the waiting bank of microphones and made a few brief remarks. Speaking in a 'soft, hoarse voice', and with his hands firmly in his pockets, the Maximum Leader declared that: 'I want to salute the people of the United States. My English, the same as last time, is not so good. All I have to say I will say to the United Nations.' And, with that, he was ushered into a waiting black Ford Sedan for the journey to Manhattan.[37]

Flanked by police cruisers, and protected by officers armed with sub-machine guns, Fidel's car had barely begun moving when, while passing by the fenced-in supporters, the Cuban leader began to wave and ordered the driver to stop. In a 'wild response', a number of his more fervent admirers now attempted to scale the wire fence; the police, armed with nightsticks, forced them back.[38] Simultaneously, a plain-clothes officer pushed Fidel's arm back into the car, while others prevented him from opening the door and getting out to greet the crowds.[39] 'The insolent police officer', ran one Cuban report, then added insult to injury by swearing at the prime minister while insisting that he remain inside the vehicle. Fidel – who had informed the Americans in advance that he wished to avoid being surrounded by security personnel and vehicles – was by now 'visibly angry', and he 'scowled and shouted to the others in his car, gesticulating that he wanted to get out, but the police were adamant'. When the Cuban driver proved reluctant to resume the journey, some twenty officers put their shoulders to the wheel and began to propel the car forward, which prompted the chauffeur to finally resume the journey.[40] The incident was quickly seized on by the Cuban press as evidence of 'barbarous' and 'insolent' treatment, and the following day the Cuban government filed an official complaint with the office of the UN Secretary General.[41] The US government, Celia Sánchez told Prensa Latina (Cuba's state news agency), wanted to avoid, at all costs, any displays of popular enthusiasm among the American population for the Cuban leader and his revolution.[42]

This was, perhaps, wishful thinking. While, for Washington, any pro-Castro sentiment was unwelcome, the deteriorating relationship between the two countries had already done a good deal to sour the public mood. Moreover, by drawing closer to Moscow, the Cuban leader had made himself *persona non grata* in the eyes of many Americans. Whereas, a year earlier, children had run around wearing toy beards during Fidel's visit to the city, now residents of Long Island decided to burn him in effigy. US officials were, then, understandably concerned about potential threats to Fidel's personal safety – General Thomas D. White, Chief of Staff of the United States Air Force, even made the wild claim that there were about 200,000 people who would quite like to assassinate him, given half a chance. For all this, though, Sánchez did have a point. Washington was keen to emphasize that Fidel was in the country under forbearance and, in secret documents, the American Secretary of State, Christian Herter, was clear that the security restrictions imposed on Fidel (who was not permitted to leave Manhattan during his stay) had been designed explicitly to 'reflect [the] attitude of US Govt toward his presence in US at this time'.[43]

The sixteen-mile journey to midtown took no time at all: citing security concerns, police had closed the Van Wyck Expressway, Grand Central Parkway and Long Island Expressway to traffic, causing chaos and frustration for Sunday motorists. For added protection, police officers were also stationed on the dozens of overpasses under which the motorcade passed. Many Castro supporters – perhaps as many as 2,000 – gathered along the route to catch a glimpse of the Maximum Leader, along with a handful of opponents, who shook their fists, shouted for Fidel to 'go home' and waved large American flags.[44] Meanwhile, the motorcade itself was followed by a raucous 'people's caravan' of supporters, honking their horns and shouting '*Viva Fidel! Viva Cuba!*'[45] 'It was', declared *Bohemia*, 'truly a Cuban afternoon in New York.'[46]

Just after 5.30 p.m., Fidel's car emerged from the Queens Midtown tunnel and, moments later, pulled up outside the Shelburne Hotel, on Lexington Avenue. Several thousand supporters had gathered there to welcome the Cuban leader, who exited the car to the sight of Cuban flags waving and raucous chants of '*Viva Fidel!*' 'The jubilation', ran one report, 'was indescribable.' After 'nodding sternly' to the waiting news reporters, he strode through the main doors and headed for his third-floor suite. Meanwhile, the 200 police officers – including mounted units – under the personal command of Police Commissioner Stephen P. Kennedy struggled to maintain order, amid violent skirmishes between pro- and anti-Cuban protesters. Then, shortly before 7 p.m., amid continuous shouts of 'Fidel, Fidel!' and 'We Will Triumph!' and renditions of the Cuban national anthem, Fidel – hatless, and now 'smiling broadly' – appeared at his third-floor window where, as cheers rang out, a giant police searchlight illuminated the scene. Three minutes later, and he disappeared into the sanctity of his plush suite.[47]

The Cuban delegation had, in fact, encountered considerable difficulties in securing accommodation in the city. Unlike some others, the country's mission to the UN did not maintain a spacious residence in New York, and the State Department's decision to confine Fidel to the island of Manhattan for security reasons ruled out the possibility of renting a large house further afield, in Long Island or Westchester. The original plan had been to stay at the Hotel Elysée, at 60 East Fifty-fourth Street, but its manager, Seymour Pinto, cancelled the reservation after learning that Fidel would be coming to New York as part of a larger than expected party. Pinto was at pains to explain that politics had had nothing to do with the decision – 'I don't care who is coming as long as they pay their bills and behave themselves,' he declared – but maintained that hosting the group would have overburdened his hotel. Cancelling other reservations, he explained, would 'kill business' and 'offend older customers'.[48] The fact that no hotel appeared willing to take the Cubans eventually became a source of some diplomatic embarrassment, and – under considerable pressure from officials from both the State Department and the UN – Edward Spatz, the owner of the Shelburne, was finally persuaded to make twenty two-room suites available to the Cubans, at a rate of $20 per night.[49] He was, though, a clearly reluctant host, telling reporters that 'we personally have strong feelings against the Cuban leader and prefer not to accommodate him' and, more bluntly, 'I hate him.'[50] Concerned that anyone might doubt his patriotism, Spatz also arranged for a large American flag to be flown from the front of his hotel on the very evening that his Cuban guests checked in. When they asked for their flag to be displayed beside it, he point-blank refused. And, after receiving complaints from some of his other residents – elderly, conservative men and women, who were evidently alarmed by the sudden influx of young, bearded revolutionaries in battle fatigues – Spatz decreed that the Cubans could not eat in the hotel dining room.[51]

As Spatz's disgruntled foreign guests were settling in for the night, another figure of whom the Shelburne's owner thoroughly disapproved was just hours away from New York, and intent on making as much mischief as possible.

# 3

## MONDAY 19 SEPTEMBER

DEAR K! DROP DEAD YOU BUM
PLACARD, ANTI-KHRUSHCHEV PICKET

The *Baltika*, a 7,500-ton, single-stack steam liner, sailed into New York Harbor on the morning of Monday 19 September, escorted by a US navy submarine and a fleet of US coastguard vessels overseen by Commander Joseph Mazotta. In a show of force, the USS *Franklin D. Roosevelt*, the fleet's most powerful aircraft carrier, was also moored nearby. It was, reported the *New York Times*, 'the greatest exercise in harbor-security measures' since the end of the Second World War. As three police helicopters buzzed overhead, the ship's passengers – who included the communist leaders of Hungary, Bulgaria and Romania as well as Nikita Khrushchev, First Secretary of the Central Committee of the Communist Party of the Soviet Union – struggled to make out the Statue of Liberty through the heavy rain. A short, rotund figure in a yellow raincoat, the Soviet leader was pacing the upper deck peering anxiously through binoculars at a motley flotilla of fishing boats and other small craft, and their cargo of jeering, placard-wielding protesters. One of the more memorable signs read:

*ROSES ARE RED*
*VIOLETS ARE BLUE*
*STALIN DROPPED DEAD*
*HOW ABOUT YOU?*

The First Secretary would later dismiss this 'carnival of fools' who wished only to 'humiliate our country and its representatives'. But aboard the *Baltika* that overcast morning, he couldn't help but recall the very different scenes that had greeted him only a year earlier, in September 1959, when 100,000 curious New Yorkers had lined the sidewalks of Midtown to celebrate his arrival.[1]

Born in 1894 in south-west Russia, of peasant stock, Khrushchev, a former metalworker, had joined the Bolshevik cause in 1918 and risen rapidly through the ranks – serving as Party boss in Moscow, and then in Ukraine, before being appointed as a political commissar with the Red Army after the Axis invasion in June 1941, winning medals for his role in the victories at Stalingrad and Kursk. By the late 1940s, Khrushchev was a key member of Stalin's inner circle, but when the dictator succumbed to a massive stroke on 5 March 1953, few people – either inside or outside the Soviet Union – imagined that, within months, Khrushchev would have outmanoeuvred his rivals to reach the very top. He benefited, in part, from the fact that so many people underestimated him – mistaking his garrulousness, buffoonery and earthiness for a lack of guile.[2] As a CIA personality report noted, on the surface Khrushchev gave the impression of being 'an impetuous, obtuse, rough-talking man, with something of the buffoon and a good deal of the tosspot in him'. But, as they had come to realize, 'behind the exterior lay a shrewd native intelligence, an agile mind, drive, ambition, and ruthlessness'. Khrushchev was, they judged, resourceful, audacious, with a 'good sense of political timing and showmanship, and a touch of the gambler's instinct'.[3]

These virtues had certainly been on display in February 1956, when Khrushchev stunned the world, and many of his own comrades, by delivering the so-called secret speech, at the Twentieth Congress of the Communist Party of the Soviet Union. Over the course of several hours, the new Soviet leader had denounced Stalin for promoting a 'cult of personality', condemned the forced confessions, show trials, executions and mass arrests of the 1930s, and rubbished Stalin's carefully crafted reputation as a great war leader. Khrushchev also embarked on a programme of liberal reform, devolving some government power, freeing hundreds of thousands of political prisoners from the gulag, placing curbs on the secret police and encouraging a greater degree of cultural freedom.[4] But this new, more liberal dispensation had its limits – both at home and abroad. Khrushchev, concerned that domestic dissent was getting out of hand, moved to rein in the criticism, making it clear that 'hostile outbursts' and attempts to blame the Soviet system itself for the excesses of Stalinism would not be tolerated. And when a popular uprising in Hungary appeared to threaten Moscow's hold on the whole of Eastern Europe, Khrushchev sent 60,000 troops, thousands of tanks and two air force divisions to crush a revolution that had, briefly, captured the imagination of much of the world.[5]

Khrushchev's 1959 visit to New York had come amid a dizzying two-week tour of the United States, during which the Soviet leader had taken tea with members of the Senate Foreign Relations Committee, inspected the size of hogs in Beltsville, Maryland, sampled his first hot dog, thrown a tantrum after being denied entry to Disneyland (due to security concerns), and enjoyed the company of Frank Sinatra, Marilyn Monroe and Shirley MacLaine. He had also discussed disarmament with President Eisenhower during a friendly summit meeting at Camp David, the presidential retreat in Maryland that was, famously, named after Ike's only grandson.[6]

Hopes for a Cold War détente, though, had quickly soured. On 1 May 1960, the U-2 pilot Gary Powers had been shot down near Sverdlovsk (Yekaterinburg), to the east of the Ural Mountains. When, a few days later, Khrushchev announced that an American spy plane had been downed, Washington – assuming that Powers had either died or committed suicide (he had been issued with a poison injection pin) – claimed that a weather plane had strayed off course. When the Soviets countered with evidence of the U-2, surveillance photographs and a CIA-trained pilot who was still very much alive, the Americans were humiliated. The bitter fallout doomed any hopes for East–West rapprochement at the

Paris summit, held later that month – which ended with Khrushchev angrily denouncing the Americans as 'thieves' and describing Eisenhower, whose invitation to visit Moscow had been summarily rescinded, as 'stinky'.[7]

In the weeks following the failed summit, Khrushchev resolved to return to the United States. Knowing full well – like Castro – that the opening of the Fifteenth General Assembly provided an unparalleled opportunity to stick it to the Americans, on their own turf, before a worldwide audience of millions, he was determined not to miss out. He was, moreover, keen to woo the new African countries and extend Soviet influence in the underdeveloped world. There was just one problem: although Khrushchev was the Soviet Union's *de facto* leader, Nikolai Bulganin, the Soviet premier, technically headed the government, while Leonid Brezhnev, as Chairman of the Presidium of the Supreme Soviet, was the titular head of state. Lacking an automatic right to speak at the UN, Khrushchev came up with an ingenious solution: he would appoint himself head of the Soviet delegation to the UN. As his son Sergei later recalled, the Soviet leader was 'simply bursting to do battle'.[8]

The news that Khrushchev was planning to return to New York was greeted with dismay in the United States: the *Cleveland Plain Dealer* accused the Soviet leader of 'sheer unmitigated gall', while *Time* magazine proclaimed that Khrushchev was 'about as welcome in the U.S. as the Black Plague'.[9] Richard Nixon was scarcely more polite. Writing privately to Llewellyn E. 'Tommy' Thompson, the American ambassador in Moscow, on 8 September, the vice president (who had famously gone toe to toe with the Soviet leader during the impromptu 'kitchen debate'* in Moscow, the previous

---

* The unplanned exchanges, which saw the two men debate the merits of their respective systems and argue about the availability of modern appliances and consumer goods for their citizens, took place at a model suburban home – replete with a generously equipped General Electric kitchen – that was housed at the American National Exhibition in Moscow's Sokolniki Park.

summer) noted that he was 'looking forward to Khrushchev's visit with interest'. Referring to the Soviet Union's recent success in sending two dogs, Belka and Strelka, into orbit (and, in contrast to their more famous predecessor, Laika, returning them safely to the earth), Nixon wondered whether the Soviet leader 'might decide to take the trip in one of their rockets. He isn't, of course, a dog, but most people think he is a son of a ———!'[10] Secretary of State Christian Herter and other senior Eisenhower administration officials also worried that the Soviet leader was planning to turn the General Assembly into a 'spectacular propaganda circus' and cause as much trouble as possible.[11] While they might have preferred him to stay at home, the authorities had no choice but to accommodate him. They did, though, decide to restrict his movements to the island of Manhattan, citing concerns for his security (this same measure was subsequently applied to Castro). Moreover, the government went out of its way to emphasize that Khrushchev's attendance at the United Nations did not 'in any sense imply that he is either a guest of the United States Government or that he is being officially welcomed to United States territory'.[12]

Khrushchev chose to make his second trip to New York by sea because, with his state-of-the art Tupolev TU-114 grounded due to mechanical issues, he could not bear the humiliation of having to take a less impressive plane that would have required a refuelling stop in London. The savage storms that had marred the first few days of the voyage doubtless caused many of Khrushchev's travelling companions to regret that particular decision, especially as the First Secretary took enormous and very obvious delight in the seasickness that afflicted almost everybody on the ship, apart from him ('I have', he later noted, 'a sturdier constitution'). Then, as the weather improved, Khrushchev took to dictating speeches and reading the latest intelligence reports from a deckchair, before whiling away the afternoons and evenings watching movies, playing countless games of shuffleboard (with the competitive ferocity, it was said, of a Florida retiree), drinking enormous quantities of wine, vodka and cognac, and poking fun at the comrades.[13]

But no one was laughing as the *Baltika* approached Pier 73, on the Manhattan side of the East River. Having balked at the rental costs, Khrushchev had ordered the Soviet ambassador to bargain hard and rent a cheaper place.[14] His instructions had been followed with rather too much enthusiasm: the pier was a wreck and, despite some last-minute attempts to patch things up, 'the roof leaked like a sieve. Plastic sheeting covered broken panes in the skylights, but the weight of water soon broke through and soaked everything below.' Both the red carpet and the rich Persian rug that had been laid out by Soviet officials earlier that morning 'soaked up the water like giant blotting paper'.[15] To add insult to injury, a boycott by the International Longshoremen's Union meant that the crew were forced to moor the ship themselves, and diplomats to lug their own baggage, as a hostile crowd looked on. Some 300 anti-communist protesters (including a number of émigrés from central and eastern Europe), 'hemmed in' behind a fenced area at the south-west corner of 25th Street and East River Drive, had waited for two hours in the pouring rain to make their displeasure known. The New York *Daily News* described how 'when Khrushchev's bald dome was seen moving from the *Baltika* to the pier the crowd let loose a volley of names – in English and assorted tongues – that would have blanched Captain Kidd'.[16]

In a calculated insult, no official representative of the national, state or city government was in attendance – and Khrushchev, who walked down the gangway to the strains of Tchaikovsky's *Swan Lake* at precisely 9:48 a.m., was welcomed formally by Jehan de Noue, along with the communist leaders of Czechoslovakia and Poland (Antonín Novotný and Władysław Gomułka), and Cyrus Eaton, a multi-millionaire financier and industrialist who, virtually alone among US businessmen, advocated friendly relations with the communist world. Eight little girls – the daughters of Soviet embassy employees – in 'pretty dresses, pigtails and white hair ribbons, greeted Mr. Khrushchev with armloads of salmon-colored, white and orange gladioli'.[17] Smiling, and tanned from his nine days at sea, Khrushchev, wearing a dark blue suit, brown Oxfords and a dark grey silk tie, strode towards the waiting microphone and, 'with his feet squarely planted on the oriental rug, he took his silver-rimmed reading glasses from a leather case' and pulled a crumpled sheaf of notes from his pocket.[18] 'The thoughts and aspirations of a majority of people in all countries', he declared, 'are now focused on one goal – how to achieve a situation in which lasting peace will be ensured all over the world.' The Soviet Union was, he emphasized, 'trying to do everything to shape the development of relations in the direction of a peaceful adjustment and the establishment of world peace'. Recalling the 'best feeling from my last year's visit to the United States', he expressed his 'great respect for the American nation' and predicted that 'the relations between our great countries will improve'. After all, he explained, 'it is common knowledge that no matter how dark a night might be, it is invariably followed by dawn.'[19] As he spoke, raindrops could be seen bouncing off his head.

For those who had been expecting fireworks, these first remarks on American soil were surprisingly emollient. Committed to the policy of 'peaceful coexistence' between the socialist and the capitalist blocs, Khrushchev – a natural optimist – could turn on the charm when he wanted to.[20] As it turned out, though, he was merely keeping his powder dry.

On finishing his speech Khrushchev was ushered into his shiny new Cadillac for the short ride to the Soviet mission.[21] As his motorcade made its way up Second Avenue, one newspaper reported, 'a waitress in a luncheonette at 72nd Street suggested to a customer that she would like to have Khrushy drop in for breakfast because she had "just the thing for him". She pointed to a can of insecticide.'[22] The mission itself, meanwhile, was targeted by Hungarian exiles who denounced Khrushchev as a 'Fat, Red Rat' who was 'Wanted for Murder'.[23]

While Khrushchev was settling into his quarters in the Soviet mission – a grand, neo-federal town house on Park Avenue – over at the Shelburne on Lexington the Cuban delegation was becoming restless.[24] Shortly before 7 p.m., after some twenty-four hours holed up in the hotel, and with wild rumours circulating that the Cubans had been plucking and cooking chickens in their rooms, extinguishing cigars on the carpets and filling the refrigerators with mouldy steaks, Fidel and his delegation stormed out. The final straw had come when Edward Spatz, having demanded an additional $10,000 as a security deposit, turned down a Cuban bond as part payment because, in his words, it 'looked wrong'. Speaking at an impromptu news conference in the hotel's (aptly named) Satire Room, Fidel complained about a general 'climate of inhospitality' in New York, declaring that if the United States was unable to treat visiting statesmen with respect then the United Nations should be moved to a different country. As for Mr Spatz's 'troublesome' demands, Fidel countered that he was 'not ready to let myself be robbed because the money I have belongs to the Cuban people'.[25] The Maximum Leader declared that he and his delegation would 'go any place, even Central Park' if necessary: after all, he explained, 'we are a mountain people . . . used to sleeping in the open air.'[26] When asked if he was not worried about being bothered by 'thieves at night', he shot back: 'How can there be thieves in this country? Don't the workers earn decent salaries? Aren't there salaries for everyone here? In Cuba anybody can sleep in Havana's Central Park without being disturbed.'

Once the laughter had died down, Fidel sought to make a more serious point. Declaring that the 'rudeness and lack of hospitality' that he had encountered was 'inexplicable', he stated that 'if a meeting as important as the General Assembly of the United Nations' took place in Cuba, 'we would double our efforts to be friendly with everyone who attended it.' After all, he explained, the embezzlers who had profited under the Batista regime, and subsequently fled into exile, had 'left us magnificent houses' that could be used to accommodate international guests. The Cuban leader now rose to his feet, placed his arm around the *New York Times* journalist Herbert L. Matthews – who had famously interviewed him in the Sierra Maestra – and, as the cameras began to flash, headed for the exit.[27]

As Fidel and a number of his aides 'piled into a black Oldsmobile', 'others in their party ran frantically into the street to get car space while the surprised police and security guards tried to maintain order'.[28] Then, amid the wailing of police sirens, and the revving of engines, the convoy was off, headed to the United Nations headquarters in Turtle Bay. Fidel Castro was taking his complaints to the top.

Following the resignation of the former Norwegian foreign minister, Trygve Lie, in November 1952, after sustained pressure from the Soviet Union over his support for the 'police action' in Korea, the United Nations had eventually turned to the little-known Swedish academic and public servant Dag Hammarskjöld as his successor as Secretary General.[29] One Dutch diplomat, who had viewed the search for Lie's replacement up close, explained that 'in spite of the reputation of ability and integrity which he had acquired among those who had met him in negotiations or at conferences, it cannot be said that [Hammarskjöld] was, at that moment, the obvious candidate for this high international function.' Rather, 'his election was much more due to the wish of the Big Powers to see – after Trygve Lie who had taken a strong position in several questions – at the head of the Secretariat someone who would concentrate mainly on the administrative problems and who would abstain from public statements on the political conduct of the Organization.'[30] Hammarskjöld himself was rather more succinct: 'I was', he said, 'simply picked out of the hat.'[31]

In Hammarskjöld, the big powers thought that they had appointed the archetypal bureaucrat: cautious, colourless, a man unlikely to cause them any particular trouble. They were wrong. As his biographer Roger Lipsey has explained, almost nobody had any 'inkling of the breadth of his political philosophy, integrity, capacity for dialogue and strategic acumen. Had his full range been better known, he would not have been elected', because 'the Big Powers would only compromise their separate interests around someone believed to be safe.'[32] Taking advantage of the greater freedom for manoeuvre provided by the death of Stalin on 5 March 1953 and the Korean War armistice agreement, which was signed on 27 July 1953, Hammarskjöld re-energized the role of Secretary General, bringing a distinctive leadership style that was rooted in his commitment to independence and impartiality, and his own personal integrity and moral courage.[33] As he settled into the role – he was re-elected, unanimously, to a second term in 1957, partly because no one wanted a fight over this issue – Hammarskjöld developed the use of 'preventive diplomacy' (negotiations to prevent conflict), invented the concept of 'shuttle diplomacy' (direct, personal, private negotiations with key protagonists), and showed a willingness to deploy UN peacekeepers to the world's trouble spots.[34]

With the accelerating pace of European decolonization fuelling the rapid growth of the United Nations, Hammarskjöld also came to see the organization as having a special role in supporting the rights of the smaller nations in a world that was still dominated by the traditional big powers. The UN had, he declared in August 1960, 'increasingly become the main platform – and the main protector of the interests – of those many nations who feel themselves strong as members of the international family but are weak in isolation'. These countries, he explained, 'look to the Organization as a spokesman and as an agent for principles which give them strength in an international concert in which other voices can mobilize all the weight of armed force, wealth, an historical role and that influence which is the other side of a special responsibility for peace and security'.[35]

Now, on the evening of 19 September, this aristocratic Swede was sitting down to dinner with his staff in the office dining room when word came through that a group of Cubans, dressed in drab-olive fatigues, had entered the UN building. While most of the group enjoyed sandwiches and bottles of rum and Mexican beer in the bar of the South Lounge, Fidel was ushered into Hammarskjöld's office on the thirty-eighth floor of the iconic Secretariat Building.[36] The Secretary General was, in the words of one of his biographers, both a 'great statesman and peacemaker . . . of unshakeable integrity', willing to stand up to the leaders of the great powers, and a 'vulnerable, questing man of spirit' – a 'sufferer, a doubter, a discoverer'.[37] The Secretary General listened patiently as Castro complained about the humiliating treatment his party had received at the Shelburne and demanded that the delegation be put up at the UN. If enough sofas could not be found for them to sleep on, Castro declared, then they would happily set up camp in the rose garden. During the course of the discussions, Fidel asked Hammarskjöld if he agreed that 'the time had arrived to move the headquarters of the United Nations to another country' (according to the Cuban press, the Secretary General simply responded with a shrug). Despite being preoccupied by the fast-moving crisis in the Congo following the coup against Lumumba only five days earlier, Hammarskjöld nevertheless gamely turned travel agent. Eventually, having worked the phones, he announced that William Zeckendorf, the prominent real estate developer and hotel owner, had offered the Cubans rooms, free of charge, at the Commodore Hotel, on East 42nd Street. But his efforts had been for nought.

The Cubans had, he now learned, arranged to stay at the Hotel Theresa in Harlem – a heavily African American area of the city, and one in which visiting dignitaries would seldom set foot, never mind take up residence – and could not be dissuaded, insisting on the 'right to choose the hotel we want'. After a discussion with John W. Hanes, Jr, State Department administrator for security and consular affairs, Police Commissioner Kennedy begrudgingly gave his approval for the Cubans to use the Theresa; and, after finishing their drinks, they vanished into the night.[38]

Some have wondered whether this was all staged; part of a carefully worked out plan to cause mischief on a grand scale. Teresa 'Teté' Casuso, the Cuban intellectual and diplomat, who defected to the United States in October 1960, certainly thought so. Casuso, who was head of the Cuban mission at the UN, later claimed that, during conversations with members of Fidel's entourage, she 'discovered the bitter truth that the whole thing had been planned beforehand':

> [Fidel] had intended from the start to complain that he
> was overcharged at the first hotel, to plant himself with his
> whole retinue and all their baggage at the United Nations
> and thus present the spectacle that they had no place to stay,
> then to move to Harlem in order to give the impression that
> it was only among the humble and despised people of the
> United States, the Negroes, that the humble and despised
> Cubans and their leader were able to find shelter.[39]

It is certainly the case that, before departing for New York, Fidel had warned that he might have 'to camp in New York's Central Park if it becomes necessary' – and had made a point of packing his backpack and hammock, just in case. But, to be fair, the Cubans had been finding it almost impossible to secure suitable hotel reservations.[40] During their increasingly frantic search for a hotel that would take them, the Hotel Theresa had been suggested to them by leaders of the New York chapter of the Fair Play for Cuba Committee (founded by left-liberal supporters of the revolution earlier in the year). This fact, in particular, would subsequently fuel conspiracy theories in the American newspapers that the entire thing was a well-planned stunt. On the other hand, if a move to Harlem had, indeed, been the plan all along, it was curious – to say the least – that Fidel had not ensured that Major Juan Almeida, one of the few leading revolutionaries of African descent, was on the trip with him. Either way, the move uptown worked a treat.

Built in 1913, the Hotel Theresa – known as the 'Waldorf of Harlem' – was an architectural wonder and a local landmark.
Photograph by Harry Hamburg/NY *Daily News* Archive via Getty Images

Built in 1913 by the Jewish American financier and manufacturer Gustavus Sidenberg, the Hotel Theresa bore graceful ornament on its all-white facade – including spandrel panels consisting of 'diamond shapes made up of crisscross lines, something like the Islamic decoration of the 14th-century Alhambra' and 'projecting panels of glazed terra cotta surrounding roughened, sandpaper-like rectangles'. 'Unlike anything ever seen in New York', the thirteen-storey hotel was located in the heart of Harlem – a neighbourhood that, for half a century, had been renowned as a centre of African American cultural innovation and political radicalism.[41] Although, by the autumn of 1960, the 'Waldorf of Harlem' had definitely seen better days, it retained a reputation for being, as the *New York Times* put it, 'a kind of village green . . . that is, politicians hold rallies in and around it, and Negro celebrities receive the acclamation of the multitudes there.'[42] In 1941, 10,000 people had turned out there to celebrate Joe Louis' latest victory in the boxing ring and, in 1959, the Theresa had hosted the annual convention of the Communist Party of the United States of America. For Castro, it was an inspired choice.[43]

As news of the Cubans' move to Harlem spread, hundreds of locals headed towards the Theresa, desperate to witness a slice of history. Some were merely curious, but Fidel's political appeal was clear enough. As the community-owned Harlem weekly, the *New York Citizen-Call*,[*] put it: 'To Harlem's oppressed ghetto dwellers, Castro was that bearded revolutionary who had thrown his nation's rascals out and who had then told white America to go to hell.'[44]

That evening, many of New York's most talented African American men and women of letters – including the historian John Henrik Clarke, playwright Julian Mayfield and the writer John Oliver Killens – had gathered in the home of poet and novelist Sarah

* The *Citizen-Call* was published by the one of the country's first black stockbrokers, John Paterson.

Elizabeth Wright for a meeting of the Harlem Writers Guild, when their proceedings were interrupted by a telephone call. It was Richard T. Gibson, the African American journalist and co-founder of the Fair Play for Cuba Committee, relaying the 'electrifying news' of Fidel's audacious 'Harlem Shuffle'. Maya Angelou, then a thirty-two-year-old poet, singer and budding civil rights activist, explained how 'in moments, we were on the street in the rain, finding cabs or private cars or heading for subways'. But, to her amazement, 'at eleven o'clock on a Monday evening, we were unable to get close to the hotel. Thousands of people filled the sidewalks and intersections, and police had cordoned off the main and side streets.' Angelou 'hovered with my friends on the edges of the crowd, enjoying the Spanish songs, the screams of "Viva Castro", and the sounds of conga drums being played nearby in the damp air'. As they looked around, Wright recalled, 'we could see people crammed onto rooftops, leaning out of thousands of windows. And a steady chanting, "Cuba, sí, Yanqui no!"'[45] At one point, 'people carried the manager of the hotel on their shoulders and he was applauded for having offered the hotel to Castro to serve as his residence during his stay in New York.'[46] The crowd was in good humour: one local observed how 'that cat and his gang may have fought in those mountains . . . and whipped that dictator Batista. But if they can stand the bedbugs in the Theresa, I'll know they're real revolutionaries!'[47] When a waving, smiling Fidel finally arrived, flanked by a heavy security presence, he was greeted by repeated cheers of 'We want Castro!'[48]

They were roaring for Fidel on the streets of Havana, too, where a hastily called rally to protest against the 'disrespectful' treatment in New York drew 25,000 to the square in front of the Presidential Palace (in the capital's movie theatres, films were stopped so that notices could be flashed onto the screen, calling on Cubans to assemble at the palace immediately). Amid a 'din of blaring auto horns', 'shouting and surging crowds' waving Cuban flags, white handkerchiefs and giant banners proclaiming, 'With a hotel or without a hotel, they will have to listen to Fidel', welcomed acting prime minister Raúl Castro and President Osvaldo Dorticós with 'clamorous applause'. Speaking first, in remarks that were broadcast nationwide via state TV and radio, Raúl (a 'sinister-looking young man' with an 'animated Pixie-like manner' whose influence on his brother was, according to the British Foreign Office, 'almost wholly bad') denounced the 'aggression and provocation' of a 'stupid US imperialism'. An imperialism that was, he said, both 'furious with, but also fearful of, the Cuban Revolution'. 'Our government', he declared, was:

> different from the North American Government. We cannot act like they act simply because we are a civilized government. We can tell President Eisenhower that if the seat of the UN were here and despite the scorn felt by our people for what he represents, we would be sure if the reverse were true and he had to come to an international meeting of this nature that our people and government would be incapable of doing to him what they there are doing to Fidel.

In the event that the US president visited Cuba, Raúl continued, 'our people would be incapable of emitting one hiss'. President Dorticós also addressed the crowds, emphasizing that, while revolutionary Cuba respected the diplomatic representatives of the United States, they did not respect – and would respect less with each passing day – 'the financial interests of North American imperialism [. . .] we are able to say with pride that we have failed to respect the American petroleum companies, the sugar companies, the public service companies and the American banks.'

The two men then presented the crowd with a formal declaration of protest at the treatment afforded to Fidel and the Cuban delegation in New York. Claiming that the United States was swimming against the tide of history, the Cuban government characterized those 'who insult and attack us, those who try to smother the voice of our people' as 'the same who walk hand in hand with the worst forces in the world: Nazi reactionism, bloody fascism, the still-remaining despots in our hemisphere . . . The company they keep unmasks them . . .' But 'those who do not want the voice of our Prime Minister to be heard at the United Nations are going to have to hear it, and with the voice of an entire people that shouts with more fervor than ever; our country or death! We shall conquer!' While the crowds in Havana roared their approval, it was reported that, out in the provinces, some of Fidel's supporters were preparing to sleep outdoors, in hammocks, in a show of solidarity.[49] Meanwhile, across town in the American embassy, senior officials – fearing a possible mob attack – were burning sensitive files.[50]

Back in Harlem, Fidel had barely had time to settle into his two-room suite on the ninth floor of the Hotel Theresa before his first guest came calling.

Born in Omaha, Nebraska, in 1925, Malcolm Little had endured a troubled youth: his father, Earl, a supporter of the Jamaican-born black nationalist Marcus Garvey, had been murdered by white supremacists when Malcolm was six years old; his mother was later hospitalized following a nervous breakdown. Separated from his siblings and discouraged from pursuing a career in law (which was, his teacher said, 'no realistic goal for a nigger'), he drifted into a life of crime – drug dealing, gambling, racketeering and pimping. In 1946 he was arrested in Boston and sentenced to ten years in prison for armed robbery. Two years later, while serving his sentence in Charleston State Penitentiary, Malcolm – attracted by its forceful condemnation of white 'devils' and its powerful message of uplift for African Americans – converted to the Nation of Islam. Abandoning his 'slave name', he now styled himself 'Malcolm X'. Paroled in 1952, Malcolm quickly moved up the NoI's ranks, becoming leader of Temple Number 7 in Harlem two years later, and helping to recruit thousands of new converts across the country.[51]

By the autumn of 1960, Malcolm X was one of the most famous black nationalists – indeed, black men – in the United States. The Nation of Islam, the organization that he had joined in 1948, and which he now served as its most charismatic spokesperson, had shot to fame the year before, following the screening of a documentary film, *The Hate that Hate Produced*, on New York's WNTA-TV. Produced by journalists Mike Wallace and Louis Lomax, the film had highlighted the NoI's unorthodox religious beliefs (which included the notion that an evil black scientist, Yacub, had been responsible for the creation of whites) and its strident criticisms of the white race.[52] The programme had begun with minister Louis X (later, Louis Farrakhan), reading an indictment of the white race as part of his play, *The Trial*, that the NoI were staging in cities across the country:

> I charge the white man with being the greatest liar on earth! I charge the white man with being the greatest drunkard on earth . . . I charge the white man with being the greatest gambler on earth. I charge the white man, ladies and gentlemen of the jury, with being the greatest murderer on earth . . . I charge the white man with being the greatest robber on earth. I charge the white man with being the greatest deceiver on earth. I charge the white man with being the greatest trouble-maker on earth. So therefore, ladies and gentlemen of the jury, I ask you, bring back a verdict of guilty as charged.[53]

Interviewed by Lomax, Malcolm had explained that followers of the group's leader, the Honorable Elijah Muhammad, believed not only that 'the black man, by nature, is divine', but that the white man was the devil. When pushed on whether white people were

capable of doing good, Malcolm responded, 'History is best qual-
ified to [judge] and we don't have any historic example where we
have found that they collectively for the people have done good.'[54]
His own sermons and speeches, meanwhile, crackled with racially
charged rhetoric. An FBI informant reported that, at a meeting
held on 20 April, Malcolm had 'asked those in the audience who
would like to see the white man go up in smoke to raise their
hands'. 'Everyone', he noted, 'raised their hand.' The fiery minister
would also regularly reassure his audiences, reminding them that
'the black man is God and the white man is the devil, so you know
who will win this last great war'.[55]

Malcolm had quickly established himself as a leading figure
in Harlem's radical scene, and had been appointed to the 28th
Precinct Community Council by its chairman, James Hicks – the
influential editor of the *New York Amsterdam News* – who had been
impressed by his masterful ability to control the crowds during a
protest against police brutality in the spring of 1957.[56] But the NoI
firebrand had also been looking for a way to further establish his
reputation as a major national – and international – figure. And
now, wrote his biographer Manning Marable, Malcolm had been
presented with 'an opportunity to crash international headlines';
one that came 'gift wrapped from the Cuban Revolution'.[57]

At around 1 a.m., Malcolm, together with his aides Captain
Joseph and John Ali, and three African American reporters –
Jimmy Booker of the *New York Amsterdam News*, the photojour-
nalist Carl Nesfield, and Ralph D. Matthews, Jr, of the *New York
Citizen-Call* – were pushing their way past the police officers who
were guarding the building. Having taken the one working elevator to the ninth floor, Malcolm's party headed down a corridor
lined with white journalists and photographers who were visibly
put out at having been refused admission. As they entered Fidel's
dimly lit suite, cigar smoke hanging heavy in the air, the Cuban
leader, still dressed in his immaculately pressed army fatigues, rose

and shook hands with each of his guests in turn. He was clearly in a fine mood – and the 'rousing Harlem welcome still seemed to ring in his ears'.[58]

After sitting down on the edge of the bed (the room was virtually devoid of furniture), Fidel beckoned Malcolm, still wearing his trench coat, to sit down beside him. The Maximum Leader's first words of broken English were lost in the hubbub, but prompted Malcolm to reply that 'downtown for you, it was ice, uptown it is warm', whereupon Fidel smiled broadly. 'Aahh yes,' he said, 'we feel very warm here.' 'Ever a militant', reported Ralph Matthews, Malcolm could not resist claiming that 'I think you will find the people in Harlem are not so addicted to the propaganda they put out downtown.' Eager to avoid missing out on a historic encounter between two figures who would come to embody opposition to American imperialism, on the one hand, and the uncompromising demand for black rights 'by any means necessary', on the other, several compañeros were now squeezing themselves into the already cramped room. Most of the Cubans smoked long cigars and, when something amused them, they 'threw back their heads and blew smoke puffs as they laughed'. As he spoke, Fidel had a habit of pointing to his temples and tapping his chest; when an interpreter translated some of Malcolm's longer sentences, though, the Cuban leader listened attentively.[59]

The conversation, which lasted for about thirty minutes, ranged widely. The two men discussed racial inequality (Fidel declared that 'we work for every oppressed person' and expressed admiration for African Americans – who had 'more political consciousness, more vision than anyone else'), the Congo crisis and the upcoming session of the UN General Assembly. At one point, Fidel paused so that he and his aides could pass round Cuban cigars, and signed copies of one of his recent speeches.[60] Then the conversation turned to US–Cuban relations. According to an FBI informant, Malcolm stated that 'usually when one sees a man whom the United States is against, there is something good in that man'. To this Castro replied that 'only the people in power in the United States are against him, not the masses'.[61]

Fidel was, Malcolm explained, 'the only white person that I have really liked'.
Photograph © Prensa Latina

With luggage now beginning to arrive at the cramped quarters, Fidel sought to draw the conversation to a close by citing Abraham Lincoln: 'You can fool some of the people some of the time . . .' he began but, visibly tiring, he simply threw up his hands while his interpreter finished the quotation for him. As the visitors stood up and prepared to leave, Malcolm delivered a parable: 'No one knows the master better than his servants. We have been servants ever since we were brought here. We know all his little tricks. Understand? We know what he is going to do before he does.' Throwing his head back, and roaring with laughter, Castro responded, '*Sí, sí!*'[62]

As Malcolm and his small entourage exited the hotel, just after 1.30 a.m., the crowd outside shouted out, '*Viva Castro!*' In remarks to the waiting, heavy-eyed journalists, he explained that Fidel had 'told me that he felt at home for the first time since his arrival in this country last Sunday afternoon'. Pressed on his personal impressions of the Cuban prime minister, Malcolm declared that 'any man who represents such a small country but who would stand up and challenge a country as large as the United States on behalf of his people must be sincere'.[63]

In subsequent comments to the *Pittsburgh Courier*, Malcolm contrasted the record of Havana and Washington when it came to racism. 'Fidel Castro', he noted, 'has denounced racial discrimination in Cuba, which is more than President Eisenhower has done here in America.' The Cuban leader had also 'come out against lynching, which is also more than Eisenhower has done . . . and has taken a more open stand for civil rights for black Cubans.' But, Malcolm continued, 'no outside man can help the "so-called" American Negro. No outside force, no outside power. It takes God to correct the situation here because it is so complicated. Muhammad represents that God. That's why I am with Muhammad.'[64] These final words were, perhaps, an attempt to smooth over disagreements with Elijah Muhammad. From their wiretap on his phone, the FBI had quickly learned that the NoI leader had been infuriated by the meeting between Malcolm and Fidel. There were several reasons for Elijah Muhammad's displeasure. Most fundamentally, the encounter challenged the Nation's strict apolitical stance: believing that racial equality within the United States was impossible, Muhammad resisted all efforts at involvement in black political issues, even opposing efforts by NoI members to register to vote – which he saw as a waste of time. The bar on political engagement was a restriction that the more politically engaged Malcolm was constantly chafing against. Additionally, Muhammad, who had seen his organization devastated by a series of FBI raids during 1942, was fearful that the authorities would seize on Malcolm's meeting with Fidel – a suspected 'Red' and foreign enemy – to justify another strike.[65] 'If I had known Malcolm was going to visit Castro', he told the *Washington Post*'s Wallace Terry in December 1960, 'I would have prevented it. The Muslim world is against Communism. I don't like it because it's atheistic.' But, he said, communism was ultimately all part of Allah's divine plan that would see the white race destroyed and blacks – God's 'original people' – reasserting themselves.[66]

The tension between Muhammad and Malcolm over the meeting with Fidel was a warning sign of a bitter conflict to come. Malcolm would eventually leave the Nation in March 1964 in acrimonious circumstances – his departure triggered by long-standing disagreements over political activism, a desire to adopt a more orthodox version of Sunni Islam, and vicious internecine scheming. The acrimony was exacerbated, moreover, by Malcolm's discovery that his beloved mentor, who was married, had fathered several children with a string of teenage secretaries. Freed from the constraints of the Nation, Malcolm founded the Organization of Afro-American Unity in June 1964. Modelled on the Organization of African Unity, the OAAU not only sought to 'bring about the complete independence of people of African descent here in the Western Hemisphere, and first here in the United States', under the slogan 'we want freedom, by any means necessary', but it also explicitly sought to internationalize the African American freedom struggle and learn from the experiences of 'our African brothers [who] have gained their independence faster than you and I here in America have'.[67] The 1960 meeting with Fidel was, then, an early signal of Malcolm's growing interest in Third World revolutionaries and his deepening conviction that the African American struggle was an integral part of the wider revolt against colonialism and white supremacy. The Cuban leader clearly made a strong personal impression, too. Fidel, Malcolm told the Cuban journalist Reinaldo Peñalver, was 'the only white person that I have really liked'.[68]

\*

Fidel's first few hours in New York City had, by any reckoning, been pretty sensational. He had first stunned his American hosts – and much of the rest of the world – by stalking out of the Shelburne and threatening to set up camp at the United Nations. Then, he and his entire delegation had relocated to Harlem – a neighbourhood few other international statesmen would have deigned to visit, never mind stay in – where he had enjoyed an iconic encounter with the black firebrand (and white America's bogeyman) Malcolm X. Inevitably, Fidel's antics dominated the following day's headlines. Writing in the *Washington Star*, the respected columnist Mary McGrory noted that 'Mr. Castro's bed has become the cause célèbre of the opening of the General Assembly' and everyone was now wondering how Nikita Khrushchev, 'who stayed quietly in the Soviet headquarters all day', would 'manage to steal the spotlight from the 34-year-old rebel'.[69]

CAPTION:

A beaming Fidel and Khrushchev emerge from the Hotel Theresa
following their historic first meeting.

Photograph by -/AFP via Getty Images

# 4

# TUESDAY 20 SEPTEMBER

I am a *Fidelista*!

NIKITA KHRUSHCHEV

At first, the reporters thought that Nikita Khrushchev was simply heading out for a lunchtime stroll when he emerged from the Soviet mission, smiling broadly, at 12.05 p.m. But then, amid a 'sudden flurry of activity by his security personnel', the Soviet leader was ushered towards his waiting Fleetwood Cadillac. As journalists shouted out, 'Where are you going?', the First Secretary of the Central Committee of the Communist Party of the Soviet Union 'leaned forward at the window, shaking his forefinger like a good-natured school teacher to his dull-witted pupils'. 'We Communists don't tell our secrets,' he exclaimed. Then the ten-car motorcade, accompanied by noisy police outriders, swung out and headed north, bound for Harlem. Newsmen, police and security personnel – all of whom had been caught on the hop – now scrambled to keep up.[1]

Khrushchev had decided on a meeting with Fidel even before the *Baltika* had set sail from Kaliningrad; midway across the Atlantic he had confided to a close aide his hope that Cuba would become a 'beacon of socialism in Latin America'. He also observed how the actions of the United States were, inexorably, pushing the Cuban leader closer to Moscow: 'Castro', he explained, 'will have to gravitate to us like an iron filing to a magnet.' The Soviet leader – who, a few months later, would pledge support for 'wars of national liberation' around the globe, as part of his efforts to extend Soviet influence and promote socialism across the Third World – well understood the romantic appeal of Castro's revolution. But he was also keen to ensure that Cuba, and its leader – whom he had never met before – caused as much discomfort as possible to the United States of America.[2]

Earlier in the day, the Cubans had suggested that they would happily travel to the Soviet mission for the meeting, but Khrushchev was having none of it. For one thing, he knew that a trip to Harlem would be a symbolic way to 'emphasize our solidarity with Cuba and our indignation at the discrimination with which Cuba was being treated'. But, just as important, the Soviet leader understood that 'by going to a Negro hotel in a Negro district, we would be making a double demonstration against the discriminatory policies of the United States of America toward Negroes, as well as toward Cuba'.[3] It was a move also guaranteed to deliver newspaper headlines, both in the United States and around the world. Given the Cold War competition for 'hearts and minds' across Asia and Africa – parts of the world where Khrushchev was determined to best the Americans – this was far too good an opportunity to pass up.

As Khrushchev's motorcade approached the Theresa, it passed by 'cut-rate department stores, cut-rate clothing, appliance, notions jewelry, and furniture stores, two huge movie theaters, the Harlem Lanes bowling alley, the Palm Café, and, on the corner diagonal to the hotel, a flashing neon sign proclaiming, "Herbert's – cash or credit. The home of blue and white diamonds".'[4] At 12.12 p.m., the Soviet leader arrived outside the Theresa. Already, the area was packed with thousands of onlookers, as well as hundreds of police (including mounted units), detectives and security personnel. One member of Khrushchev's entourage recalled how the noise was unbelievable. Antonio Núñez Jiménez, who had been waiting patiently in the Theresa's lobby, ran out to greet the Soviet leader and escort him inside. But as they made their way through the Theresa's cramped, rather dreary lobby towards the rickety, manual-operated elevator, scuffles between Cuban, Soviet and US security agents broke out. As the New York *Daily News* put it, in typically breathless style:

> Khrushy's burly security chief, Lt. Gen. Nikolai Zakharov, 6-foot-3, 220-pounder, became unaccountably irked with the way the city police were trying to squeeze his pudgy boss through the jampacked lobby.
>
> Zakharov flailed away with fists and elbows, landing mostly on police uniforms, until a uniformed motorcycle captain clamped a restrictive collar on the mad Russian.[5]

As he was ushered into Castro's corner suite, which overlooked Seventh Avenue and 125th Street, Khrushchev was appalled by the poor state of the hotel: it was shabby and the 'air was heavy and stale. Apparently the furniture and bedclothes had not been aired out sufficiently, and perhaps they were not, as we say, of the first degree of freshness – or even the second.' He was further shocked by the state of Fidel's quarters: the bed was covered with books, and the floor littered with records, maracas and cigar butts.[6] But while his suite reminded Khrushchev of a pigsty, the Cuban leader himself made a much more favourable impact: 'This was the first time that I had ever seen him in person, and he made a powerful impression on me: a man of great height with a black beard and a pleasant, stern face, which was lit up by a kind of goodness. His face simply glowed with it and it sparkled in his eyes.'

They talked only briefly – Fidel 'expressed his pleasure at my visit, and I spoke words of solidarity and approval of his policies.' 'That was', Khrushchev recalled, 'all there was to it. . .'[7] The Soviet newspaper *Izvestia* reported that, during the 'sincere and brotherly meeting', the two men had 'noted with great satisfaction' that their views on a number of issues that were to be discussed at the Fifteenth General Assembly happily coincided.[8] As the meeting broke up, Fidel introduced Khrushchev to other members of the Cuban delegation, which included the journalists Luis Gómez

Wangüemert and Carlos Franqui, as photographers snapped away.[9]

Fidel and Khrushchev may have said very little during their twenty-two-minute encounter, but the symbolism was everything. For their part, the Cubans took enormous delight from the fact that the Soviet leader had come to them. An editorial in the Cuban daily *El Mundo*, for instance, noted that a year earlier, the President of the United States had refused to meet with Castro (Ike had, in fact, made sure to be out of town rather than risk tarnishing the 'dignity' of his office). But now, one year on, the leader of the world's other superpower had made a point of visiting Fidel 'in his modest Harlem suite'. 'Thanks to the Cuban revolution', they continued, 'our little country is the center of world attention today because it is expressing the desire and hopes of all small and weak countries.'[10] *Revolución*, meanwhile, declared the visit to be 'the most prominent historical event' to have taken place during the General Assembly, thus far – and a welcome reaffirmation of Moscow's 'friendship' towards 'Cuba and its Revolution'.[11] Not every Cuban, though, was delighted by the news of Castro and Khrushchev's growing rapport. In a report filed from Santiago de Cuba, a couple of days after the meeting at the Hotel Theresa, the American consul G. H. Summ noted that he had seen people 'arguing openly on the streets for the first time since I have been here [. . .] In particular I saw one argument right in front of a local INRA office, where a man was gesticulating violently while pointing to the Havana paper showing Castro and Khrushchev embracing.'[12]

Washington, meanwhile, was even more irked by the meeting. By going to Harlem, Khrushchev had exposed America's greatest weakness – racial discrimination – and underlined the USSR's support for racial equality, before the entire world, at the very moment when more than a dozen new African countries were poised to join the United Nations. Back on 2 September, shortly after Khrushchev had announced that he would be travelling to New York, US

Air Force Colonel John Robertson had written to Roy Rubottom, Assistant Secretary of State for Inter-American Affairs, with a proposal. 'Let us tell Khrushchev and the world', he said, that the Soviet leader is 'persona non grata on our soil'. Urging the State Department to ensure that 'no accommodations are available in any first-class hotel', Robertson – in remarks that betrayed his own racial prejudice – suggested that if Khrushchev 'should have to reside in Harlem during his visit he would be better able to comprehend the Congo problem. Let's make his visit a howling success for us – not for him.'[13] In the event, Khrushchev's sojourn in Harlem was a propaganda triumph – for America's enemies.

When the two leaders emerged onto the sidewalk, shortly after 12.30 p.m., they were greeted by crowds of cheering spectators, excited journalists and hundreds of police, who were desperately trying to maintain order. It was, declared the *New York Times*, 'the biggest event on 125th Street' since the funeral of W. C. Handy, the 'father of the blues', two years earlier.[14] As the photographers snapped away, Khrushchev and Castro embraced. Given the physical disparities between them, it was a moment fraught with danger. As Khrushchev put it, 'we enclosed each other in an embrace . . . He bent over me as though covering my body with his. Although my dimensions were somewhat wider, his height overpowered everything. Besides, he was a solidly built man for his height.'[15] Writing in *Izvestia*, special correspondents Nikolai Karev and Nikolai Polyanov noted how 'the head of a great state had cast aside the conventions of diplomatic etiquette and had come to Harlem to call on the national hero of Cuba, a man whom capitalist America treated without ceremony [. . .] Never before', they declared, 'had anything like this happened in Harlem.'[16]

While Castro returned to his suite, to feast on T-bone steak (medium-rare), candied yams, French fries and a thick chicken soup (all prepared by the Theresa's chef, Marion L. Burgess, under the watchful eye of two Cuban officials), Khrushchev headed back to the Upper East Side, the cheers of the crowds still ringing in his ears.[17] Turning to his aides, the Soviet leader – well aware that Cuba was not, yet, fully within Moscow's orbit – exclaimed, 'Castro is like a young horse that hasn't been broken.' In public, Khrushchev was more fulsome. Pressed by newsmen, the Soviet premier declared that Fidel was a 'heroic man' who had freed his people from 'the tyranny of Batista and who has provided a better life for his people'. Later that afternoon, while heading to the UN for the formal opening of the General Assembly (where he would share a second fraternal hug with Fidel, and see his favoured candidate for Assembly president, Jiri Nosek of Czechoslovakia, lose out to the Irish diplomat Frederick Boland by forty-six votes to twenty-five), Khrushchev was asked whether the Cuban leader was a communist. The Kremlin boss demurred, but proclaimed that he was, for his part, a *Fidelista*! The Soviets' enthusiasm for the Cuban Revolution was gathering pace.[18]

While the formalities of the UN General Assembly were getting underway in Turtle Bay, a very different meeting was taking place just a few blocks away. At 3 p.m., senior British and US officials, including Sir Frederick Hoyer Millar, Permanent Under Secretary at the Foreign Office, and Livingston Merchant, Under Secretary for Political Affairs at the State Department, gathered in suite 2707 at the Waldorf-Astoria on Park Avenue to discuss the Cuban situation. Amid discussions about the relative strength of anti-Castro forces on the island (the Americans were hopeful of an 'early ripening of opposition') and a brief appraisal of the threat that the revolutionary government posed to the US naval base at Guantánamo Bay, Sir Frederick cautioned that it would be 'dangerous for the United States to make any premature move against Castro'. If the Cuban premier 'were given rather more time', he suggested, then Castro 'might bring about his own downfall'. The Americans, he said, should proceed carefully.[19]

London had had concerns about the approach being taken in Washington for some time. Harold Macmillan, who had succeeded Sir Anthony Eden as prime minister in the aftermath of the Suez debacle, had worked assiduously to restore the 'special relationship' with the United States. On 25 July 1960, he had written to Ike – with whom he had forged a firm friendship during the Second World War – to urge caution in the Antilles. Macmillan was at pains to stress that 'we fully share your concern at the way in which Castro has allowed his country to become ever more open to communist and Soviet influence' and agreed that a communist-controlled Cuba would pose an 'obvious menace' to the 'security of the Western hemisphere and so to the whole free world'. He also recognized that, though Britain had a valuable export trade with Cuba and political interests in the region vis-à-vis the West Indies (where it sought what it viewed as a smooth and orderly transition to independence), this was a matter on which the Americans 'must clearly play the hand'. Nevertheless, the prime minister believed that there was a real danger that, by increasing the economic and diplomatic pressure on the island, 'many Cubans who might otherwise have gradually drifted into opposition to Castro will instead be inclined to regard him – and themselves – as martyrs'. Might it not be wiser, Macmillan suggested, to 'let the yeast rise of its own accord . . .' In ending, he mentioned how it would 'make it easier for us to help if we had a rather clearer understanding of your actual intentions. I know, and fully sympathize with, your purpose – the unseating of Castro and his replacement by a more suitable regime – but I am not very clear how you really mean to achieve this aim.' After all, Macmillan explained – the failed attempt to unseat Egypt's Gamal Abdel Nasser still a source of pain – 'we have been through it all ourselves and know the difficulties and dangers . . .'[20]

The British, who, it transpired, would remain in the dark, were right to be worried.

*

On the afternoon of Sunday 19 April 1959, a 'somewhat nervous and tense' Fidel Castro had met with Richard Nixon at his office in the US Capitol building for the best part of two and a half hours. After the encounter, the vice president drew up a lengthy memorandum for senior administration officials, including Eisenhower, Christian Herter and the CIA director Allen Dulles, summarizing his impressions. Nixon confessed that his own evaluation of Castro was 'somewhat mixed'. There was no doubt that the Cuban prime minister 'has those undefinable qualities which make him a leader of men', and that 'whatever we may think of him he is going to be a great factor in the development of Cuba and very possibly in Latin American affairs generally'. But, Nixon cautioned, 'he is either incredibly naïve about Communism or under Communist discipline – my guess is the former . . .' In the final analysis, though, Castro's leadership abilities meant that Washington had 'no choice but at least to try and orient him in the right direction'.[21]

By early 1960, however, the administration (including Nixon) had decided that the revolutionary government in Havana was beyond redemption. In January, at a meeting of the top-secret Special Group – which had the responsibility for approving and overseeing covert operations – Allen Dulles 'noted the possibility that over the long run' the United States would 'not be able to tolerate the Castro regime in Cuba'. He suggested, therefore, that 'covert contingency planning to accomplish the fall of the Castro government might be in order.'[22] A month later, following the high-profile (and highly successful) visit to Cuba of Anastas Mikoyan, Khrushchev's right-hand man, the US embassy in Havana informed Washington that there was 'little hope' that 'we can work out a satisfactory relationship with the Cuban Government'.[23] On 17 February, the CIA director presented President Eisenhower with a plan of action to harass the Castro regime. Its focus was on sabotaging sugar refineries in order to deny Castro the lucrative and indispensable revenue from the 1960 sugar crop, thereby – it was hoped – eroding Fidel's popularity and destabilizing his regime.[24] After listening patiently, Eisenhower – who, in private, deemed Fidel a 'madman' who was 'going wild and harming the whole American structure' – expressed some doubts about the efficacy of what was being proposed. More broadly, though, he questioned 'why we were thinking of something on such a narrow basis. He said that he wondered why we weren't trying to identify assets for this and other things as well across the board, including even possibly things that were drastic.'[25] Dulles, who was one of America's most enthusiastic Cold Warriors, did not need to be asked twice. Just weeks later, the president was presented with a far more expansive plan, which aimed to bring about the 'replacement of the Castro regime with one more devoted to the true interests of the Cuban people and more acceptable to the U.S.' It consisted of four main elements: the creation of a 'responsible, appealing and unified opposition to the Castro regime, publicly declared as such and therefore necessarily located outside of Cuba'; the building of a radio broadcasting facility on Swan Island (ninety-five miles off the coast of Honduras) to beam opposition propaganda into Cuba; the establishment of a covert intelligence organization inside Cuba that would 'arrange for the illegal infiltration and exfiltration of individuals', help distribute propaganda and facilitate the defection of key personnel; and the assembling and training of a paramilitary force outside of Cuba and the development of logistical support for covert military operations. An initial budget of $4.4 million (equivalent to something like $30 million in 2018 prices) was proposed.[26]

Although he did not know it at the time, in signing off on Dulles's plan, Ike had planted the seeds of a national humiliation.

CAPTION:

Police officers struggle to restrain the crowds outside the Hotel Theresa.
Placards read, 'U.S. Jim Crows Fidel Just Like U.S. Jim Crows Us Negroes!'
and 'Fidel is Welcome in Harlem Anytime! Cuba Practices Real Democracy.
No Race Discrimination.'

Photograph by Andrew St. George. Courtesy of Yale University Manuscripts and
Archives / Andrew and Tom Szentgyorgy

# 5

# WEDNESDAY 21 SEPTEMBER

My impression of Harlem is that it's wonderful. We are very happy here.

FIDEL CASTRO

On the afternoon of 21 September, Havana radio broadcast an open letter to Love B. Woods, the owner of the Hotel Theresa, praising him for accommodating the Cuban delegation.[1] Woods, who was born on a farm in the little town of Union, South Carolina, in 1887, had shown an early interest in business and, after working as a Pullman porter to fund his education, opened a clothing store and later a restaurant in the state capital, Columbia. After moving to New York City in the early 1920s, he entered the hotel business and, a few years later, opened the Woodside, on Harlem's Lenox Avenue and 147th Street. Popular with musicians, including the Mills Brothers and Count Basie – who wrote 'Jumpin' at the Woodside' in its honour – and members of the 'fast crowd', the hotel, with its hustlers and gangsters, had an unsavoury reputation. But it made its owner rich. Before long, Woods, a lifelong bachelor who did not smoke and refrained from drinking alcohol, was 'a familiar figure riding around Harlem in his chauffeured limousine'. Just four months before Fidel arrived in New York, Woods – whose cash cow had been purchased by the city as part of a redevelopment scheme – had taken on the Theresa's lease. He dreamed of restoring its reputation as the Waldorf of Harlem.[2]

In taking in the Cuban delegation, Woods was at pains to point out that 'we don't discriminate against anybody.' 'I just accept them', he said, 'just like anybody else. They're just like any other guests.' Despite the prominence of his new tenants, Woods, the

*New York Times* reported, 'remained unruffled, almost indifferent. He did not bustle officiously. He did not wear a carnation in his button-hole', although he was – briefly – spotted wearing a new light grey hat, rather than his trademark cap. ('I sort of needed a new hat anyway,' he explained, almost apologetically.) Amid persistent rumours in the tabloid press that the Cubans were littering their rooms with cigar butts and half-eaten food, Woods was clear: 'Their rooms are clean as a pin. No litter, no mess, nothing'; the Cubans had behaved like gentlemen. When it came to the more salacious rumours – such as the steady stream of 'blondes, brunettes [and] redheads' who were allegedly paying late-night calls to the Cubans – Woods smiled ruefully, before declaring that, while he did not intend to run his hotel 'like a church', it was a 'decent place' and, in any case, ladies were not allowed in the lobby after 9 p.m.[3]

By opening the doors of his hotel to Fidel, Woods briefly became something of a folk hero in Cuba. The employees of the luxurious – and recently nationalized – Havana Riviera (opened by the American mobster Meyer Lansky in 1957) temporarily renamed it the 'Havana Theresa'; and their counterparts at the St John's Hotel, in Havana's Vedado district, followed suit. A workers' representative declared that:

> The employees who work in the old St. John's Hotel,
> adopting this resolution to change its name, believe that
> it is one of the many tributes of gratitude that the Cuban
> people will pay to the twenty million blacks discriminated
> against in the United States, for the enthusiastic displays of
> sympathy and solidarity with the Cuban Revolution and its
> supreme leader, Major Fidel Castro.[4]

Meanwhile, the leadership of the March 13 Revolutionary Directory, a student organization, cabled the Theresa a message of thanks for 'opening wide its doors to comrade Fidel' and acting 'without hesitation and without fear'.[5] From the streets of Havana, the African American journalist William Worthy reported how 'practically every Cuban who has recognized me as a "Norte Americano" has asked with delight if I had heard that "Fidel" is staying in Harlem at the Hotel Theresa'. There was, he explained, 'enormous satisfaction that their Prime Minister found sanctuary, as it were, among that part of the United States population with which they most readily identify'.[6] Telegrams of congratulation poured into the Theresa, from Castro sympathizers across the United States, and the hotel's switchboard lit up with calls from well-wishers – some from as far away as London.[7] Meanwhile, for its part, Cuban radio emphasized 'the profound gratitude of the Cuban people' to Woods for his 'valiant and worthy gesture in offering lodging to Fidel Castro'. Declaring that the names of Love B. Woods and the Hotel Theresa had been etched into the pages of history, they informed Woods that liberty had now been transferred symbolically from Bedloe Island, home of the Statue of Liberty, to 'the top of your hotel'.[8]

But it was not only Woods who had offered the Cubans a generous welcome; for the duration of their stay at the Theresa, Fidel and his compañeros were greeted with enthusiasm and genuine warmth both by the local community and from further afield. Some admirers of the Cuban Revolution made a special effort to show their appreciation. The writer and social activist Margaret Randall – twenty-three years old and heavily pregnant – was so desperate to see her hero in the flesh that she prepared her special paella recipe for him, replete with giant langoustines, chicken wings, sausage, bell peppers and saffron. She carefully transported her tin-foil-wrapped platter from her Lower East Side apartment on the subway, only for the NYPD to turn her away outside the Theresa: 'no amount of pleading convinced the police officers to let me through.'[9] Residents of East Harlem, with its large Puerto

Rican population, also came to the Theresa to cheer this new icon of Latin American liberation, as did a smattering of beatniks from Greenwich Village – one carried a placard, declaring 'Man, like us cats dig Fidel the most. He knows what's hip and bugs the squares.'[10] It was, though, the welcome afforded to Fidel by Harlem's African American population that really stood out.

Night after night, thousands gathered in the streets around the Theresa to show their support for Fidel and the Cuban Revolution.
Photograph by Gerard Gery/*Paris Match* via Getty Images

On coming to power in January 1959, Fidel had committed the revolutionary government to dismantling the racism and racial segregation that had long marred Cuban society. Within weeks, a flurry of new laws had been passed that sought to integrate previously all-white schools, beaches, swimming pools, restaurants and other facilities – both public and private – and wage war against racial discrimination in the workplace.[11] Later, historians would question the effectiveness of (and even the motivation behind) the revolutionaries' loudly proclaimed attempt to fashion a unified Cuba, free from racial divide or demarcation.[12] It was, after all, unrealistic to imagine that a system of racial prejudice that had been entrenched over centuries – and the ideology and attitudes that underpinned it – could be eradicated, in just a few months, via government decree.[13] At the time, though, the government's crusade caused a palpable sense of excitement for many – both inside Cuba and overseas. The presence of a government, less than a hundred miles off the coast of the segregated South, that was committed – in both word and deed – to ending the colour bar inevitably attracted the attention of African Americans. The New York congressman Adam Clayton Powell, Jr – one of only two African Americans in the US House of Representatives – flew to Havana just weeks after Fidel had taken power and, standing alongside the Maximum Leader before a million-strong rally in the capital, lavished praise on the new government's racial policies.[14] Much of the black press in America was also effusive. Writing in the *Baltimore Afro-American*, on 7 February 1959, Ralph Matthews (Sr) famously declared that: 'Every white man who cuffs, deprives, and abuses even the lowest colored person, simply because he is white and the other colored, should have seared upon his conscience the fact that it is possible for the tables to be turned. Castro has proved it in our time.'[15]

Five years after the US Supreme Court's ruling, in *Brown* v. *Board of Education*, that segregated schools were unconstitutional, only 0.2 per cent of black children in the Deep South attended classes alongside whites. Meanwhile, millions of African Americans across the states of the former Confederacy were still excluded from first-class citizenship – including the right to vote – through a combination of legal impediments, economic coercion and violence. And, although the cities of the north might have lacked the 'Whites Only' signs of the Jim Crow South, a powerful combination of poverty, prejudice and segregation (both formal and informal) worked to keep black Americans firmly 'in their place'. As one historian has it, 'Northern blacks lived as second-class citizens . . . trapped in an economic, political, and legal regime that seldom recognized them as equals . . . In nearly every

arena, blacks and whites lived separate, unequal lives.' Public policy and discriminatory market practices confined African Americans to the worst neighbourhoods (real estate agents routinely
refused to sell properties, and banks declined to issue loans, to
African Americans seeking to purchase homes in 'white' areas);
bars, social clubs and restaurants were often off limits, or simply unwelcoming; police brutality was a fact of daily life; and
segregated education and employment discrimination kept the
full promise of the American dream out of reach for many.[16] It
was hardly surprising, then, that the apparently radical changes
underway in Cuba – an island that had long captivated the African American imagination – inspired such interest among black
Americans.[17] Urging his fellow African Americans to 'take a close
look at the Cuban revolution', the playwright Julian Mayfield –
who had travelled to Cuba back in July – noted that, while there,
he 'saw proof that it doesn't take decades of gentle persuasion to
deal a death blow to white supremacy'. 'Great social change', he
explained, 'need not wait on the patient education' of segregationists.[18] The contrast with the Eisenhower administration's approach
was stark: speaking to a group of black leaders in May 1958, the
president had explained that 'no one is more anxious than I am
to see Negroes receive first-class citizenship in this country . . .
but you must be patient.'[19] With Ike continuing to offer a counsel
of patience and gradualism in the face of growing demands for
meaningful change, it was little wonder that many black Americans glimpsed, in revolutionary Cuba, the possibilities of a new,
and much better, world.[20]

One of those black Americans was Robert F. Williams who,
by 1960, had forged a reputation as one of America's foremost
black freedom fighters. He was an uncompromising champion of
racial equality, and the right to use armed self-defence in order to
achieve it. As president of the Monroe, North Carolina branch of
the NAACP, he had led by example – facing down the Ku Klux

Klan with machine guns and dynamite. Williams visited Cuba twice in the summer of 1960; the absence of 'white only' signs, the integrated schools, and his ability to stroll, unhindered, along the streets of Havana, all made a powerful impression on him. Writing in his weekly newsletter, *The Crusader*, Williams – who had been censured by the NAACP national leadership the year before over incendiary comments about the need to 'meet violence with violence' and 'stop lynching with lynching' – told his followers how 'on the streets of Cuba I learned for the first time in my life what it feels like to be respected as a fellow human being, and to be accepted in the human race'. It was in Cuba, he explained, that 'I realized that I was born and have lived all my life in a land that was never home'.[21] As for the swirling accusations in the American press that Cuba was going 'red', Williams had a pithy retort: 'If this is communism', he told journalists, 'I vote for communism. Cuba is an inspiration for me.'[22]

Williams was not alone. From the Havana Riviera, Richard Gibson, the head of the New York chapter of the Fair Play for Cuba Committee – and the first African American journalist to be employed by CBS – dashed off a postcard, sending 'greetings from a really free country, where our kind of people are given a tremendous welcome'. 'The progress here', Gibson declared, was 'incredible'.[23] For the historian John Henrik Clarke, meanwhile, the Cuban Revolution had 'challenged all oppressive regimes throughout the world and given hope to people still longing to be free'. William Worthy, the foreign correspondent for the *Baltimore Afro-American*, hailed Fidel's 'bold measures that overnight established equality as the law of the land' while also warning that the punitive economic measures being taken in Washington, together with a press campaign vilifying the revolution, suggested the possibility of an American military intervention. Such a prospect was, he declared, entirely without justification: there was absolutely 'nothing going on' in Cuba that should 'scare anyone except those

Yankees and wealthy Cubans whose ill-gotten profits are being taken away [. . .] The State Department', Worthy claimed, 'knows this as well as I do.'[24]

Mainstream public opinion in America began to move against the Cuban Revolution during the early months of 1960, amid accusations of growing communist influence on the island. But African Americans were, as one leading historian has pointed out, 'much slower to turn away from Castro'.[25] After all, they had grown used to hearing that supporters of civil rights were, in fact, 'reds', and were all too aware that some of Castro's biggest critics just happened to be vociferous southern segregationists. In the autumn of 1960, there was likely no more receptive location for Fidel and his fellow revolutionaries in the whole of the United States than Harlem – the unofficial capital of black America.

Founded in 1658 as a Dutch village (and named after Haarlem in the Netherlands), nineteenth-century Harlem was a predominantly Italian and Jewish neighbourhood until the onset of the Great Migration, which saw some 1.6 million African Americans leave the rural South between the First and Second World Wars, headed for the cities of the north. New York was, unsurprisingly, one of the most popular destinations and, between 1916 and 1930, tens of thousands of African American migrants settled in Harlem, whose population went from being ten per cent black in 1910 to seventy per cent in the space of just two decades.[26] This dramatic population influx was accompanied by an explosion of political organizing, with the NAACP (which was committed to eradicating racial prejudice and promoting equal rights) and Marcus Garvey's Universal Negro Improvement Association (whose slogan, 'Africa for the Africans, at home and abroad', encapsulated its Pan-African orientation) leading the fight for civil rights.[27] The neighbourhood was also home to a remarkable cultural flowering, which has come to be known as the 'Harlem Renaissance'.

From the end of the First World War through the start of the Great Depression, artists such as Aaron Douglas, poets including Langston Hughes and Countee Cullen, writers like Claude McKay and Zora Neale Hurston, and musicians, including Duke Ellington and Louis Armstrong, were at the forefront of the 'New Negro' movement, which challenged racial stereotypes, celebrated black pride, and promoted racial 'uplift'. It was one of the most exciting and consequential periods in modern African American history.[28]

By 1960, Harlem's renaissance heyday lay more than three decades in the past. You could still catch a show at the Apollo (Fred Barr and 'Doc' Wheeler's Gospel Caravan were playing there the week of Fidel's visit) and, after a hard night at Club Baron on Lenox and 132nd Street, enjoy soul food at Jenny Lou's, where James Baldwin and Sidney Poitier liked to eat; but the ravages of the Great Depression had taken a heavy toll.[29] Many of Harlem's famous tenement buildings were now little more than rat-infested slums; garbage was too often piled up in the streets; crime was endemic, and drug addiction on the rise; rates of asthma, venereal disease and tuberculosis were shamefully high (in 1952, the mortality rate for TB in Harlem was fifteen times that for Flushing, the largely white neighbourhood of Queens).[30] Forty-eight hours before Fidel descended on Harlem, the *New York Amsterdam News* ran a story on the plight of one Lillie M. Bradley, a mother of four who was paying an extortionate rent for what was little more than a dilapidated firetrap a mile or so north-west of the Theresa. The six-room apartment, which was in desperate need of a fresh coat of paint, was blighted by alarming cracks in the walls, gaping holes in the floors and ceilings, and doors that were hanging off their hinges. The ceiling in one of the bedrooms had recently caved in (luckily no one had been sleeping at the time), and the bathroom had at times been rendered unusable by overflows from the dwellings above. Although a spokesperson for the landlord claimed that Bradley, a 'trouble maker who is always starting something', must have been responsible for ruining the 'beautiful' apartment, other tenants confirmed that the entire block was in a dire state.[31]

Moreover, despite post-war New York's reputation as a bastion of liberalism, Harlem was no oasis of racial equality. The neighbourhood's black children, for instance, had to settle for a substandard education in poorly funded, overcrowded and segregated public schools that were staffed by unqualified or under-qualified teachers. Meanwhile, police brutality and corruption were rife – with many officers implicated in the 'numbers game' (an illegal daily lottery) and others in the pay of organized crime. And while the white NYPD officers who walked the beat in Harlem were all too willing to turn a blind eye to crime, they nevertheless insisted on respect, and were quick to demean, humiliate and brutalize any individual who – as they saw it – had been insufficiently deferent, or had deigned to challenge their authority.[32] Writing in 1960, Harlem native James Baldwin gave voice to the community's feelings when it came to New York's finest:

> None of the Police Commissioner's men, even with the best
> will in the world, have any way of understanding the lives
> led by the people they swagger about in twos and threes
> controlling. Their very presence is an insult, and it would
> be, even if they spent their entire day feeding gumdrops
> to children. They represent the force of the white world,
> and that world's real intentions are, simply, for that world's
> criminal profit and ease, to keep the black man corralled
> up here, in his place. The badge, the gun in the holster, and
> the swinging club make vivid what will happen should his
> rebellion become overt. Rare, indeed, is the Harlem citizen,
> from the most circumspect church member to the most
> shiftless adolescent, who does not have a long tale to tell of

police incompetence, injustice, or brutality. I myself have witnessed and endured it more than once. The businessmen and racketeers also have a story. And so do the prostitutes.

The verdict of local NAACP leader L. Joseph Overton was equally scathing: Harlem, he said, was a 'police state'.[33]

But as the black feminist intellectual Michele Wallace, who grew up in Harlem in the 1950s and 1960s, has pointed out, 'Harlem isn't what you think it is'. It is 'not merely one seething ghetto but a place where people, black people of all different sorts, actually live and choose to live'. With its burgeoning black middle and professional class, Harlem was 'mink coats and two-car families . . . as well as no hot water and welfare checks'. When walking down Seventh Avenue with her grandmother on Sunday mornings, she later recalled, 'all along our way to the opulence of Abyssinian Baptist Church, the old men would tip their hats and old women in mink stoles and smart black suits would stop to say hello.'[34] The neighbourhood's diversity and nonconformity were captured by the African American poet, and Fidel admirer, LeRoi Jones (who later changed his name to Amiri Baraka). In his essay 'City of Harlem', he described a 125th Street that was 'jammed with shoppers and walkers', with the record stores 'scream[ing] through loudspeakers at the street': 'Young girls, doctors, pimps, detectives, preachers, drummers, accountants, gamblers, labor organizers, postmen, wives, Muslims, junkies, the employed: all going someplace – an endless stream of Americans, whose singularity in America is that they are black and can never honestly enter into the lunatic asylum of white America.'[35]

The neighbourhood certainly retained something of its old cultural magnetism. Romare Bearden and Norman Lewis, for instance, continued to produce internationally acclaimed art, even as a new generation came to the fore (Harlem native Faith Ringgold, for instance, was poised to create some of the most remarkable and provocative art of the 1960s).[36] The Harlem Writers Guild, founded by John Oliver Killens, Rosa Guy and John Henrik Clarke in 1950, was still going strong. Growing from modest origins in a small storefront office, over the years the group nurtured the talents of Maya Angelou, Alice Childress, Lorraine Hansberry, Audre Lorde, Julian Mayfield and numerous other distinguished poets, novelists and playwrights.[37] It was jazz, though, with which Harlem was synonymous. During the early 1940s, a generation of young musicians, including Dizzy Gillespie, Charlie Parker and Thelonious Monk, had pioneered the bebop style in Harlem's jazz clubs, especially Minton's Playhouse and Monroe's Uptown House. (In contrast to the popular swing style of big band jazz, bebop was characterized by rapid chord progression, a fast tempo, improvisation, dissonance and harmonic richness.[38]) In the decade that followed, jazz retained its appeal among the denizens of Harlem.[39] On Friday 23 September 1960, for instance, Wells' Restaurant – famous for its chicken and waffles, said to be the best in the world – launched a new addition to Harlem's night-time scene, 'Jazz at the Upstairs'. The vibraphonist Dave Pike and his Quartet were booked for the launch.[40] Meanwhile, the legendary nightclub Smalls' Paradise offered live performances from the likes of Charlie Mariano and the King Curtis Quintet.[41] Just around the corner from the Theresa, at 319 West 125th Street, was the Baby Grand, a legendary art deco saloon bar that featured some of the hottest acts of the day – including Charles Mingus and stars from rhythm and blues like Big Maybelle, Etta James and Mary Ann Fisher. Fisher, who had toured with Ray Charles (he wrote the hit song 'Mary Ann' about her), was on the bill during Fidel's stay.[42] Harlem was not, though, all high-end jazz, abstract expressionism and literary sophistication. As the community's numerous bowling leagues prepared to resume, following the summer break, the excitement of the new season was augmented by the announcement that, at the end of September, Harlem Lanes – a beautiful new state-of-

the-art 'bowling palace', featuring thirty AMF automatic pinspot-
ters, as well as a cocktail lounge, restaurant and snack bar – would
be opening its doors, seven days a week.[43]

In addition to its cultural richness, Harlem had an exceptionally
strong sense of political vitality, and its streets fizzed with political
activism. Rallies, protests, fundraisers and boycotts were common
features of the local political culture, as black Harlemites, often
excluded from formal political and economic power, mobilized in
impressive numbers to protest inequalities, and organized at the
community level to demand their rights.[44] In September 1955, for
instance, 10,000 people had turned out for a rally protesting the
brutal lynching of fourteen-year-old Emmett Till, in Mississippi,
while, in the spring of 1960, as the lunch-counter sit-ins rocked the
Jim Crow South, the New York-based Congress of Racial Equality
organized sympathy protests outside the F. W. Woolworth's Store
on 125th Street.[45] That autumn, Ornette Coleman, the controversial
pioneer of free jazz, was one of the main draws at a 'Jazz for Sit-In'
concert that was held to raise money for the southern movement.[46]
But while there was plenty of sympathy for the southern struggle,
black Harlemites were also engaged in a fierce civil rights fight of
their own. One of the more high-profile campaigns involved a
battle against segregated schools (the situation in New York was
just as bad as in southern cities like Atlanta, Memphis and New
Orleans), led by the 'Harlem Nine'. In the autumn of 1958, this
group of black mothers – whose number included the activist Mae
Mallory – outraged by the poor quality of the education on offer,
kept their children out of the three all-black junior high schools to
which they had been assigned, and demanded that they be allowed
to enrol them in better schools, elsewhere in the city. That December, Judge Justine Polier ruled that the three schools in question
offered an 'inferior education' as a result of racial discrimination
and, in a compromise settlement, the children were enrolled in a
better school elsewhere in the neighbourhood.[47] Police brutality,

meanwhile, sparked growing pressure for meaningful reforms, as well as angry protests on the streets. More than five hundred gathered outside the West 123rd Street police station on 13 July 1959, for example, after Charles Samuel, a black postal clerk, was beaten – and then arrested – after intervening in the brutal arrest of Carmela Caviglione. The boxing champion Sugar Ray Robinson was summoned to help calm the crowd – eventually persuading them to disperse quietly only after assuring them (wrongly) that Caviglione and Samuel had not been beaten.[48]

Harlem was also, as one scholar has put it, the historic 'incubator for black nationalism in the United States'. *The Hate that Hate Produced* might have made the Nation of Islam famous, but the Muslim Brotherhood, the United African Nationalist Movement (led by James B. Lawson) and the Universal African Nationalist Movement were just some of the organizations that were competing with it for followers, for money and for influence. 'Harlem Square', the area in front of Lewis H. Michaux's National Memorial African Book Store (nicknamed 'the House of Common Sense and the Home of Proper Propaganda') on Seventh Avenue and 125th Street – just around the corner from the Theresa – served for decades as an informal meeting place. Under the watchful eye of Michaux – himself an assured, rapid-fire speaker, who typically sported a fez – activists pushed newspapers, enterprising vendors hawked pies and cakes, and street orators, including the legendary Edward 'Pork Chop' Davis and Carlos Cooks, soapboxed their particular versions of black nationalism. Amid all the diversity of opinion and debate, the nationalists agreed that, as Clarke put it, 'the Afro-American constitutes what is tantamount to an exploited colony within a sovereign nation. Their fight is for national, and personal liberation. No people are really free until they become the instrument of their own liberation.' They were also united in disparaging the 'respectable', middle-class spokesmen of the mainstream NAACP and National Urban League: a 'crumb-crunching, cocktail-sipping Uncle Tom leadership' that was 'paid by colonialists', according to Abbey Lincoln, the jazz singer, activist and founder of the Cultural Association for Women of African Heritage.[49]

Black Harlemites – whether Christian or Muslim, nationalist or integrationist – together with their fellow African Americans across the country, shared a keen interest in political developments across Africa and Asia, where the pace of decolonization was quickening. In May 1960, the NAACP's official magazine, *The Crisis*, editorialized that 'American Negroes take courage and hope from an independent Ghana and Guinea; revolts in the Congo stiffen the resolve of Africans in South Africa'. 'Everywhere', it proclaimed, 'the colored peoples are resolved that the arrogance and domination of whites must go.'[50] At the end of July, Jaja Anucha Wachuku, the speaker of the Nigerian House of Representatives, visited Harlem to address leading figures from the worlds of business, education and politics. At a meeting held at the offices of the United Mutual Insurance Company on Lenox Avenue, Wachuku declared that 'We in Nigeria want to know you, your men, your women, your business women. We want you to help us build our country,' and proclaimed that 'the people in Nigeria will not be satisfied until the whole of Africa is liberated.'[51] In the run-up to the opening of the UN General Assembly, meanwhile, the *New York Citizen-Call* ran a series of articles on African leaders, including the Congo's Patrice Lumumba, Togo's Sylvanus Olympio, Tanganyika's Julius Nyerere, and Kenneth Kaunda of Northern Rhodesia.[52] For its part, the influential *Chicago Defender* heralded the arrival of the 'voice of New Africa' at the United Nations: an 'Africa which is seething with nationalism and whose speedy rise out of the dust of colonialism has bewildered the white world'.[53] As they watched European colonialism crumble and a new generation of black Africans take power in their own right, many of Harlem's African Americans not only took inspiration from these movements for national liberation, but asserted that their own fight for justice, dignity and freedom was a part of the same, global struggle. In Harlem, then, Fidel was among friends.[54]

There was no hiding the fact that, from the moment that he arrived at the Theresa, Fidel was greeted as a hero by the local community. It seemed, the Cuban magazine *Bohemia* noted, as if Harlemites now lived 'permanently outdoors' as day after day, and night after night, thousands gathered in the streets around the hotel, shouting 'Viva Castro, Viva Cuba!' and carrying placards. As one slogan had it, 'Fidel is Welcome in Harlem Anytime. Cuba Practices Real Democracy. No Race Discrimination.' When some opponents of the revolution attempted to drive past the Theresa, FIEL radio reported how 'the "lads" of Harlem responded to this insolence with a shower of rotten eggs'. Many locals strained to catch a glimpse of the Theresa's most famous guest, and raucous cheers broke out whenever Fidel appeared at the window to wave or emerged from the hotel's lobby onto the street.[55] Writing from London, the activist Eslanda Robeson declared that she and her husband, Paul – who was in England to record a BBC radio series – felt 'especially proud that we are colored Americans' in light of the warm and very public welcome that Fidel had received from Harlem. The friendliness of the reception had, she explained, made for 'a very heartwarming sight on television, and it reads beautiful in the newspapers . . .'[56] Speaking to the African American journalist Alfred Duckett, one taxi driver encapsulated the reaction of many locals: 'them downtown white folk didn't treat him right so he come up here to Harlem where he could feel at home.' This warmth was explained, in part, by the Cubans' commitment to racial equality.[57] Just in case anyone doubted this commitment to racial justice, though, Fidel made a point of flying in his Army Chief of Staff, Juan Almeida, less than twenty-four hours after checking in at the Theresa. When, on the evening of Wednesday 21 September, Almeida took a (much-trailed) stroll around the neighbourhood before dropping in to Teddy's Shanty for a cup of coffee, he 'received wild applause from many of the estimated 20,000 spectators in the vicinity' who viewed him as one of their own.[58] In fact, he had hardly managed to get halfway down the block before being surrounded by hundreds of locals, who greeted him with shouts of '*Viva Almeida!*' and 'Brother!' Soon the army chief and Antonio Núñez Jiménez, who accompanied him on the walk, were caught up in a 'whirlwind' of several thousand supporters. Almeida, who took the opportunity to flirt with the waitresses, appeared to enjoy the attention.[59]

Although Fidel himself spent much of 21 September holed up in his suite, working on his speech for the United Nations, sustained by nothing more than a ham-and-egg breakfast and a lunch of fried chicken, he let it be known that he was keen to meet with local black leaders.[60] However, when word reached NAACP headquarters at 20 West 40th Street, just south of Bryant Park, it immediately set alarm bells ringing.

The NAACP had survived the McCarthyism of the late 1940s and early 1950s by expelling the small number of known communists from its ranks, distancing itself from the American Communist Party, Communist Front organizations and suspected 'fellow travellers', and burnishing its patriotic credentials. Theirs was to be a fight against American racism waged in strict accordance with America's own constitutional framework. As the ideological struggle between the Soviet Union and the United States intensified, the organization had adopted a policy of what historian Mary Dudziak has termed 'Cold War civil rights': Washington, it argued, would be better able to meet the challenge of leading the 'free world', counter Soviet propaganda that emphasized American hypocrisy, and win the 'hearts and minds' of the newly independent peoples of Africa and Asia by delivering on the promise of first-class citizenship and democratic freedom for all of its citizens.

The destruction of Jim Crow segregation, then, was a patriotic act that would help the nation to win the Cold War.[61] On hearing of Fidel's overtures, Gloster Current, the NAACP's staunchly anti-communist director of branches, promptly fired off a telegram to the organization's entire New York leadership: 'Understand Castro seeking conference with NAACP leaders in New York. Urgently request that you check with National Office before accepting any invitations for such a meeting.'

One NAACP leader who did not get the message was Joe Overton, president of the New York City branch – he was not at his Lenox Avenue home when the courier called.[62] Overton, a longtime civil rights and labour leader, had been elected to office in November 1958, promising to revitalize the branch. His preference for direct action, rather than committee meetings, had already led him to clash with the NAACP national leadership when a campaign on behalf of Harlem's black liquor salesmen – who were restricted to working in African American neighbourhoods – had led to embarrassing accusations of 'cheap demagoguery' and 'racial chauvinism' amid claims that, by seeking 'preferential treatment' for black salesmen, the organization was promoting 'reverse discrimination'.[63] Overton knew full well that his willingness to meet with Castro would cause palpitations among the Association's top brass and, when pressed by a reporter on whether he was offering an official endorsement of the Cuban Revolution, he 'beat a hasty retreat'.[64] Little surprise that, just a few weeks later, Roy Wilkins, the NAACP's executive secretary, and Gloster Current eased their errant colleague from office.[65] For the coming generation of activists – who were less worried than their parents about being red-baited, who evinced a refreshing enthusiasm for taking the battle to the streets and were pretty relaxed about the politics of radical or even revolutionary change – at times the NAACP appeared hopelessly out of step.

*

While some Harlemites were undoubtedly fans of Fidel's politics, many more simply took pride in the fact that their community – a 'maligned ghetto', typically hidden away from public view and off limits to foreign dignitaries* – was now the centre of worldwide attention.[66] As Duckett put it, the locals were 'plainly, simply and understandably flattered and appreciative' that Fidel Castro had paid them the compliment of staying 'uptown'.[67] Jackie Robinson – the baseball star who had integrated the major leagues back in 1947 – decried the 'obvious attempts' by communists to curry favour. But even he was forced to concede that Castro's decision to stay at the Theresa had given Harlem 'a real lift – a sense of pride'.[68] It was a sentiment echoed in the pages of the *New York Citizen-Call*, which noted how several Harlemites had 'expressed hostility for some daily papers who were saying "nasty" things about Castro. One man said, "they just don't want us to have nothing. I'm glad Castro came up here to show these people we are somebody".'[69]

It was, though, hard to escape the broader consequences of Fidel's stay. According to one Havana radio station, Harlem was 'boiling', and – by relocating to the Theresa – Fidel had 'pulled aside the screen, showing the world that the Negroes, kept apart in a quarter as if they had the plague', wanted freedom and – as their cheers demonstrated – liked him. Harlem's African Americans, whose 'only crime is not to be white in a country like the United States, know that only a revolution can save them'. 'Every day', they claimed, 'it is harder for the . . . masters to contain the slaves.'[70]

Fidel's move to the Hotel Theresa was especially embarrassing for the US government precisely because it challenged directly the story about race relations that they liked to tell – both to Americans and to the wider world. They sought to frame segregation and

* When Khrushchev had insisted on visiting Harlem during his 1959 visit to New York, he had been whisked along the neighbourhood's near-deserted streets in his limousine, at seven o'clock on a Sunday morning, on his way to the airport.

institutionalized white supremacy as a regional problem, largely confined for historic reasons to the South and – thanks to a combination of court rulings, federal legislation and carefully crafted initiatives – in the process of being eradicated in a peaceful and democratic manner, as mandated by the country's constitutional form of government. By shining the world's media spotlight on Harlem, Fidel exposed this as little more than a self-serving myth: the stain of segregation was alive and well in the urban north, including in New York, one of the country's most famous and important cities, and a citadel of mid-century American liberalism (the city's mayor, Robert F. Wagner, Jr., was a champion of organized labour, who supported affordable housing and healthcare, and presented the Big Apple as a thriving, tolerant and cosmopolitan city).[71]

Many commentators agreed that Fidel's move to the Theresa constituted a 'direct slap in the face of US racial practices'.[72] The 'stiff-necked' officials at the State Department, proclaimed one, were likely chewing 'their linen cuffs to shreds'.[73] Writing in the *New York Amsterdam News*, James Hicks described racial discrimination as the point where the US was 'most vulnerable to foreign attack. It is our Achilles heel – our soft, unprotected underbelly.'[74] Meanwhile, Drew Pearson – one of America's best-known journalists – declared in his syndicated column that Fidel's 'sudden flutter from a midtown New York Hotel to one in Harlem, leaving chicken feathers behind, was part of a carefully calculated move to hit the United States where the Communist world considers us weak – with our Negro population'. It was also, Pearson claimed, intended to appeal to the new African countries that had joined the United Nations, whose leaders had noted 'the spectacular manner' with which Fidel had 'planted his entourage in Harlem'.[75]

Even better – as far as many African Americans were concerned – Harlem's gain had come at the expense of 'The Man'. As one bystander put it, Castro 'sure made a fool out of them white folks'.[76] There was particular delight at widespread (though untrue) rumours that the government had been so desperate to prevent the Cubans from moving to Harlem that they had offered to put them up, for free, in midtown. Little wonder, then, that – as Duckett put it – Harlem was 'laughing up its sleeve at the clumsy goof which this country has made in international diplomacy'.[77]

Much of Harlem might have been laughing, as well as cheering, but not everyone was quite so enamoured with the Cubans. Several hundred Baptist ministers voiced their displeasure and, speaking at a reunion of the 369th Veterans Association – the famed 'Harlem Hellfighters' – on Sunday 25 September, Adam Clayton Powell, Jr, deplored what he viewed as 'Fidel Castro's use of Harlem as a battleground for his own political ends'. The congressman – who had soured on Fidel amid concerns about growing communist influence and, perhaps more important, wounded pride that his own advice to Cuba's new leader had been consistently ignored – exclaimed that 'we, the Negro people, have enough problems of our own without the additional burden of Dr. Castro's confusion'.[78]

While Powell was content to launch verbal missiles, Cuban opponents of Castro, including former Batista supporters who had fled after the revolution, took to the streets to challenge the *Fidelistas* directly. Inevitably, these interactions occasionally boiled over into physical confrontation: pro- and anti-Castro groups jostled each other in the streets, threw eggs and traded punches.[79] But a far more serious altercation took place on the afternoon of 21 September at the El Prado restaurant, eight blocks south of Central Park. At about 3.20 p.m. a dozen or so supporters of the Cuban Revolution descended on the 'dimly lit' restaurant, famous for its Creole food, to confront five members of the leading anti-Castro organization, the Cuban Democratic Revolutionary Front, who were wearing buttons that declared 'Khrushchev Kastro Not

Wanted'. Amid a hail of insults and beer bottles, shots suddenly rang out. Luis Rodriguez, a twenty-five-year-old opponent of Castro, was hit in the shoulder. But in the chaos, a far greater tragedy unfolded. A bystander, nine-year-old Magdalena Urdaneta, was shot in the right side of her back. The young Venezuelan was holidaying in New York with her family: a treat, it was said, for 'getting good marks in school'. Magdalena underwent emergency surgery at a nearby hospital, but succumbed to her injuries the next day. As her distraught parents made plans to fly her body back to Caracas, the Cuban Democratic Revolutionary Front issued a statement from its office at 1650 Broadway. Little Magdalena was, they declared, 'the innocent victim of a blood-hungry tyrant'. The State Department, meanwhile, declared that the young girl was the victim of 'an aggressive attack by adherents of the Castro regime'. While the Cubans railed against this 'monstrous' lie, much of the US press seemed to agree with Washington's version of events.[80] As one provocative headline writer had it: 'Because Castro Is in Harlem, A Child Is Dead'.[81]

# 6

# THURSDAY 22 SEPTEMBER

... the President does not intend, under any circumstances, to be present at the UN while Khrushchev is there and will not address the General Assembly during the opening general debate. This is a final decision.

US STATE DEPARTMENT, 2 SEPTEMBER

For President Eisenhower, Thursday 22 September began early, with a 6 a.m. breakfast at the White House, before heading to the helicopter that was stationed on the South Lawn for the short flight to Andrews Air Force Base in Maryland. There, he boarded the presidential VC137 Boeing 707 Stratoliner that would fly him to New York for the UN meeting. Eisenhower's plane touched down just after eight o'clock and, after he was welcomed by the city's mayor, Robert Wagner, and the Secretary of State, Christian Herter, the presidential motorcade set off for Turtle Bay. Eisenhower's astute and long-serving secretary, Ann C. Whitman, accompanied the president on the trip, and was struck by the 'wonderful' crowds who had turned out and the 'charged' atmosphere in the city. 'As the president's limousine emerged from the Manhattan end of the Queens Midtown Tunnel', reported the *New York Times*, 'it was greeted by cheering office workers and residents.' It was a welcome sight for the sixty-nine-year-old, who had less than four months left in office, and his 'pleasure was apparent as he responded by standing up in the half-open car to wave'.[1]

At the start of September, when Nikita Khrushchev formally announced his intention to lead the Soviet delegation, the president's initial instinct was to 'totally ignore the fact that he was coming'. Rather than risk going toe to toe with a man whom he now derided, in private, as a 'murderer', Eisenhower decided instead to attend the Assembly in December to deliver a vale-dictory address.[2] In Washington's opinion, it was clear that the Soviets intended to create a sort of 'grandiose propaganda circus'[3] in New York, and it was therefore considered 'inappropriate and undignified for heads of state or government to lend themselves to such [an] exercise'. On 2 September, the State Department issued a circular to all US diplomatic posts, clarifying that Eisen-hower would neither 'participate in UN General Assembly or be there while Khrushchev is', nor would he address the General Assembly during its opening general debate.[4] It was a position that was supported by some of America's closest allies: Paris, for instance, concurred that it was 'wise not to attempt to compete with Khrushchev in demagoguery'.[5]

Within days, though, everything had changed. In addition to announcing his own attendance at the UN, Khrushchev had, behind the scenes, been busily urging the leaders of the so-called non-aligned countries to join him at the Assembly, in order to dis-cuss disarmament and 'world peace'.[6] Made up of nations, mainly in Asia and Africa, that challenged the bipolar framework of the Cold War (they offered fealty to neither Moscow nor Washing-ton and supported peaceful coexistence), the neutralist bloc rep-resented a sizeable proportion of the world's population, and was capable of exercising real influence in the United Nations.[7] In short order, Yugoslavia's Josip Broz Tito, Gamal Abdel Nasser of the United Arab Republic, Indonesia's Sukarno, Ghanaian pres-ident Kwame Nkrumah and India's Jawaharlal Nehru all intimated that they, too, would be travelling to New York – in addition to the leaders of Poland, Hungary, Czechoslovakia, Romania and, of course, Cuba. Washington's stance of cool indifference was no longer tenable.

Just before noon on Thursday 8 September, Andrew Goodpaster – who, as Eisenhower's Staff Secretary, was one of the most powerful men in the White House – reported to Herter that:

> the UN meeting had been on the President's mind and the President was inclined to think he should go up . . . He feels that if he waits and then goes up that Khrushchev has gotten the jump here. Khrushchev could stay around for some time working up the situation and snarling and accusing the U.S. The President thought he should make the opening speech. He said it would probably be attacked and rebutted by Khrushchev but it would be better that than the other way around.[8]

On 14 September James Hagerty, the White House Press Secretary, announced that the president would now be travelling to the United Nations on the morning of 22 September, for the purpose of addressing the General Assembly.[9] For Washington, it now became imperative to ensure that there would be 'a number of strong voices' in New York, able to 'speak out' in defence of the West and to counter the anticipated communist offensive.[10] It was a position with which London agreed wholeheartedly: on 15 September, for instance, the prime minister informed his cabinet that there was now 'a serious danger' that Khrushchev would 'dominate' the General Assembly and, by impressing the new African members of the United Nations, 'secure [a] considerable political advantage'. Sir Patrick Dean, Britain's ambassador to the United Nations, called for the 'big guns' to help take on the 'Communist barrage'.[11] The prime ministers of Canada and Australia, John Diefenbaker and Robert Menzies, were primed and, on 20 September, Eisenhower wrote to his old friend Harold Macmillan (who had already floated the prospect of attending), stating that 'I now believe that your attendance at the General Assembly would be a real service to the West'.[12] After discussing the matter with the

Queen at Balmoral and with his cabinet in London, the British prime minister readily agreed to fly to New York.[13]

The game was on.

President Eisenhower might have decided to speak at the UN, but he had absolutely no intention of circulating on the floor of the General Assembly – where he risked running into the Soviet leader.[14] At 10.46 a.m., in a piece of pre-arranged choreography, Eisenhower arrived at the General Assembly Building. Based on a Le Corbusier design, this impressive trapezoid structure featured concave, windowless longitudinal facades and a north wall constructed of translucent glass, set between broad marble columns. Pulling up outside the building's public entrance, he was met by Jehan de Noue, who escorted him to the Secretary General's office, tucked away behind the podium of the giant, domed General Assembly chamber. Although the US president had initially hoped to give the first of the day's speeches from a member state, Brazil had proved reluctant to give up its traditional slot at the top of the bill.* And so, while Foreign Minister Horacio Lafer was finishing his remarks, Eisenhower chatted amiably with Dag Hammarskjöld and Frederick Boland.[15]

At 11.12 a.m., Eisenhower stepped onto the podium to address his fellow leaders, and the wider world.[16] Speaking against the backdrop of the UN's iconic olive branch emblem, the US president began by welcoming those nations – including Cameroon, the Central African Republic, Congo, Ivory Coast and Niger – who were 'represented here for the first time'. Noting that the 'drive of self-determination and of rising human aspirations' was producing 'ferment' across great swathes of the globe, Eisenhower called for

---

* Asked about the origins of this tradition in 2010, Desmond Parker, UN Chief of Protocol, explained that 'in very early times, when no one wanted to speak first, Brazil always offered to speak first. And so they . . . earned the right to speak first at the General Assembly.'

a 'renewed attack on poverty, illiteracy, and disease', and promised substantial additional American aid for Africa, Asia, Latin America and the Middle East. After urging the international community to commit to the exclusively peaceful exploration of outer space, the president called on the communist nations to resume efforts to create a 'workable system of disarmament', pledging that the United States was prepared to 'submit to any international inspection, provided only that it is effective and truly reciprocal'.

Imploring that 'narrow national advantage' be set aside in favour of positive and constructive international action, Eisenhower declared that it was 'only through the United Nations and its truly democratic processes' that humanity would be able to make 'real and universal progress toward the goal of peace with justice'. The president ended his address by looking to the future:

As we enter the decade of the 1960s, let us launch a renewed effort to strengthen this international community; to forge new bonds between its members in undertaking new ventures on behalf of all mankind.

As we take up this task, let us not delude ourselves that the absence of war alone is a sufficient basis for a peaceful world. I repeat, we must also build a world of justice under law, and we must overcome poverty, illiteracy, and disease.

'Let us go forward together', he said, 'leaving none behind.'[17]

As Eisenhower left the rostrum, both Nikita Khrushchev and Fidel Castro ostentatiously refused to join with the customary applause.[18]

Writing in the British *Guardian* newspaper, James Morris complained that the president's speech lacked 'vision, inspiration, emotion'; 'Hardly a heart, a fear, did he stir, hardly a tear of gratitude did he raise, not one flickering vision of conciliation did he evoke among his yearning listeners.' Instead, Morris declared, the leader of the free world 'spoke like a man who has shrugged his shoulders'.[19] But, while *Le Monde* described the speech as 'a bit pale' and the Soviet news agency TASS dismissed it as containing 'nothing new', not everyone was quite so harsh in their judgement.[20]

The British Foreign Office, rather predictably, praised the speech as 'one of the most constructive and important' in the history of the United Nations, while Andrew Cordier, executive assistant to Dag Hammarskjöld, privately welcomed what he characterized as 'by far the most sweeping support that the United States has given to the United Nations in fifteen years'. Perhaps more important, representatives of the so-called uncommitted nations appear to have been genuinely impressed by what one Indonesian diplomat described as the 'temperate and restrained quality' of Eisenhower's remarks, as well as with some of his specific proposals to support the developing world.[21]

Some commentators, too, were supportive. *The Times* of London, for instance, editorialized that 'the great merit of President Eisenhower's speech is that it was not an attempt to answer Mr. Khrushchev's points before they were made but a direct appeal to the Assembly to take the measure of its capabilities' and see the UN as 'at least an effective nucleus of world government'.[22] There was a positive reaction in Turkey, Greece, Italy and India, while the *New York Times* columnist James Reston hailed the speech as a master stroke, commending the president for playing 'this country's strongest card . . . that the ideals and national interests of the United States are closer to the ideals and interests of the small nations than are the national interests of the Communist world.'[23] When pressed by reporters, even Nikita Khrushchev was forced to concede that Eisenhower's proposals on disarmament contained some 'good aspects', and that the speech, overall, had been 'conciliatory'.[24]

When it came to US–Cuban relations, however, there was precious little evidence of conciliation. On finishing his speech at the

UN, Eisenhower returned immediately to the Waldorf-Astoria where, at 1 p.m., in an effort to improve regional relations, he hosted a lavish luncheon for the heads of eighteen Latin American delegations to the United Nations.[25] In brief remarks, the president declared that 'our nations are bound together not merely by inescapable ties of geography. We are strong, and we are worthwhile only because we are bound together by things of the spirit. The dedication we have to imperishable values, of human dignity and liberty, and the sovereignty of our respective nations – these are the things that are worthwhile.' 'But,' Eisenhower continued, 'because we do believe in these values . . . we must devote ourselves' to ensuring a better life 'not merely for such people as sit around this table, but for the lowliest peon, the lowliest farmer' and – in a clear sign that the antics at the Hotel Theresa were playing on his mind – 'the lowliest dweller in Harlem . . .'[26]

Four miles away, Harlem's most famous new resident was treating twelve employees of the Theresa to steaks and a round of beers in the hotel's downstairs coffee shop. In a deliberate and, as it turned out, spectacularly counterproductive White House snub, Fidel had not been invited to join his fellow Latin American leaders at the president's table. But the Cuban premier was in a magnanimous mood. 'We are not sad,' he said. 'We are going to take it easy. We wish them a good appetite.' In any case, he declared, he was 'honored to lunch with the poor and humble people of Harlem'.[27] For their part, the surprised employees declared themselves more than satisfied to be hosting the Maximum Leader in their hotel, and chatted with Fidel and other members of the Cuban delegation 'in a friendly and cordial tone'.[28] The whole thing was a brilliant PR retort. *Revolución* led with front-page photographs of the two, very different lunch gatherings, pointing out that while 'The shark and the sardines eat together' Fidel had deemed it an 'honour to eat with humble'.[29] Cuban radio, meanwhile, disparaged the 'rude and idiotic' behaviour of the US government.

Rather than being offended, they declared, Cubans should feel 'proud'. After all, why break bread with the 'imperialist rulers' and their 'Latin American lackeys', when one could eat, instead, with the 'Negroes in Harlem . . . who are denied their rights and who live in horrible conditions'.[30]

While President Eisenhower might not have wanted to party with Fidel Castro (whose 'public performances', the commander-in-chief privately suggested, 'appeared to be the acts of a man mentally unbalanced'), others proved more enthusiastic. That evening, while Ike was enjoying a stag dinner in his Waldorf-Astoria suite with friends – including Clifford Roberts, chairman of Augusta National (home of the Masters golf championship), and the businessman George E. Allen – Fidel and his compañeros were honoured guests at an altogether different party, which was held in the Theresa's ballroom, the Skyline Room.[31]

Organized at short notice by the New York chapter of the Fair Play for Cuba Committee, the reception drew the great and the good of Harlem – the sort of 'high-rated' figures, quipped the *Baltimore Afro-American*, who could usually be found 'swarming at such events' – as well as black activists and a host of left-liberal celebrities, actors, artists and intellectuals.[32] Among the 250 or so guests were the black freedom fighter Robert F. Williams, the black poet, playwright and activist LeRoi Jones/Amiri Baraka, the New Left intellectual and Columbia University sociologist C. Wright Mills and the radical campaigning journalist I. F. Stone. The Beat poet Allen Ginsberg, who had achieved international fame with the publication of 'Howl' in 1956, managed the extraordinary feat of rendering the Cubans momentarily speechless when, after shaking Fidel's hand, he explained to them that 'Marijuana is revolutionary, but the imperialists have invented all kinds of stories about it so no one will smoke and rebel.' What, he wondered, did they think about pot, and when were they going to legalize it? Caught off guard, the Cubans mumbled that they did not want anything to interfere with the important revolutionary work that remained to be done. Ginsberg, who believed that no 'good society' could be successfully founded 'on the basis of old-style human consciousness', was not convinced. Reflecting on the encounter a year later, he explained that, while he was 'NOT down on the Cubans or anti their revolution', no revolution could succeed in truly liberating the masses unless it also challenged 'the rules of identity forced on them by already outmoded means of consciousness' and rejected 'puritanical censorship'.[33]

Carleton Beals, who had travelled from his home in Clinton, Connecticut, to attend the party at the Theresa, was something of a hero in Cuba for his 1933 exposé of the Machado dictatorship (and American complicity with it), *The Crime of Cuba*. Although he had initially been dismissive of Castro's 26 July Movement (they were, he said, 'rebels without a cause'), he had been won around, and in February 1960 became a founding member of the Fair Play for Cuba Committee. When Fidel had arrived in New York on 18 September, a telegram from Beals was waiting for him: 'Welcome', it said. 'I am ashamed of my people's lack of courtesy, so generous with gold for its lackeys, but so poor in generosity of spirit.' Other prominent figures circulating in the Skyline Room were Claude Bourdet, a one-time member of the French Resistance, an opponent of colonialism and co-founder of the French weekly *France-Observateur*; and the British theatre critic Kenneth Tynan. Tynan, who was just finishing up a successful stint at the *New Yorker*, had visited Cuba back in April 1959, where he had turned down the opportunity to view a public execution (despite having had tickets) but had readily met with Fidel, who struck him as 'excellent, ebullient and a real radical'. Tynan had returned to the US captivated by the 'libertarian fervour' of Havana and the possibilities of this 'genuine do-it-yourself revolution'. His support for the Cuban Revolution, though, eventually drew unwelcome attention from the US authorities. In May 1960 he found himself hauled before the Senate Internal Security Subcommittee, where he was – among other things – asked about why he had signed the Fair Play for Cuba Committee's statement in support of Fidel and the revolution, which had appeared in the *New York Times* the previous month, 'in defiance of the views of President Eisenhower'. Recalling this episode in the pages of *Harper's Magazine* that autumn, Tynan observed that he had 'brooded over' the question 'for a long, incredulous moment' before responding 'that I was English, and that I had been forming opinions all my life without worrying for a second whether or not they coincided with those of the President of the United States.'[34]

Security for the reception was tight: admittance was strictly by invitation only, and, as the *New York Daily News* reported, 'detectives frisked each person on the way in.'[35] Julian Mayfield, who attended with his wife, the Puerto Rican doctor and political activist Ana Livia Cordero, was asked whether he was carrying a pocket-knife, prompting one fellow writer to declare that the pen was mightier than the sword.[36] The checks did, though, yield a few weapons: two penknives and an automatic revolver.[37] The latter belonged to Commander José Moleón Carrera, military attaché at the Cuban Embassy, who objected vehemently to the confiscation of his weapon. If the gun was not returned, he fumed, then all of the Americans living in Cuba would be disarmed, with anyone who resisted thrown into jail.[38]

Carrera might have been in a foul temper, but everyone else appeared to be in a fine mood – despite the somewhat 'desolate' surroundings (the Theresa, Mayfield wrote, 'is about as dingy a place as you can find').[39] As the legendary Magnum photographer Henri Cartier-Bresson snapped away, and the guests sipped on their cocktails and enjoyed the home-made cakes and cookies that had been provided, Fidel made himself 'available to everyone present, talking animatedly to individuals and to groups and predicting changes in his native land that were to benefit the "humble and poor", which he vowed were long overdue'.⁴⁰ Michael Conant, the young student editor of Columbia University's *Owl*, managed, 'after much pushing', to make his way to Fidel's table, where he secured a brief interview (they discussed agrarian reform, Cuban tourism and a possible student exchange programme).⁴¹ Others swarmed around the Maximum Leader, eager to secure their hero's autograph.⁴²

At a reception in the Theresa's ballroom Fidel was – naturally –
the centre of attention.
Photograph © Henri Cartier-Bresson/Magnum Photos

During a short, informal ceremony, Fidel presented Love B. Woods with a small statue of the famed nineteenth-century Cuban revolutionary José Martí, inscribed: 'He who incites and propagates racial hatred and opposition is sinning against mankind.'⁴³ For his part, Fidel was presented with a bust of Abraham Lincoln by Fair Play for Cuba Committee leader Richard Gibson, who quipped: 'from one liberator to another.' Visibly moved, the Cuban leader 'made a brief talk about how difficult it is for people to accept new ideas, but how, in the end, if the ideas are good they prevail'. He felt, he said, 'like a man travelling through a desert who suddenly reached an oasis. We know how capable it is of producing propaganda, but we also know that, in spite of this, we have many friends in the United States, and that the more propaganda they make against us, the stronger we are.' Someone shouted out, 'Fidel for President of the U.S.!', and a great cheer erupted.[44]

Although at times he appeared a little fatigued, Fidel was, Mayfield recalled, 'in great form'. In a letter written a couple of days later, Mayfield described the Cuban leader as 'a beautiful man':

> He is a hero, we know – one of the few of our times,
> almost anachronistic – but his manner is that of a young
> fellow who has done what had to be done and he cannot
> understand what all the excitement is about. They are all
> so young! And when we think of what they have done to
> change the world and make the Washington golf-player
> tremble in his boots – well, it's something to think about.[45]

Mayfield was not the only one to come over all star-struck. The Polish-born journalist K. S. Karol was in the Skyline Room – seated at the same table as Bourdet, Cartier-Bresson, Stone and Maria Winn, the young assistant to the British documentary filmmaker Richard Leacock – and he captured the mood of the occasion brilliantly. 'I shall always remember that evening', he wrote, 'not least for its fraternal and free-and-easy atmosphere, which formed a glaring contrast to that of all the diplomatic receptions . . . I had attended on previous evenings in Manhattan':

> The proletarian staff of the hotel, the olive-green uniforms
> of the *guerrilleros*, the general lack of formality, all helped
> to emphasize the gaiety and the stimulating, if not
> revolutionary, character of the meeting. Fidel Castro arrived
> rather late, and was immediately surrounded by a group

of Negroes, each as imposing in stature as Fidel himself. They flung themselves into his open arms. Everyone else then wanted to follow their example, and there were a few moments of pandemonium . . .[46]

Ten years later, this sort of thing would be satirized memorably by Tom Wolfe, whose 'Radical Chic: That Party at Lenny's' – an account of a fundraiser for the Black Panthers hosted by Leonard Bernstein and his wife, Felicia, at their Park Avenue penthouse – appeared in the 8 June 1970 edition of *New York* magazine. In his celebrated essay Wolfe poked fun at the fashionable, *au courant* sensibility of the artists, socialites and intellectuals who, it seemed to him, were all too keen to fawn over a group whose ideology, tactics and goals were wildly divergent from their own life experience (as well as inimical to their own social, economic and political interests). At one point he wondered,

> what the Black Panthers eat here on the hors d'oeuvre trail? Do the Panthers like little Roquefort cheese morsels wrapped in crushed nuts this way, and asparagus tips in mayonnaise dabs, and *meatballs petites au Coq Hardi*, all of which are at this very moment being offered to them on gadrooned silver platters by maids in black uniforms with hand-ironed white aprons.[47]

The party at the Theresa, though, took place in rather more innocent times. Castro's uncanny ability to attract the support of young, liberal middle-class Americans had been observed by the historian and public intellectual Arthur Schlesinger, Jr, a year earlier, when the Cuban leader had drawn a crowd of 8,700 on a visit to Harvard University. Schlesinger, who as a special assistant to President John F. Kennedy would have a ringside seat as Washington sought to deal with the 'Castro problem' once and for all, noted that 'the undergraduates saw in him, I think, the hipster who in the era of the Organization Man had joyfully defied the system, summoned a dozen good friends and overturned a government of wicked old men'.[48]

As the presence of Bourdet, Cartier-Bresson, Karol and Tynan at the Theresa attests, Fidel's appeal was by no means restricted to Americans. Haunted by Khrushchev's revelations about the crimes of Stalin and appalled by the Soviet Union's brutal response to the Hungarian uprising, a generation of European progressives and left-wing artists and intellectuals also looked to the Cuban Revolution for inspiration. As the renowned Marxist historian (and lifelong communist) Eric Hobsbawm observed, the revolution could hardly have been better designed to appeal to Western leftists. 'The Cuban Revolution', he noted, 'had everything: romance, heroism in the mountains, ex-student leaders with the selfless generosity of youth – the eldest was barely past thirty – a jubilant people, in a tropical tourist paradise pulsing with rumba rhythms.' And, lacking (at this stage) a fixed ideological position,* it could be welcomed enthusiastically by revolutionaries from across the political Left.[49] Just a few months before the reception at the Theresa, the French intellectuals Jean-Paul Sartre and Simone de Beauvoir had travelled to Cuba, in order to see, with their own eyes, a revolution that was actually unfolding.[50]

The couple had arrived in Havana on 22 February, during the midst of the Carnival celebrations, and were immediately smitten: 'the gaiety of the place', declared de Beauvoir, 'exploded like a miracle under the blue sky.'[51] Based in the Hotel Nacional – the 'fortress of luxury' – on the Malecón, the city's historic esplanade, the couple were shown the sights of the old town, introduced to leading revolutionaries, spoke at the University of Havana, appeared

---

* Fidel declared Revolutionary Cuba to be a socialist nation on 1 May 1961; on 2 December that same year he came out as a Marxist-Leninist, proclaiming that 'Marxism or scientific socialism has become the revolutionary movement of the working class'.

on Cuban television and were fêted by some of the island's most prominent novelists, artists, poets and playwrights.[52] On one famous occasion, immortalized by the legendary photographer Alberto Korda, they paid a midnight visit to Cuba's National Bank, where they were ushered through the lobby, past rebel soldiers – including, at the reception desk, a young rebel officer 'curled up . . . his long black hair spread on his shoulders, his cap on his nose, his eyes closed . . . snoring very lightly' – into the director's office. There, over coffee and cigars, they chatted for more than two hours with Che Guevara, who had been appointed as the bank's director the previous autumn: 'I am first of all a doctor,' Che said, 'then somewhat of a soldier, and finally, as you see, a banker.'[53] Sartre and de Beauvoir were also given a personal tour of the island by Fidel, who drove them around in his jeep. They visited sugar cane fields, new agricultural cooperatives and tourist developments on the newly public beaches, as well as a former rebel hideout, and Santiago, Cuba's second city. They also took a memorable fishing trip in the waterways of the Península de Zapata, where – dumbfounded – they watched the Maximum Leader blast a shotgun into the water before scooping out the stunned fish.[54]

The visit of the French existentialists was headline news. Carlos Franqui described how 'Sartre came into town like an *enfant terrible* . . . and within a week both he and Simone de Beauvoir were incredibly popular, in large measure because the people got to see the both of them – Sartre, ugly but *simpático*, and Simone, more reserved but interested in everything Cuban.'[55] Wherever they appeared, they were greeted with chants of '*Saltre, Saltre, Saltre. Simona, Simona, Simona*,' and jostled by cheering, boisterous crowds. Their names were even incorporated into a popular carnival refrain: '*¡Saltre, Simona: un dos tres! / ¡Saltre, Simona: echen un pie!*'*[56]

* This translates as 'Sartre, Simone, one two three! Sartre, Simone, get on the dance floor!'

For their part, Sartre and de Beauvoir were clearly impressed by what they found in Cuba. De Beauvoir later recalled a revolution characterized not by bureaucratic machinery 'but a direct contact between leaders and people, and a mass of seething and slightly confused hopes. It wouldn't last forever, but it was a comforting sight. For the first time in our lives, we were witnessing happiness that had been attained by violence', and it 'restored a pleasure in just being alive that I thought I had lost forever'.[57] She wrote that: 'To watch the struggle of six million men against oppression, hunger, slums, unemployment, illiteracy, to understand the mechanisms of the struggle and discover its significance was a passionately interesting experience.'[58] Sartre was, if anything, even more effusive. In a series of articles entitled *Hurricane over the Sugar* (*Ouragan sur le sucre*) and published in the leading French daily *France-Soir* later that summer, he lauded Cuba's organic, bottom-up revolution, free from ideological hang-ups; it was an exercise, he said, in 'direct democracy'.[59] Sartre was not at all perturbed by the purges and public trials that had led to scores of former Batista supporters being sent to the firing squad during the early months of the revolution. Indeed, he understood perfectly well that revolution was, by definition, '*une médecine de cheval*' (a phrase that translates, rather disappointingly, as 'strong medicine'). 'A society breaks its bones with hammer blows, demolishes its structures, overthrows its institutions, transforms the regime of property and redistributes its wealth, orients its production along other principles, [and] attempts to increase its rate of growth as rapidly as possible,' Sartre told the conservative, middle-class readers of *France-Soir*. But then, 'in the very moment of most radical destruction, [it] seeks to reconstruct, to give itself by bone grafts a new skeleton.' Sartre acknowledged that the remedy was extreme, 'and it is often necessary to impose it by violence'. While the 'extermination of the adversary and of several allies is not inevitable', it was, he declared, 'prudent to prepare for such an event'.[60]

As for the Cuban revolutionaries themselves, they had formed a 'cult of energy'. Liberated from the 'latifundias of sleep', they 'live energy, they exercise it, they invent it, perhaps'. Che – at least in Sartre's telling – was the archetypal existentialist hero: a man defiant in the face of injustice and absolutely committed to action.[61] And as for Fidel? This fearless opponent of injustice, 'who fought, who is fighting, for a whole people' with 'no other interest than theirs', was a sort of everyday superman 'prepared even to give the people the moon if they asked for it, because, he tells Sartre, "If someone asked me for the moon, it would be because someone needed it".'[62] The desire of the Cubans to defend their hard-won freedom and to maintain the revolution had Sartre's full support: 'I do not see', he wrote, 'how any people can propose today a more urgent goal nor one more worthy of its efforts.' 'The Cubans must win', Sartre declared, 'or we will lose all, even hope.'[63]

There were, to be sure, some voices of caution in the air during the second half of 1960. Visiting the island in July, LeRoi Jones/Amiri Baraka was moved by the collective struggle of the Cuban people and, like so many of his contemporaries, was captivated by Fidel's personal charisma. But, on the eve of his departure to Havana, his good friend and fellow Greenwich Village poet, Gilbert Sorrentino, had exclaimed that 'I don't trust guys in uniforms'.[64] And while Ginsberg may have viewed Fidel as an 'honest rat', his fellow Beat poet Gregory Corso felt compelled to remind his friend that, for all their apparent good humour and playfulness, the *barbudos* did also carry Sten guns. It was a prescient observation: during a 1965 trip to Havana, Ginsberg would witness first-hand the Cuban government's repression of homosexuals. And, after speaking out once too often ('well, the worst thing I said was that I'd heard by rumour that Raúl Castro was gay. And the second worst thing I said was that Che Guevara was cute'), Fidel had him placed on the next plane out of Havana, which just happened to be travelling to Prague.* [65] In 1971, Sartre and de Beauvoir would themselves denounce Havana's 'use of repressive measures against intellectuals and writers', in the process making themselves *personae non gratae* ('Cuba's door', Fidel declared, 'is definitely, definitively and eternally closed to you').[66] That, though, lay in the future. In the autumn of 1960, Castro, who combined the rebelliousness of a James Dean character with a programme of social and political reform that appeared untainted by communist totalitarianism, seemed to many on the literary and artistic Left to be the ideal revolutionary for a generation that was chafing against the drab consensus of the 1950s.

As 22 September drew to a close, Fidel had good reason to feel cheerful. He had, first of all, turned the snub of being excluded from the luncheon for Latin American leaders into a (very funny) PR triumph, and taken the opportunity – yet again – to place his government on the side of the 'poor' and 'humble' people of Harlem. Then, he had spent the evening basking in the adoration of intellectuals, artists and leftists, during an event that augured the close connection between the Cuban Revolution and the 1960s New Left, anti-war and student movements that would animate the coming decade.

Fidel's appeal, though, was not restricted to the coming generation of American writers, poets and radicals. In one of history's ironies, he also quickened the pulse of many of the old men in the Kremlin.

---

* An anxious and somewhat bewildered Ginsberg soon recovered his poise. Putting his disappointment with the Cuban 'police state' behind him, he made the most of his time in the Czechoslovakian capital – visiting Kafka's grave, writing some new poems, reciting 'Howl' to 500 students at Charles University and enjoying the adulation of his many admirers.

FRIDAY, 30 SEPTEMBER

CAPTION:

In a pugnacious speech at the UN General Assembly, Nikita Khrushchev
urged his fellow world leaders to 'bury colonialism'.

Photograph by Bettman via Getty Images

# 7

# FRIDAY 23 SEPTEMBER

Cuba makes us feel like boys again.
ANASTAS MIKOYAN

Standing outside the entrance to the Soviet mission, glancing repeatedly at his watch, Nikita Khrushchev looked, said one observer, 'like a bride who had been left at the altar'. Fidel, who liked to keep people waiting, had also misjudged the evening traffic and was running seriously late; Khrushchev, having mistaken the sound of a passing fire truck for the Cuban motorcade, had come down from his rooms and now found himself trapped out on the sidewalk. As the minutes ticked by and the Cuban leader failed to appear, the Soviet leader began joshing with reporters. When one reporter asked where Castro was, Khrushchev replied, 'He will come. Meanwhile, we will take some air. It is not quite fresh,' he said, in a reference to the city's pollution, 'but still, it's air.' Pressed on how long he intended to remain in New York, the Soviet leader responded, with a grin, 'I feel like staying, so I'm not going . . . but apparently I will not be granted citizenship.' At one point an election campaign truck, featuring a rocket bearing the slogan 'Nixon In, Khrushchev Out', passed by, and Khrushchev 'grinned from ear to ear, put his arms up, and pretended to shudder in terror'.[1]

Earlier that day, in a 'fighting speech' at the United Nations, the Soviet leader had called for Dag Hammarskjöld, whom he accused of siding with the colonial powers, to be replaced with a 'triumvirate' – representing the Western, communist and neutral blocs – and suggested that the UN headquarters itself be moved to either Austria or Switzerland.[2] Picking at the open sore that was the U-2 incident, Khrushchev accused the United States of 'piracy' and 'perfidy' and suggested that Washington was stoking an atmosphere in which the nations of the world were forced to live in constant fear of war. Moscow, in contrast, stood ready to 'do everything we can so that general and complete disarmament becomes reality and mankind is saved from the arms race and the threat of a new destructive war'. But the Soviet leader was quick to dismiss Eisenhower's plans for a system of international control as nothing more than a subterfuge for international espionage. Khrushchev also reaffirmed the Soviet Union's support for peaceful coexistence. 'Relations between all states should', he said, be allowed to 'develop in a peaceful way, without resort to force, without wars, without interference in the internal affairs of another'. If not, the alternative was coexistence 'at dagger's point'.

Welcoming the admission of the new African states to the United Nations, Khrushchev celebrated the rolling back of colonialism as 'a great hallmark of our epoch' and declared that the world was entering a new era, in which the countries of Africa, Asia and Latin America were 'beginning to take an active part in the determination of the destinies of the whole world'. Much, though, remained to be done: as well as calling for a return to order in the Congo under the 'legitimate leadership' of Patrice Lumumba, Khrushchev saluted the 'heroic selfless struggle' for independence in Algeria (where the Front de Libération Nationale was engaged in a bitter struggle against the French), as well as the fight for national self-determination in Kenya, Tanganyika, Uganda and other colonies. 'When the peoples rise up to struggle for their freedom, for a better life', Khrushchev declared, 'no force in the world can stop this mighty movement.'

After speaking for some two hours, Khrushchev ended his peroration with a rallying call: 'let us talk, argue, but let us solve the questions of general and complete disarmament. Let us bury colonialism that has been condemned by mankind.' The peoples of the world, he declared, 'are expecting the United Nations General Assembly . . . to adopt decisions meeting the aspiration of the peoples'.[3]

Khrushchev's speech did not win any friends in Washington (although Eisenhower joked that he did agree with the Soviet leader on one thing: the desirability of moving the UN out of New York*). The criticism of Hammarskjöld caused particular consternation, with Secretary of State Herter declaring that it amounted to 'an all-out attack, a real declaration of war against the structure, the personnel, and the location of the United Nations'.[4] In a meeting with Jawaharlal Nehru, held in the Waldorf Hotel, Eisenhower confided that he was 'astonished' by the 'virulence' of Khrushchev's remarks. With some commentators speculating that the Soviet Union might even quit the UN, Ike worried that the collapse of the organization would be a 'terrible disaster for the world', above all for the smaller nations. As for how long Khrushchev intended to remain in New York, the president was resigned to the fact that he would likely 'remain as long as he can make trouble'.[5] Herter, meanwhile, urged the president to refrain from making any public statement for the time being. Telephoning the White House from New York on the morning of 24 September, he advised that, for all of Khrushchev's bluster, the situation was 'riding along very

* When the United Nations voted in 1945 to locate its headquarters in the United States, rather than in Europe, other American cities – notably San Francisco and Philadelphia – were considered the front runners. The eventual triumph of New York owed much to the energetic lobbying of city officials and the donation, by the financier and philanthropist John D. Rockefeller, Jr, of an eighteen-acre property, formerly the site of a row of slaughterhouses, along the East River. When reminded of this gift, Ike quipped that he would happily give it back. He commented that 'the only virtue . . . of having the UN in New York is that by being so located it does not unduly exacerbate the balance of payments problem in the light of the amount of money we pour into it.' For more see Charlene Mires, *Capital of the World: The Race to Host the United Nations* (New York: New York University Press, 2013).

well . . . Mr. K did not make many friends yesterday.' The attack
on the UN appeared to have gone down badly with many of the
Afro-Asian nations (a resolution sponsored by seventeen of them,
which was broadly supportive of Hammarskjöld's handling of the
Congo crisis, had been passed 70-0 on the eve of the Assembly),
triggering what the *New York Times* called 'something like a sympathetic counter-reaction'.[6] It was clear, though, that Khrushchev
had succeeded in needling the president. Writing in her diary on
25 September, his secretary, Ann Whitman, recorded how:

> The other night, talking about Mr. K and his threats, the
> President told me what Lord Home [the British foreign
> secretary] said, with sarcasm, that sometimes he wished
> 'the world could go back to the old methods of diplomacy.'
> . . . meaning of course the big stick. The President strongly
> intimated that he wished there was no moral restriction that
> prevented him from one night pushing the proper button
> and sending all of our atomic bombs in the direction of the
> Communist bloc. This is the strongest statement I have ever
> heard him make on the subject.[7]

Reporting from Moscow a couple of days later, the British
ambassador noted that Khrushchev's speech had been covered in
the Soviet press 'in terms of semi-religious adulation and awe. It
has supposedly confounded the warmongers and shown the way
to a brighter cleaner world.' It was an impression that was, though,
undermined by the first newsreels of the General Assembly proceedings that were subsequently screened in Moscow's cinemas.
As the British embassy reported, 'an opening shot of the United
Nations skyscraper drew "ooh's" of admiration' and 'later on there
was a shot of Soviet factory workers avidly drinking in the radio
broadcast of Khrushchev's . . . speech.' Unfortunately, though, the
sound quality was 'under par and the Soviet leader's voice came
over as a high-pitched gabble' – prompting widespread laughter.[8]

In any case, commentators in the West were far from impressed by Khrushchev's performance: 'a dreadful speech [. . .] dishonest, rude, threatening, drab, unyielding, and far too long', concluded the *Guardian*'s James Morris (who was evidently hard to please).[9] The *Washington Post* described the speech as 'chilling', while the *New York Post* concluded that 'mankind's hopes for a better day were hardly brightened by anything the Soviet leader said.'[10] Commenting on Khrushchev's 'harangue' in the *New York Times*, James Reston wondered whether the new Soviet strategy was 'to bore us to death'.[11] The speech fared little better in continental Europe: *La Giustizia*, the newspaper of the Italian Social Democratic Party, characterized Khrushchev's remarks as an 'insult to truth'; Frankfurt's *Abendpost* declared that the Soviet leader had 'run out of ideas'; and the Scandinavian press was, unsurprisingly, scathing about his attack on the Secretary General.[12]

Khrushchev's speech did, though, have one high-profile fan. Indeed, Fidel Castro had leaped to his feet and offered vigorous and very public applause merely at the sight of the Soviet leader entering the Assembly Hall. During Khrushchev's actual remarks, Fidel had led the Cuban delegation in enthusiastic clapping and other demonstrations of support; and, as he left the assembly – wearing a 'freshly pressed fatigue uniform and highly polished boots', reported the *New York Times* – he declared the speech to have been 'good. Very good.'[13] The Cuban press followed suit, giving what the US ambassador in Havana described as 'prominent and panegyric play to Khrushchev speech in U.N.' *Revolución*, for instance, praised Khrushchev for having 'expressed in precise terms ideas of great force and clarity' and lauded the Soviet leader as 'just and valiant . . . a firm but serene statesman'.[14] Many Cubans, it was said, had even taken the trouble to listen to the speech, which was broadcast live on all Cuban radio and television stations.

During his address to the UN General Assembly, Nikita Khrushchev had made sure to single out his new friends from the

Antilles. 'Courageous Cuba' had, he declared, 'become the object of all kinds of attacks, intrigues and subversion, economic aggression and finally, poorly concealed threats of intervention'. After years of exploitation by the 'American monopolies', the Cuban people had now, thanks to a popular revolution, 'freed themselves' and 'taken their fate into their own hands firmly declaring to the United States monopolists: No more plundering of our country. We ourselves shall utilize the wealth of our labour and our land!' Referring to the US-sponsored coup that had overthrown the leftist government of Jacobo Árbenz in Guatemala back in the summer of 1954, Khrushchev declared that it was vital that the United Nations 'do all it can to remove from Cuba the overhanging threat of interference from outside'.[15]

The close relationship between Cuba and the Soviet Union was not preordained. As Khrushchev's biographer has noted, 'when Fidel Castro's forces came sweeping out of the Sierra Maestra and seized Havana in January 1959, Moscow had no clear idea of who they were and what they stood for.'[16] Although Raúl had joined the Cuban Communist Party (Partido Socialista Popular, or PSP) in 1953, Fidel seemed committed to pursuing a more independent course, and, in the early days of the revolution at least, it was not inconceivable that some sort of *modus vivendi* with the United States could have been worked out.[17] But, in the face of implacable American opposition to its radical economic policies, the government in Havana began to reach out to the Soviet Union.[18] Encouraged by enthusiastic reports from Aleksandr Ivanovich Alekseyev, the KGB's new *Rezident* (station chief) in Havana – who had, he later recalled, immediately 'fallen in love' with the revolution – the leadership in Moscow responded positively.[19] To begin with, Fidel was keen to impose limits and to keep the extent of the relationship secret (not least because of the island's ingrained culture of anti-communism, fuelled in part by the Catholic Church). Havana was prepared to purchase arms from Eastern bloc countries, including Poland and Czechoslovakia, and welcomed seventeen Spanish republican army officers, who had been living in exile in the USSR, as military advisers. But Fidel would not countenance requesting weapons directly from Moscow, partly because he feared provoking a response from Washington, which had long opposed any 'interference' by foreign powers in an area of the world that they viewed with proprietorial zeal.* He did, though, concede that the Soviets could play 'a decisive role in the strengthening of our revolution by helping us economically'.[20]

A key moment in what one leading historian has called the 'Cuban-Soviet minuet' arrived in February 1960, when Anastas Mikoyan, the number two in the Kremlin and Nikita Khrushchev's favoured international troubleshooter, arrived in Havana at the head of a technical and cultural mission.[21] The son of an illiterate village carpenter, Mikoyan – a native Armenian – had joined the Bolsheviks in 1915 and quickly risen through the ranks, serving as people's commissar for trade and becoming a leading member of the politburo. Having survived the bloody purges of the 1930s, he emerged as one of Khrushchev's key allies following Stalin's death in 1953, as a champion of greater freedoms and liberal reforms. In February 1955, Khrushchev appointed him First Deputy Chairman of the Council of Ministers.[22]

Mikoyan arrived in Cuba on 4 February, where he was greeted by a 'throng of people', including musicians who serenaded him with Cuban melodies. For the next ten days, he barely had time to pause for breath. Mikoyan laid a wreath at the memorial to José

---

* Under the 'Monroe Doctrine', originally formulated in 1823 by the Secretary of State, John Quincy Adams, and articulated by the country's fifth president, James Monroe, European attempts to exert control over any independent state in the Americas would, by definition, be viewed as an 'unfriendly act', 'dangerous to our peace and safety'.

Martí on the Paseo del Prado; opened the Soviet Trade Exhibition; watched the cabaret at the famed El Tropicana; met with economists, government officials, businessmen and leading revolutionaries (including Che Guevara, Raúl Castro and Raúl Roa); visited cooperative farms; chatted with Ernest Hemingway (the old Bolshevik, it turned out, was a big fan); viewed the construction of new workers' housing in Havana; visited the Isla de Pinos, where Fidel had spent two years in prison; swam in the warm waters off Cayo Largo; enjoyed a fishing trip with the Maximum Leader; toured around Santiago de Cuba; and spent a night roughing it in the Gran Piedra mountains. On his final day in Cuba, the First Deputy Chairman signed a major commercial agreement, providing Havana with $100 million in trade credits, and agreeing to purchase significant quantities of Cuban sugar and to supply the island with oil.[23]

Mikoyan was won over. Speaking before a rally of textile workers on 7 February, he declared, to raucous cheers, that 'the Cuban revolution can accomplish miracles too', and ended his speech by proclaiming, in 'heavily accented Spanish', 'Long live the Cuban People!'[24] Ever since his arrival, he had felt surrounded by 'kindred spirits', and was struck by 'the Cuban leaders' youth and revolutionary ardour, their enthusiasm, complete sincerity, faith in their cause, as well as the belief in the Revolution and the enthusiasm among large segments of the population – all this indicated that the Cuban Revolution answered the hopes and expectations of the working masses'.[25]

The spirit of enthusiasm was infectious: Mikoyan's thirty-year-old son, Sergo, who accompanied him on the trip, watched his father deliver an impassioned speech at a rice-hulling plant, standing on an improvised podium constructed of bags of rice. 'Everything in Cuba', he noted, 'had its own special, inimitable flavour', and he had, he confessed, 'fallen in love with this country, its Revolution, its leaders and its people'.[26]

For Mikoyan senior, meanwhile, Cuba had stirred powerful memories of his own youthful idealism and revolutionary fervour.[27] Reporting to Khrushchev on his return to Moscow, the old Bolshevik assured his boss that, yes, Castro was 'a revolutionary. Completely like us.' In Cuba, he explained, 'I felt as though I had returned to my childhood.'[28]

Soon, Khrushchev – encouraged by Fidel's increasingly strident anti-Americanism – was preparing to throw his weight behind the revolutionary government in Havana. In early July, he warned publicly that if the 'aggressive forces in the Pentagon' dared to launch an intervention against Cuba, 'Soviet artillerymen' would be able to 'support the Cuban people with their rocket fire'.[29] A few weeks later, on 26 July – the anniversary of the eponymous attack on the Moncada Barracks – the Soviet leader declared that 'the cause of heroic Cuba . . . has today become the banner of all progressive forces in Latin America which are rising to the struggle for liberation from the imperialist yoke.' Arguing that 'the Cuban people are not alone', he pledged Moscow's support for their 'just struggle'.[30] Scoring propaganda victories, gaining the tactical upper hand and securing strategic advantage via third-party states were all prominent features of the global superpower rivalry, and Khrushchev knew full well that the establishment of a successful socialist republic in America's own backyard promised to cause no end of trouble for Washington. Just as important, it would allow the Soviets to steal a march on the Chinese, with whom tensions had been rising ever since Khrushchev's denunciation of Stalin's 'cult of personality' during his 'secret speech' of 1956 (a critique that was viewed, in China, as a thinly veiled attack on Chairman Mao). Beijing, believing Moscow to be insufficiently revolutionary (too cautious, they said, when it came to the political uses of violence; too committed to the 'bourgeois' goal of peaceful coexistence), was vigorously challenging its leadership of international communism and competing with it for hearts and minds in the

Third World – including in Cuba, where, Mao declared, the battle had been carried 'to the imperialist rear'.[31] Now, in the autumn of 1960, Khrushchev had the chance to display the strength of Soviet–Cuban friendship before the whole world. The temptation was irresistible.

So it was that, just hours after his speech at the UN, and following his own pilgrimage to Harlem three days earlier, Khrushchev was preparing to receive Castro and his entourage as honoured guests at the Soviet mission on Park Avenue.

The Cuban leader eventually arrived just after 7.30 p.m. – almost forty minutes late. Brushing aside the Cubans' profuse apologies, the Soviet leader 'flung his arms' around Fidel and ushered him inside. 'Protocol', he declared, putting any personal irritation to one side, 'has no importance.'[32]

Amid the plush surroundings of the mission – with its thick rugs, fine paintings, white linen and delicate porcelain – Khrushchev broke the ice by removing his jacket and inviting his guests to do the same. The dinner, which lasted for four hours, featured consommé, caviar, salmon, stuffed pigeon and roast lamb, with fruit and chocolate for dessert, all washed down with countless shots of Khrushchev's favourite Ukrainian pepper-infused vodka – which made the Cubans 'feel their throats': Carlos Franqui recalled that, by the end of the night, more than one of his fellow countrymen found himself 'shipwrecked in a sea of vodka and cigars'. Although Fidel would have preferred to stick to politics, the Soviet premier was in a playful and jovial mood. He ribbed his foreign minister, Andrei Gromyko, for having afforded official recognition to the Batista regime in the 1940s (the Cubans, he said, should put him on trial for treason), and even poked fun at the Maximum Leader himself by recalling a joke that, he said, was doing the rounds: Fidel, he explained, was standing among a group of people outside the Pearly Gates. When St Peter called for all communists to step forward, Fidel remained motionless. 'Hey, what about you!' St Peter shouted out. 'You must be deaf!' Khrushchev, at least, appeared to find it funny.

Around midnight, gifts were exchanged, and the Soviets were presented with cigars, alligator-skin wallets, small wooden statues of Camilo Cienfuegos – a hero of the Cuban Revolution who had sailed with Fidel aboard the *Granma* (and who had died in an unexplained plane crash on the night of 28 October 1959) – and a bust of José Martí with the inscription 'Now, war is the last resort, and in the future war will be a crime.' On a slightly lighter note, Fidel also presented Khrushchev with a pair of maracas for his granddaughter, Julia* – which Khrushchev immediately began to play – as well as a tumbadora (or conga drum). The two leaders emerged onto the sidewalk for another photocall at 12.10 a.m.: 'smiling broadly, they brushed past security guards and strode to a microphone.' Fidel was effusive. In pointed remarks, given his treatment by the Americans, he thanked his hosts for their 'great hospitality'. The Soviets were 'very polite and respectful people', and he declared that he and his companions had gained a 'wonderful impression' of Khrushchev and the whole Soviet delegation. When asked what the two leaders had discussed, he responded that they had 'talked about peace'. Pressed on whether Khrushchev would now travel to Cuba aboard the *Baltika*, the Maximum Leader refused to be drawn.[33]

In the words of Carlos Franqui, 'the honeymoon between Fidel and the Russians had begun.'[34]

---

* Khrushchev had adopted Julia following the death of her father, Leonid (his eldest son), during the Second World War.

Nikita Khrushchev holds an impromptu press conference outside the USSR's Glen Cove retreat, on Long Island.

# 8

## SATURDAY 24 SEPTEMBER

The victory of a small revolutionary force over the much
larger forces of the imperialist puppets in Cuba shows . . .
that the imperialists are 'paper tigers'.

MAO ZEDONG

For the editorial writers of *Rodong Sinmun*, the official organ of
North Korea's Workers' Party, the 'insulting provocations' that
Fidel Castro had endured at the hands of his American hosts
revealed that the 'U.S. imperialists' were little more than 'shame-
less beasts' with 'human faces'; 'gangsters', opposed to the cause
of world peace.[1] In similar vein, Beijing radio observed that, on
arriving in New York, the Cubans had 'received the kind of rifle-
butt welcome that the State Department gives all those who work
for peace, national independence, and social progress'. Declaring that 'those who try to insult Fidel are joining up with all the
foulest things in the world', the Chinese communists expressed
confidence that 'the people – united, vigilant, and refusing to be
insulted, deceived, or disunited' would ultimately 'defeat imperialism, reaction, and war . . .'[2]

Given these expressions of support, and the evident growing
closeness between the government in Havana and their counterparts in Beijing and Pyongyang, it was not particularly surprising when, late on the evening of 24 September, news broke that
the Cuban government had decided to offer formal diplomatic
recognition to the communist governments of the Democratic
People's Republic of Korea and the People's Republic of China.
Neither was a member of the United Nations – China's seat would
continue to be occupied by representatives of the nationalist

government-in-exile, based in Taiwan, until 1971; North Korea did not join the organization until 1991. Although Havana had held back from formally recognizing the government in Beijing earlier in the year, to avoid further straining relations with the US, by the autumn such considerations had been brushed aside; the final decision was reached during a late-night cabinet meeting that Fidel chaired by telephone from his suite in the Theresa, and which concluded in the early hours of Saturday morning.[3]

Cuba's decision to extend official recognition to the People's Republic of China was, the *New York Times* declared, 'like the explosion of a time bomb. We all knew it was coming, but could not know just when.' But there was no doubt that this was a move of great international significance – giving Communist China 'its first diplomatic foothold in the Western Hemisphere'. Even more important, the *New York Times* noted, Castro's latest act of defiance was 'symbolic of the completeness with which he is waging what amounts to an all-out cold war against the United States'. Convinced that Washington was determined to 'overthrow them and the Cuban revolution . . . their policies have taken on a "do or die" quality. They are risking all in the belief that the United States is demanding unconditional surrender.' 'For the sake of Cuba as well as the United States', the *Times* editorial cautioned, 'one must hope that the struggle is not carried much further.'[4]

Keen to secure international allies, and win diplomatic, economic and military backing for their revolution, William Gálvez, Inspector General of the Cuban armed forces, had been despatched on a goodwill trip to China four months earlier. During a private meeting with Chairman Mao on 10 May, he explained that the Cuban people wished to strengthen their 'intimate relationship' with the Chinese people, in opposition to the 'imperialists of the U.S.'[5]

Gálvez was pushing at an open door. A year earlier, Mao and other Chinese communist leaders had gone out of their way to schmooze with the Latin American delegates who were in Moscow for the Twenty-first Congress of the Communist Party of the Soviet Union. They had also invited a group of them – including Juan Marinello, president of Cuba's Communist Party, the PSP – to visit Beijing immediately afterwards. Latin America, which was economically underdeveloped and had a history of exploitation by 'the imperialists', was viewed by Mao as fruitful terrain. Like the Soviets, the Chinese were keen to extend their global influence, and this was a region where they spied an opportunity to wrest the initiative from Moscow. Mao expressed his hopes that concerted action by communists, and an accompanying increase in international tensions in the region, would 'distract and disperse the imperialist forces over a vast area', thereby enabling communist insurgents to take the fight to them. In the months that followed, Chinese propaganda efforts in Latin America were stepped up, and a training programme for Latin American communist leaders was intensified.[6]

Moreover, the Chinese were increasingly enthusiastic about the Cuban Revolution. Mao, who had championed guerrilla warfare during the Chinese Revolution ('the guerrilla', he wrote, 'must move among the people as a fish swims in the sea'), argued that 'the victory of a small revolutionary force over the much larger forces of the imperialist puppets in Cuba' had revealed the imperialists to be nothing more than 'paper tigers'.[7] In June 1960, Peng Zhen, a leading member of the Chinese politburo, declared that 'the valiant people of Cuba have given a brilliant example for the peoples of Latin America'.[8] But China was prepared to offer more than warm words: technicians were despatched to advise the Cuban armed forces and to work with the Institute for Agrarian Reform; the Peking State Opera Company and delegations from student, trade and labour organizations followed soon after.[9]

Then, on 23 July, Cuba and the People's Republic of China signed a landmark trade deal, under which Beijing agreed to buy up to 500,000 tons of Cuban sugar per annum, at world prices, for the next five years, with promises of further economic aid and technical assistance to come. This was, concluded the American intelligence services, concrete evidence of Beijing's 'willingness to back anti-US movements with considerable material support'.[10] Fidel agreed, telling the National Congress of Cuban Women, during a speech in August, that 'we shall be friends with the . . . Chinese People's Republic because they have proven to be our friends, while the imperialists attack us and want to destroy us.'[11]

Having overseen the economic reconstruction of his country following the ravages of the Korean War, Kim Il Sung was also keen to establish alliances across the Global South. A champion of the Third World, which he viewed as a 'powerful revolutionary force', Kim, who had waged guerrilla warfare against Japanese colonialists in Manchuria during the 1930s, also identified personally with the new generation of anticolonial revolutionaries who emerged during the 1960s.[12] Developing a strategy that historian Benjamin R. Young has termed 'guerrilla internationalism', Pyongyang sought to nurture and strengthen anti-imperialist solidarity across Africa, Asia and Central America.[13] Cuba – which, like North Korea, was on the front line of the struggle against American imperialism – was an obvious potential ally, and ultimately provided Kim with a bridgehead into the rest of Latin America.[14] On 29 August, just a few weeks before establishing formal diplomatic relations, Cuba and North Korea had signed an agreement for the exchange of scientists, educators, artists and athletes.[15] Che himself would visit Pyongyang in November 1960, while on a global tour of socialist countries. He was, he later said, immensely impressed by this 'tiny country' that had been 'resurrected from the ashes of American bombardment and invasion'.[16] In the coming years, the two countries would offer each other ideological, diplomatic, military and economic support* – as well as warm words of friendship.[17] Kim Il Sung described the Korean and Cuban peoples as 'comrades-in-arms and intimate brothers who are fighting shoulder to shoulder on the front of the struggle for the revolutionary cause of the international working class and of the struggle against U.S. imperialism, our common enemy'. Fidel reciprocated. Piling on the flattery in good communist fashion, he lauded Kim's 'eminent, outstanding [and] heroic' leadership of the socialist cause.[18] Although no one knew it at the time, then, the autumn of 1960 marked the beginning of what would become a 'long and enduring friendship' between Cuba and the Democratic People's Republic of Korea; a friendship that has survived into the twenty-first century.[19]

The granting of official recognition to 'Red China' and North Korea might have generated headlines but, for Fidel, Saturday 24 September passed relatively quietly. After sleeping late, he spent most of the day holed up in his suite at the Theresa, working on his UN speech. The *New York Times* reported that the Cuban premier 'sent out for a lunch of chicken and rice' and left it to his aides to oversee the raising of the Cuban flag outside the hotel. Just after 12.30 p.m. a dozen pro-Castro Cubans, headed by Jorge Orihuela – a diamond-cutter, and New York-based member of Castro's 26 July Movement – had marched up Seventh Avenue and entered the Hotel Theresa, carrying a Cuban flag. After obtaining permission from Love B. Woods and consulting with members of the NYPD – who advised that, according to protocol, the American flag had to fly to the right of any foreign flag – they held a modest

---

* In the aftermath of Hurricane Flora, which wreaked havoc on Cuba in the autumn of 1963, for instance, the North Korean government sent thousands of tons of rice, as well as five tractors, construction equipment and medicine. Later in the decade, some 700 volunteer fighters, together with weapons and equipment, arrived in Havana, as part of North Korea's commitment to defend Cuba against possible armed aggression.

ceremony on the hotel's mezzanine. At 1 p.m., after the American flag had been moved, the two-by-four-foot Cuban banner was raised and, as the blue-and-white-striped ensign, with its distinctive red triangle and white star, fluttered in the breeze above the Theresa's main entrance, members of the Cuban delegation stood for their country's national anthem: 'do not fear a glorious death', they sang, 'for to die for the homeland is to live.' The Maximum Leader made a brief appearance at a ninth-floor window at around 6 p.m., to wave to the crowd of 500 or so cheering supporters who had gathered outside; there was also a brief flurry of excitement when two Spanish-speaking ladies 'of uncertain status' – one a 'plump redhead, the other a tall, slim brunette with an artificial streak of gray in her locks'; both from Coney Island – were given 'the bounce' by the hotel's owner, who was keen to avoid 'any irregularities'. But for the reporters who, hoping for more 'dramatic public behaviour by Havana's bearded revolutionaries', had 'lingered lazily among the large detail of security forces', it had been a disappointingly quiet day.[20]

Nikita Khrushchev, too, was keen to relax. A little after 11 a.m., the Soviet leader – 'his usual ebullient self' – walked out of the mission towards his waiting limousine. The New York *Daily News* reported how, on opening the rear door, he beckoned to 'several satellite leaders to join him. Bashfully, the underlings went through an Alphonse-and-Gaston routine before . . . Antonín Novotný of Czechoslovakia, Gheorghe Gheorghiu-Dej, Communist Chief of Romania, and a third Red VIP, name unknown, entered the car.' Khrushchev took the front seat, next to the driver, and in short order the motorcade was off, headed for Glen Cove on the north shore of Long Island – the mansion-dotted 'Gold Coast', whose opulence had been immortalized by F. Scott Fitzgerald in his 1925 novel, *The Great Gatsby*.[21]

Built in 1912–13 by the American oil magnate George Dupont Pratt, Killenworth – a thirty-nine-room house, designed in the

Tudor Revival style – had been purchased by the Soviet Union in April 1946 as the country retreat for its UN delegation.[22] With its wood panelling, beautiful fireplaces and low retaining garden wall 'embedded with broken pieces of white statuary' that, it was claimed, had been sourced from Pompeii, Glen Cove certainly provided the Soviets with a place to relax in style.[23] The State Department had initially insisted that Khrushchev would have to remain confined to Manhattan for the duration of his stay in New York City but, after sustained protests from the Soviet Union and a personal intervention from the UN Secretary-General himself, it had relented.[24] Having kicked up such a fuss, Khrushchev was now determined to take advantage of his new freedom.

Khrushchev's motorcade – which reportedly consisted of forty-three cars and a fifty-man motorcycle escort – made its way through Queens to Nassau County, the joy of the 'sparkling sun-shine' offset only by the occasional small group who gathered at street corners to jeer or shout out 'Go back to Siberia!' or 'Murderer!' Glen Cove's mayor, Joseph A. Suozzi, annoyed that the Soviets cited diplomatic exemption to avoid paying local property taxes, had urged residents to ignore their high-profile guest. But as many as seventy-five children, many of them teenagers, though some as young as six, had gathered on Dosoris Lane, about a hundred yards from the entrance to the estate. 'They stood along a rustic fence where late fall flowers were growing, and strewed their bicycles about the grass', eagerly awaiting the arrival of the Soviet leader – for whom they had 'pencilled small placards with derisive greetings and made up rhymes to shout'. Maria Rybka, nine-year-old daughter of a Ukrainian immigrant, carried a sign – in Russian – that declared, simply, 'Murder.' As a police helicopter, complete with sharpshooter, hovered overhead, the motorcade swept through the imposing iron gates and into the sanctuary of the sprawling thirty-four-acre compound.[25]

Late in the afternoon, Gamal Abdel Nasser arrived at Glen Cove for talks. Although he had not originally planned to attend the General Assembly, the lure of the international spotlight had proved too strong. Like other neutralist leaders, Nasser believed that he could play a moderating role in the Cold War, thereby helping to ease global tensions, and he also saw an invaluable opportunity to extend his influence – and that of the UAR – among the new African nations. Having long since given up hopes of receiving an official invitation from the White House, Nasser was also keen to pay a first visit to the United States (the furthest west that he had previously travelled was Yugoslavia). During an audience with the American ambassador, G. Frederick Reinhardt, at the Barrage Rest House, a government residence on the out-skirts of Cairo, on 21 September, Nasser had explained that he was keen to develop a greater understanding of, and sympathy for, the 'Arab point of view' among the American public.[26] His meeting with Khrushchev – on his first full day in New York – was part of a breathless schedule that also saw the Arab leader confer with the prime minister of Lebanon, Saeb Salam, Tito of Yugoslavia and Nkrumah of Ghana.[27]

Ninety minutes later, after posing for photographs and waving his guest off, Khrushchev stood on the driveway where, for more than an hour, he chatted amiably with journalists.[28] On the dis-cussions with Nasser, he explained that they had 'mainly talked of disarmament and the effort for a stronger peace'. The two men were, he said, 'old acquaintances and we maintain good relations' and, yes, the meeting had been fruitful (although, according to Nasser's confidant, Mohamed Heikal, nothing of any great seri-ousness had been discussed because, on arrival, Khrushchev had immediately warned his guest that 'this place is bugged and we have discovered the bugging.')[29] When asked why he had travelled to Glen Cove, Khrushchev responded that 'there are no hares in Manhattan, whereas they can be found here. I like them a lot.' In response to an invitation to reflect on 'your stay here, in the heart of capitalism, so to speak', the First Secretary explained that 'this is the heart of capitalism and I have the heart of a Communist. Evidently, we can coexist on one planet.' Then, to laughter, he continued, 'in the capitalist world it often happens that an old but rich widow marries a young man. And they live together, though he evidently doesn't thirst for the old woman's love. Still he lives with her.' 'In the same way', Khrushchev explained, 'capitalist and socialist states must coexist even though there is no love lost between them.' When asked why he was not holding his press conference from the balcony, as he had been doing while staying at the Soviet mission, Khrushchev prompted further mirth when he shot back, 'There is no need for that here. You felt offended that then we were talking "on different levels". Now I can talk with you on the same level, on the ground.' Then, after making a lengthy defence of his plans to reform the United Nations (which were not, he stressed, motivated by any personal animosity towards the Secretary General himself), Khrushchev called a halt to proceedings. Noting that it was getting dark and increasingly difficult to make notes, he assured the 'gentlemen of the press' that he was merely concerned about saving their eyesight.[30]

While Khrushchev was retiring for the evening, Nasser was still in talks with Nkrumah at the Ghanaian mission.[31] It is not known whether the subject of Fidel Castro had come up in conversation – according to a joint statement the two men had discussed 'matters of mutual concern, including those of concern to Africa'. But the next morning, Nasser would emulate Khrushchev by making his own pilgrimage to Harlem.

# 9

# SUNDAY 25 SEPTEMBER

Like Egypt, Cuba Will Triumph
*REVOLUCIÓN*

At 10.45 a.m. on Sunday 25 September, Gamal Abdel Nasser, his entourage of police detectives, FBI agents, government aides and personal security guards 'flanking him like barnacles on a battle-ship', arrived outside the Hotel Theresa. The forty-two-year-old president of what was now the United Arab Republic* – known to his colleagues as *al-raïs*, or 'the boss' – radiated energy: as one historian has put it, in somewhat exotic terms, 'tall and muscular, he moved like a panther. His olive-skinned countenance, white teeth gleaming between aquiline nose and prognathous jaw, was spellbindingly expressive.'[1] After flashing his famous smile for the cameras and waving to the 3,000-strong crowd that had swarmed around the hotel to greet him, the Egyptian leader was hustled into the Theresa. The Arab world's most famous revolutionary was about to meet the *enfant terrible* of Latin America for the very first time.[2]

Four years earlier, Nasser – the first native Egyptian to rule the country for more than two and a half millennia – had stunned the world, as well as members of his own government, by nationalizing the Suez Canal. His audacious move proved wildly popular across the Middle East and North Africa but caused outrage in Britain, the former colonial master, and France – each of which owned a

* The United Arab Republic was formed out of the merger of Egypt and Syria in 1958. Although Syria seceded from the union in 1961, Egypt continued to be known as the UAR until 1971.

fifty per cent stake in the company that ran the waterway. Prime ministers Anthony Eden and Guy Mollet quickly determined that this act of 'aggression' could not be allowed to stand. Eden, who viewed Nasser as a sort of Arab Mussolini, was determined not only to force Nasser to 'disgorge his spoils' and to recover the canal, on which Western Europe was dependent for two-thirds of its oil supplies, but to sweep aside the Egyptian regime itself. On 5 November, Britain and France launched a coordinated military operation against Egypt under the pretext of protecting the Suez Canal from an Israeli invasion that had begun a week earlier, and which had been secretly encouraged by, and coordinated with, London and Paris. For a time, it looked as if Nasser was finished: after taking to the roof of his suburban villa to watch Royal Air Force bombers pound Cairo, he briefly considered surrendering in a 'final sacrifice' for his country. But he quickly recovered his poise, rallying the Egyptian people with a pledge to 'defend our country, our history and our future'. 'We will fight', he had declared, 'to the last drop of blood.'

The Anglo-French attack prompted widespread outrage across the Middle East and Africa and brought heavy condemnation from the communist world. Moscow and Beijing denounced the aggression of the Western colonialists and pledged solidarity with the Egyptian people, and Khrushchev even threatened to send in the Red Army. Tellingly, there was strong criticism from close allies, too, including Canada, Australia and the United States. President Eisenhower, furious that he had been 'double-crossed' by the British (who had kept him entirely in the dark about their plans), insisted on a ceasefire, even threatening London with oil sanctions if they persisted. On 7 November, with the so-called special relationship between the United Kingdom and the United States under unprecedented strain, Eden ordered that the allied advance be halted. Two months after this humiliating climbdown, and with his health broken, Eden resigned the premiership.[3]

By successfully facing down the combined military might of Britain and France, Nasser – the son of a postal clerk from Alexandria – had emerged as a genuine hero of the Arab world and a global icon of anticolonial resistance.[4] In addition to his considerable personal magnetism, Nasser's main strengths – according to a biographical sketch drawn up by the US State Department – were 'self-confidence, willingness to take great risks, tactical skill, drive, a flare [*sic*] for intrigue, and a strong will'. Since coming to power, he had also proven remarkably consistent in promoting 'the independence of Egypt and the Arab states, increased Arab military strength, and assertion of Egyptian leadership in three concentric zones – the Arab world, Africa, and the Moslem world'.[5] Given his unparalleled status, it was hardly surprising that the new Cuban government had turned to Nasser in their quest for international legitimacy, ideological support and material assistance.

Even before their dramatic seizure of power in January 1959, the young Cuban rebels had admired the Egyptian leader for his agrarian reforms (which saw fifteen per cent of the country's viable agricultural land redistributed to the peasantry, or *fellahin*) and for his dramatic standoff with the former colonial powers over Suez.[6] Eager to win new friends (a task made more urgent by Cuba's growing isolation in the Western hemisphere), in June 1959 Fidel sent Che Guevara on a major international tour that, over the course of three months, took in India, Pakistan, Ceylon, Japan, Indonesia and Yugoslavia. His first stop was Egypt.[7]

Che, accompanied by his personal bodyguard and two government officials, arrived in Cairo on 12 June. Nasser, who had initially dismissed the Cuban rebels as 'a bunch of Errol Flynns, theatrical brigands but not true revolutionaries', nevertheless rolled out the red carpet. Che was given a tour of the pyramids and spent a night at the stunning Montaza Palace, in Alexandria. He also visited the Suez Canal, Port Said (a site of fierce fighting during the 1956 war) and Aswan, where construction of the High Dam had begun in January, thanks to Soviet technical and financial support.[8] The Cuban revolutionary also met with Nasser for face-to-face talks, during which – extraordinarily – he challenged the president directly. When Nasser explained that relatively few Egyptians had been compelled to leave the country as a result of his reforms, Che retorted, 'that means that nothing much happened in your revolution.' 'I measure the depth of the social transformation', he explained, 'by the number of people who are affected by it and feel that they have no place in the new society.'[9] Che also spoke 'in bitter terms' about the United States, though Nasser reportedly cautioned the young firebrand 'that if one dealt with the imperialists, one would suffer a five per cent loss in one's resources. However, if one dealt with the Communists, one would lose one hundred per cent of his assets.'[10]

Despite their differences, the trip was a success: as one historian has explained, Nasser 'recognized Cuba as the only anticolonial, anti-imperialist nation in Latin America' – a status that was confirmed when the Egyptian government invited Cuba to attend the next meeting of the Afro-Asian Congress. (Che was 'thrilled', writing that Cuba was now officially 'part of an historical convergence of all the oppressed peoples in the world at this hour of their liberation'.) During a public show of support in Gaza (the strip was occupied by Egypt between 1959 and 1967), Palestinians declared that, just as Nasser had become a symbol for the Arab people, so Fidel had become a symbol of Latin American liberation. Cuba and Egypt also began discussions on future trade relations (Cairo was particularly keen to sell cotton to the Cubans).[11]

The exchange of high-level dignitaries continued apace. In March 1960, one of Nasser's key foreign policy lieutenants, Hussein Zulficar Sabri, was in Havana, in another sign of the growing warmth between the two governments. Sabri made clear Cairo's support for the Cuban Revolution. 'We are', he stated, 'ready to help the people of Cuba by giving them assistance against any possible foreign aggression.'[12]

In August, the Cuban minister of defence, Raúl Castro, was in Alexandria, where he attended the official celebrations marking the eighth anniversary of the expulsion of King Farouk. Speaking to a rally at the city's municipal stadium, he told the crowds that his country was facing the same challenge that Egypt had – opposition from 'monopolists'. What was needed, he said, was a united front to 'fight against imperialism in Asia, Africa, and Latin America'. Nasser in turn urged the Cubans to resist the 'intimidation and pressure' and issued a powerful rhetorical statement of support, declaring that 'we, the people of the United Arab Republic, fully support the cause of liberty throughout the world; we support the cause of liberty in Cuba; we support the fight put up by Fidel Castro.'[13]

Now, finally, Nasser and Fidel were meeting face to face.

Upstairs at the Theresa, the two men conferred for an hour and a half – initially alone apart from Regino Boti, Cuba's minister of the economy, who served as interpreter, and then accompanied by aides. The discussion was wide-ranging, with Nasser making frequent references to the similarities between Egypt and Cuba in terms of their history of colonial exploitation, their recent revolutions and the challenge that they faced in seeking to modernize what were, essentially, one-crop economies. The two leaders chewed over the pros and cons of trading raw materials (namely cotton and sugar) to the communist bloc in exchange for long-term credits, technical assistance and weapons. Fidel listened eagerly as Nasser recounted the Egyptian experience during the Suez Crisis. The UAR leader also cautioned Fidel against being drawn into a military conflict with the United States over the naval base at Guantánamo Bay, and emphasized the importance of 'the idea of Arab unity' to the Egyptian revolution, prompting a discussion about the situation in Latin America. While Fidel said that there were some shared bases, namely religion, language and an 'oppression of the peasants' that was common to all Latin-American countries, thus far 'there had been no unifying factor as strong as the idea of Arab unity'. As for the leadership of the so-called Third World nations, Nasser invited Cuba to join the neutralist camp and help to 'construct a diplomatic alliance to stand between East and West' (Fidel was polite but non-committal at this stage, though in 1961 Cuba would be a founder member of the Non-Aligned Movement, which sought to organize the neutralist countries on a more formal basis). Asked whether he planned to attend Fidel's speech at the UN the following day, Nasser expressed his regrets. Much as he would have liked to be there, the Egyptian leader explained, his meeting with President Eisenhower 'had been fixed for precisely the time that Castro would be talking'; a revelation that prompted Fidel to mutter that the Americans were deliberately trying to hinder the development of good relations between their two countries (in truth, the timing was probably just a coincidence).[14]

At 12.30 p.m. the two men emerged from the Theresa, 'a study in contrasts'. In his light blue suit, starched shirt and dark blue tie, Nasser had the appearance of 'a prosperous Cairo salesman', while Castro, wearing his 'open-throat fatigues', stood uncharacteristically shyly alongside him. As the assembled crowds chanted 'Viva Nasser!' and 'Viva Castro!' and waved blown-up pictures of the Arab hero, the two leaders 'thrust through the security men' and posed for the cameras, smiling and shaking hands.[15] Speaking to reporters, Fidel declared that Nasser's visit had been a 'source of great inspiration for our delegation, which finds itself practically confined and surrounded by the hostility of an imperialist power like the United States'. 'They have had to make many sacrifices', Fidel continued, 'but in the end they triumphed, and we, like the Arabs, will also win. We are fighting against a ferocious imperialism, just as Nasser faced.' The two men also affirmed their desire to trade visits to Havana and Cairo, although no dates had yet been fixed.[16]

In a statement to Egyptian radio, which was also published in the Cairo-controlled daily *Al Gomhuria* (*The Republic*) on 28 September, Fidel was effusive. He had, he said, been 'pleased to have the opportunity to meet with the Arab leader whose struggle embodies a beautiful meaning – the liquidation of imperialism. The personality of the great Arab leader is loved not only in the Arab countries but is also a great hope for all the peoples of the world who seek freedom, dignity, and independence.' During their historic encounter at the Theresa, Fidel explained, he had felt Nasser's 'great personality, which was shaped by his wonderful accomplishments. The great effect of this meeting on me intensifies my conviction that the growing peoples of the world will achieve all their victories and aspirations.' And he looked forward to Nasser's visit to Cuba, promising that 'The Arab people will see that their leader has had a great place and a greater love in every heart.'[17]

For his part, Nasser was keen to put his support for the Cubans on record: 'the government and the people of the United Arab Republic', he declared, 'express their solidarity with the Cuban revolution.'[18]

Despite the warm words and public expressions of support, the *New York Times* journalist Max Frankel noted that Nasser and Castro had 'avoided the demonstrative hugging and backslapping that has been a feature of Castro–Khrushchev encounters'.[19] It was a sharp observation. Nasser had, in fact, found their encounter rather uncomfortable: he was repulsed by the 'terrible smells' and general squalor of the Cubans' accommodation. Even worse, he had taken great offence when, upon presenting Fidel with a beautiful silver tea service, the latter had expressed his disappointment at not having been given a crocodile. An astonished Nasser explained that there were precisely four crocodiles in Egypt, all of them to be found in the zoo; for days after, the Egyptian leader could be heard muttering, 'A crocodile . . . a crocodile.' Meanwhile, reports soon reached both British and American diplomats that, in private, some members of the UAR delegation were making disparaging comments about 'Castro's show in Harlem'.[20] In fact the poor personal chemistry was an early sign of the somewhat discordant relationship that would develop between the two leaders, who disagreed from the outset about how best to construct a transnational movement of the left. When Cuba sent guerrillas to Zaire – formerly the Republic of the Congo – in 1965 in an attempt to overthrow the US-backed government in Léopoldville, for instance, Nasser dismissed the whole enterprise as futile.[21]

After some prodding by his security guards, Nasser gave a final wave to the crowds before climbing into his sleek, black Cadillac for the journey back to his Sands Point estate.[22] His visit to Harlem had been a public relations triumph, and the huge crowds that had gathered were testament to his 'star status', particularly among black nationalists who admired his unwavering opposition to colonialism. But, while local taxi driver Paul Smith conceded that 'Nasser is a great man. There's no doubt about that', he was getting 'tired of the traffic jams these leaders are making'. 'Streets are blocked off', he explained, which 'slow up my business'.[23]

As the crowds began to thin out and the traffic around the Theresa got back to normal, Castro returned to his suite. A group, largely good-natured, remained on the streets, banging bongo drums and chanting, 'Yellow press, yellow press, cha, cha, cha.' The good mood was interrupted briefly when, as the *Daily News* put it, 'pro- and anti-Castro factions clashed in a battle royal – fists and baseball bats' outside the hotel (fifteen people were arrested, and several protesters and two police officers suffered minor injuries). 'Except for occasional, flitting appearances of a beard in a ninth-floor window' – which drew loud, enthusiastic cheers from the hundreds of 'flag-waving supporters' on 125th Street – the Cuban premier remained largely out of sight. One rumour – which, if true, was highly ironic – had it that Khrushchev had advised the Cuban leader to 'stop his clowning so that he would be taken more seriously when he addresses the UN'.[24]

Fidel's address before the General Assembly was now less than twenty-four hours away.

CAPTION:

According to one wag, Fidel's four-and-a-half-hour speech to the UN General
Assembly covered everything except the dispute between Britain and Iceland
over the sardine harvest.

Photograph by Bettman via Getty Images

# 10

## MONDAY 26 SEPTEMBER

Today, Fidel, 2 p.m.
*REVOLUCIÓN*

'Although it has been said that I speak at great length', Fidel declared, 'you may rest assured that we will endeavor to be brief.' It was not to be. Even some of his closest supporters had to concede that the Maximum Leader had a tendency to 'go on for hours and hours'. 'Even in Cuba', noted Carlos Franqui, 'people fell asleep during Fidel's harangues. And this despite their affection for Fidel and their interest in what he had to say.'[1]

Asked the day before about rumours that the Cuban leader was planning to speak for four hours, Khrushchev had responded, animatedly, that even if Fidel ended up talking for six hours, 'I shall still be listening to him with pleasure'.[2] In the event, Fidel's four-and-a-half-hour speech (still a UN record) would sorely test the stamina of his new, sixty-six-year-old fan. Earlier that morning, the Soviet leader had attended the General Assembly, where he heard the Canadian prime minister, John Diefenbaker, mount a robust defence of the West. In contrast to the 'restrained, wise and conciliatory' address that had been delivered by Eisenhower, Khrushchev had, he claimed, offered little more than 'a gigantic propaganda drama of destructive misrepresentation'. The Canadian leader also offered a categorical rejection of 'the unjust and intemperate attacks' that had been made on the 'office and person' of the Secretary General. As for Khrushchev's call for the final elimination of colonialism, Diefenbaker contrasted the thirty or more nations who had achieved independence from Britain and France since the end of the Second World War with the 'record of Soviet domination over peoples and territories, sometimes gained in the name of liberation, but always accompanied by the loss of personal and political freedom'. How, he wondered, would member states be able to reconcile the 'tragedy' of Hungary (whose revolution Moscow had crushed) with Khrushchev's support for the right of nations 'to establish systems of their own free will and choosing'?[3]

Then, much more agreeably, Khrushchev had headed to the Biltmore Hotel's palatial ballroom, for a luncheon hosted in his honour by Cyrus S. Eaton and his wife, Anne. Three years earlier, the philanthropist couple had hosted the first Pugwash Conference on Science and World Affairs, which sought to encourage international dialogue between scientists, intellectuals and public officials, with the eventual aim of creating a world free from nuclear weapons.[4] In his welcoming remarks, Eaton expressed his hopes that 'this luncheon [will] not only lead to strengthened friendships, but also serve as a forum for discussion of ways and means to increase business between the Soviet Union and North America, and to secure cooperation to the mutual advantage of all three nations in the markets of the world'. Expressing his faith in the Soviet leader's 'complete sincerity in desiring peace', he looked forward to the time when 'the United States, Canada and the Soviet Union will declare for collaboration on a program dictated by common sense'.[5] For his part, Khrushchev told the audience of some two hundred bankers, industrialists and public officials, drawn from both the United States and Canada, that 'the representatives of the capitalist and the socialist states have to learn to understand one another in order to settle questions between states by peaceful means' and avoid the prospect of another world war. The Soviet government would, he reiterated, spare no effort in seeking to achieve disarmament. 'After all,' he noted, 'the people both in the socialist and in the capitalist countries want to live in friendship.'[6]

After lunching on consommé, *filet de boeuf* and *tartes aux fraises*, served on elegant gold-crested china and washed down with finest claret and champagne, Khrushchev was back in the General Assembly to see Fidel take centre stage.[7]

Fidel's black Chevrolet, escorted by motorcycle outriders, had pulled up outside the General Assembly building at precisely 3.40 p.m. The Cuban leader, accompanied by Major Juan Almeida, Ramiro Valdés and Antonio Núñez Jiménez, was met by his foreign minister, Raúl Roa, and escorted inside. After taking the escalator to the first floor, he entered the chamber and took his seat at the head of the Cuban delegation, near the front of the hall. Fidel 'listened attentively' to the Albanian prime minister, Mehmet Shehu, as he wrapped up his own speech, although the Cuban leader was observed nervously touching his shirt pocket from time to time.[8]

Fidel, wearing neatly pressed battle fatigues, took to the floor at 3.50 p.m.[9] Striding purposefully to the podium, he carried a brown leather briefcase, containing a number of documents and aides-mémoire, which he opened and placed on the lectern. Then, after taking two sips of water, he was off.[10] 'At first', the *New York Times* reported, 'he spoke slowly, his hands behind his back . . . But later, at key junctures, he waved papers and gesticulated with a powerful hand.' Although he had promised to speak slowly in order to assist the interpreters, the writer and Fair Play for Cuba Committee activist Waldo Frank – who in 1959 had been hired by the Cubans to write a history of their revolution – observed how, after just a few minutes, Fidel's 'words were so flowing and so flooding that the interpreters could attempt no more than minute digests, snatched as from a torrent'.[11]

The four and a half hours that Fidel spent at the rostrum were, Frank concluded, a study in contrasts. Almost everything about the UN Assembly Hall was, he explained, designed to instill a sense of coolness:

the walls – gold, black-ribbed – are immense half-opened
fans, faintly a-sway in the airs of the orations. The two
rostrums, one above the other . . . suggest marble, bluish
and aquamarine . . . the lounge and the bar are cool. The six
women telephone operators near the bar cool the delegates
with cool voices.

But the coolness and calm of the General Assembly were now
thrown into sharp relief by the presence of Cuba's fiery and unorthodox young leader. Even Fidel's beard – bushy, and black 'suffused
with overtones of red wherever sun or the hall's light struck it'
– served to 'disturb the decorous delegates, many of whom wear
dapper goatees and Van Dykes'. There was, Frank declared, 'a
radical difference of *heat* between the passionate Cuban and the
Assembly. And although they listened, more patient than rapt . . .
the difference of temperature excluded comfort on both sides: the
delegates' and Castro's.'[12]

The speech to the UN – ostensibly the reason for his trip to New
York in the first place – offered Fidel an incomparable platform
from which to assert his legitimacy as a revolutionary leader, to
claim a leadership role in the wider struggle against imperialism
and to make a pitch for support from the newly admitted nations
of Africa. He was also able to address his fellow world leaders
(although neither Christian Herter nor his British counterpart,
Lord Home, was in the Assembly Hall while Fidel spoke) as well as
those, especially across Africa, Asia and Latin America, who were
listening via television or radio or following the coverage in the
newspapers.[13]

Fidel began by complaining about the 'degrading and humiliating treatment', including 'efforts at extortion', that he had
endured at the Shelburne Hotel, and expressing his gratitude to
the Theresa – a 'humble hotel in Harlem' – for its hospitality.
Then, after a lengthy account of US–Cuban relations over the

previous six decades (during which Cuba had been 'an append-age . . . a virtual colony of the United States'), he celebrated the triumph of his revolution: 'we are proud that we can now say', he declared, that 'our people govern themselves!' Justifying his government's programme of economic nationalization and land reform, Fidel lashed out at the hysterical reaction of the United States, which had, he claimed (with some justification), engaged in all sorts of punitive actions – including sabotage against sugar refineries, black propaganda and economic coercion – in an attempt to 'punish the revolutionary government' in Havana.[14]

Fidel was keen to highlight the success of his new government before the world. Despite the hostility of the United States, the revolution had already achieved much: it had created 10,000 new schools and built 25,000 houses, agricultural production was rising, teams of doctors had been sent into the countryside to battle disease and improve sanitary conditions, corruption was being rooted out and industrial production was up, he claimed, by thirty-five per cent. What 'was yesterday a land without hope, a land of misery, a land of illiteracy', Fidel declared, 'is gradually becoming one of the most enlightened, advanced and developed nations of this continent'. Turning to his fellow Latin American leaders, Fidel stated baldly that they should 'welcome a revolution like the Cuban revolution, which has forced the monopolies to return at least a small part of their profits from the natural resources and the sweat of the peoples of Latin America'.[15]

After speaking for some two hours, Fidel turned his attention to the US naval base at Guantánamo Bay. Secured by the United States under a 1903 lease giving Washington 'sole jurisdiction' over roughly forty-five square miles of Cuban territory, the naval facility was a permanent reminder of America's exploitation of the island. It was little wonder that the new revolutionary government wanted it gone. But while Fidel admitted that his government was 'seriously considering requesting, within the framework of international law, that the naval and military forces of the United States be withdrawn from the Guantánamo base', he was determined to proceed with caution. Aware that Admiral Arleigh Burke, Eisenhower's Chief of Naval Operations, had pledged that if the Cubans 'would try to take the place by force, we would fight back', Fidel made it absolutely clear that his government had 'never spoken a single word that could imply any type of attack' on the American facility. After all, he explained, 'it is clearly in our interest not to give imperialism the slightest pretext to attack us.' According to Fidel, all the recent talk in Washington about defending the base was merely designed to 'create a climate of hysteria and to set the stage to attack us'.[16]

Turning next to the global stage, the Maximum Leader explained that 'the case of Cuba' was not 'an isolated one'. 'It is the case of the Congo, it is the case of Egypt, it is the case of Algeria . . . the case of Cuba is the case of all the underdeveloped and colonized countries.' All across Latin America, he declared, the economic resources were in the control – directly or indirectly – of 'the monopolies'. And he warned his sister republics that, if they attempted to enact agrarian reform, 'any representative coming here to the United Nations will be confined to Manhattan; they will have hotel rooms denied to them; they will have insults poured on them and they may, possibly, be mistreated by the police themselves [. . .] How long', he asked, 'must Latin America wait for its development? As far as the monopolies are concerned, it will have to wait *ad calendas Graecas* [forever].'[17]

Revolutionary Cuba was, Fidel declared, fully behind Patrice Lumumba – the only Congolese leader who had 'stood firm against the interests of the monopolies and shoulder to shoulder with his people' – and on the side of the Algerians, who were engaged in a 'heroic' struggle against the French. Indeed, Cuba was on the side of all the African countries that remained subject to colonial control, as well as 'the blacks who are discriminated against in the

Union of South Africa'. 'We are', Fidel proclaimed, 'on the side of the people who wish not only to be politically free – because it is very easy to raise a flag, choose a coat of arms, sing an anthem and put another color on the map – but also to be economically free.' There could be no true political independence, he stated, 'unless there is economic independence'.[18]

On this, Fidel certainly had a point. While many in Washington were happy to give rhetorical support to decolonization, and welcomed the independence of former colonies, there was a distinct lack of empathy when it came to economic reforms that either threatened America's existing interests (including access to markets as well as to strategic resources such as oil and uranium) or smacked of communism (a distinction that often appeared to exist only on paper). Government officials – under the sway of modernization theorists, and keen to see off the communist threat – sent billions of dollars in development aid to the Global South during the 1950s, covering everything from agricultural assistance to the development of a consumer society, in the belief that the economic development of the region, along capitalist lines, would serve to strengthen the dynamism and overall stability of the so-called Free World. Alongside aid, more robust measures were also available to protect what America believed to be its vital national interests: the CIA, for instance, helped to sponsor regime change in Iran (1953) and Guatemala (1954); while, by the end of 1960, there were some 700 US military advisers in South Vietnam, helping to shore up the government of Ngo Dinh Diem. The Soviet Union, to be sure, was no paragon of virtue: having imposed 'people's democracies' in Eastern Europe through the ruthless application of force and police terror, Moscow was now attempting through military and economic aid to draw newly independent states in Africa and Asia into the Soviet orbit.[19]

Fidel, though, was not about to start criticizing his new friends in the Kremlin. After speaking in support of Khrushchev's proposals for disarmament and calling for the admission of the People's Republic of China to the United Nations, he turned his attention once more to the United States. The government in Washington 'cannot', he declared, 'be on the side of the peasants who want land because it is an ally of the landowners. It cannot be on the side of workers seeking better living conditions, in any part of the world, because it is an ally of the monopolies. It cannot be on the side of the colonies seeking liberation, because it is an ally of the colonizers.' World opinion, including public opinion in the United States, needed to look afresh at the world's problems: the underdeveloped countries (who were, after all, in the majority) 'cannot always be painted as the aggressors; revolutionaries cannot always be presented as . . . enemies of the US people.' Cuba, meanwhile, was, 'and will always be, on the side of the just. We are, and always will be, against colonialism, against exploitation, against the monopolies, against warmongering, against the arms race and against the playing at war. That is, and always will be, our position.'[20]

As the clock approached 8.15 p.m., Fidel ended by quoting from the recent Declaration of Havana. The Cuban people, he explained, stood for nothing less than:

> The right of the peasants to the land; the right of the workers
> to the fruit of their labor; the right of children to education;
> the right of the sick to medical treatment and hospital
> attention; the right of youth to work; the right of students to
> free education . . . ; the right of Negroes and Indians to full
> dignity as human beings; the right of women to civil, social
> and political equality; the right of the elderly to a secure old
> age; the right of intellectuals, artists, and scientists to fight,
> with their work, for a better world . . . the right of nations to
> their full sovereignty; the right of peoples to turn fortresses
> into schools, and to arm their workers, peasants, students,

intellectuals, blacks, Indians, women, the young and the old, and all the oppressed and exploited people, so they themselves can defend their rights and their destiny.

'Some of you wanted to know what line the revolutionary government in Cuba was following,' Fidel proclaimed. 'There it is!'[21]

Exaggerating just a bit, *Bohemia* reported that Fidel's speech had been:

interrupted thirty times by outbreaks of applause, which in certain moments became ovations. In the press-box, to the surprise of those who were accustomed to UN sessions, claps were often heard. First the Latin American journalists clapped, caught up in the stirring and true words of the speaker. Then their European colleagues joined the wave of enthusiasm that was gaining ground with every paragraph of the denouncement launched against the very face of the northern colossus.

He stepped from the podium and returned to his seat at 8.20 p.m. *Bohemia* reported that 'numerous delegates . . . approached Fidel . . . to shake his hand'; 'whilst the Assembly members in league with imperialism left in frosty silence, there was a human whirlwind around the Cuban Prime Minister.'[22]

The delegates from the Soviet Union and the Eastern bloc had offered repeated applause throughout (Khrushchev was particularly demonstrative – at one point standing up and raising his fist), and representatives from Ghana and Guinea now crowded round Fidel, shaking his hand enthusiastically. Others, though, appeared rather less enamoured. As Fidel's speech passed the two-hour mark, some in the audience had begun looking at their watches, while others shifted restlessly in their seats. Nehru even appeared to take a nap (though, in fairness, he was seventy years of age), while others discreetly left the chamber; by the time Fidel finished speaking, reported the *New York Times*, the hall was half empty. At one point, Celia Sánchez, Castro's loyal confidante and a dynamic figure within the 26 July Movement, turned to her cousin, Julio Girona, who was sitting beside her in the Assembly Hall, and declared, 'Fidel is talking too much.' Afterwards, one friendly Italian journalist 'observed that Fidel had said all he had to say in the first hour, and that it was a shame he had gone on so long'.[23]

In Cuba, the entire country had shut down for the afternoon. People gathered in parks and public spaces to hear the speech, including 500 who congregated outside the National Capitol building, where a television screen and speakers had been rigged up; those with a radio or TV set in their home were asked to leave their windows and doors open, so that those without access to one would not miss out.*[24] Fidel's historic address before the General Assembly was greeted with acclaim: 'FORMIDABLE! A DAY OF GLORY FOR CUBA', proclaimed the front page of *Revolución*, which hailed his 'sensational' and 'brilliant' speech. By using his speech not only to defend the Cuban Revolution, but to launch a wider attack on US imperialism and to champion the rights of the peoples of the so-called underdeveloped world to seize control of their own destinies, Fidel had laid claim to a wider, global role.[25] His voice, declared one commentator, had 'transformed a small Caribbean people into an example for America, Asia and Africa'; it was a 'voice that was the bane of imperialists, monopolists, of bastard egos, of feudal mentalities, of historical banalities, and of myths and prejudices manufactured in the workshops of Wall Street by jugglers of the dollar'. It was a voice that 'continue[d]

---

* At the time, only the United States boasted more televisions per capita than Cuba – where the rate was one in twenty-five – while radio ownership, at one for every six inhabitants, was broadly similar. Figures from Lillian Guerra, *Visions of Power in Cuba: Revolution, Redemption, and Resistance, 1959–1971* (Chapel Hill: The University of North Carolina Press, 2012), 41.

to shout in the name of all those who . . . had long suffered from the hunger and thirst for justice'.[26] As one Latin American diplomat is said to have remarked, 'the presence of Cuba has disrupted the geography of America. The Caribbean island now seems like a continent, and the continent seems like an island.'[27] Cuba's Radio Mambi, meanwhile, declared that 'no one has ever spoken so precisely, so clearly, so sincerely, and so patriotically at any international event as Fidel Castro did . . . in the U.N. General Assembly'. Anyone who 'really desires freedom' and 'every true Cuban' would, they said, 'feel proud of the role that our country and our leader are playing in the future of humanity'.[28]

Not everyone was convinced. In Costa Rica, whose centre-right government led by Mario Echandi had no time for Fidel, the press condemned the speech as 'disordered, incoherent and vulgar invective'; nothing but 'words, words, and more words'.[29] American commentators were scarcely more enthusiastic: *Time* magazine dismissed Fidel's 'anti-U.S. farrago', while the *New York Herald Tribune* poured scorn on a 'boorish four and a half hour talkathon' that 'not only imposed on his distinguished listeners' time and patience, but insulted their intelligence'. The United Nations, they declared, deserved 'more respect'.[30] In comments to the Cambodian leader, Prince Sihanouk, President Eisenhower noted, wryly, that 'despite their passion for complete coverage' the American television networks had finally given up and pulled the live feed of Fidel's speech.[31]

Writing in the London *Observer*, Cyril Dunn lamented how Fidel's speech had been treated by the US press 'only with derision' – according to one wag, it had covered everything except 'the [recent] row between the British and Iceland over the sardine harvest'. This was, Dunn argued, profoundly unfair: despite its great length, it had presented 'an impressively coherent version of Cuba's sad history, as seen by a revolutionary Socialist as old-fashioned as Keir Hardie'.[32] It was a view shared by the left-wing

*France-Observateur*: in attacking US imperialism Fidel had, they declared, 'touched on something that is very sensitive for Latin Americans and for the rest of the colonial peoples', something that, far from simply being a matter for rational discussion, was 'part of their history, part of their blood'.[33]

In private, some senior Western diplomats agreed. Sir Patrick Dean, Britain's Permanent Representative at the United Nations, cautioned against underestimating Castro's speech: 'repetitive and tedious though it became', he wrote in a report filed on 12 November, 'his diatribe found many anti-American echoes among Latin American representatives here – echoes which will presumably be heard in less muted tones among the populations of the Latin American countries.'[34] While some delegates had 'objected to being addressed in the General Assembly as if they were a Cuban crowd in the streets of Havana', British officials noted privately that 'later, when this impression also had faded somewhat, they admitted grudgingly that he had said many things that wanted saying . . .'[35] It was a view that was shared on the other side of the Atlantic: in a briefing paper submitted in advance of the cabinet meeting of 7 October, Richard F. Pederson – a senior American diplomat at the UN – noted that Castro had 'made an effective verbal attack on the United States which impressed many delegates, including the new Africans, at the time'.[36]

Fidel's over-preparation, lack of self-discipline and natural loquaciousness had made it easy for his enemies to dismiss the speech as nothing more than an over-long tirade.[37] But this – his only real misstep of the entire trip – appeared to do him, and the Cuban cause, no great harm. Notably, the Fair Play for Cuba Committee was quick to declare his speech 'one of the most outstanding political documents of a generation', while I. F. Stone praised it as a 'tour de force'.[38] Indeed, Fidel's powerful critique of what he viewed as American empire was one that would resonate increasingly among the emerging New Left. Inspired by the revisionist scholarship of William Appleman Williams – whose *The Tragedy of American Diplomacy*, published in 1959, argued that the search for overseas markets and commercial expansion had been the driving force behind US foreign policy since the closing of the frontier in 1890 – a new generation of intellectuals, students and activists were increasingly vocal in their disillusionment with Washington's support for a series of repressive anti-communist dictatorships overseas (including in South Korea, South Vietnam and the Dominican Republic). They were also ever more willing to criticize their country's deployment of military, economic and cultural power in an effort to secure global hegemony.[39] It was a critique that would reach its apogee just a few years later, during the mass protests against America's military involvement in Vietnam, when many leading opponents of the war argued that, rather than defending South Vietnamese 'freedom' against communist aggression, the United States, in seeking to crush a legitimate struggle for national liberation, was instead playing the role of a colonial power.[40] Meanwhile, Fidel's affirmation of the 'rights of nations to their full sovereignty' and of the right of 'all oppressed and exploited people' to 'defend their rights and their destiny' foreshadowed Havana's robust, even daring support for revolutionaries across Latin America and Africa in the years ahead.

# 11

# TUESDAY 27 SEPTEMBER

The process of liberation is irresistible and irreversible.
UN RESOLUTION 1514

Early on the morning of Tuesday 27 September, Harold Macmillan – who had flown in to McGuire Air Force Base, New Jersey, aboard an RAF Comet thirty-six hours previously – sat down for an informal catch-up in President Eisenhower's Waldorf-Astoria suite. As the two old friends ate breakfast, Ike outlined his wish to pay a three- or four-day visit to Great Britain in November, after the US election, so that he might 'pay his respects to the Queen', and also hold useful talks with senior politicians 'on the prospects for continued collaboration under the new administration'. Then, at 9 a.m., the two men were joined by senior officials, including Lord Home and Christian Herter, for a more formal review of recent foreign policy developments.[1]

Macmillan noted that the mood of the General Assembly appeared to be improving and 'there is a feeling that Khrushchev has overplayed his hand'. The mere mention of the Soviet leader's name, though, prompted an interjection by Eisenhower, who denounced the recent luncheon that had been hosted by Cyrus Eaton as 'about as despicable a thing as he knew of'. Steering the conversation back to the UN, Herter 'said that Hammarskjöld has told him that it begins to look as though the United Nations had imported from the Congo some of the political chaos that now exists there'. But Eisenhower was optimistic that 'after Khrushchev, Castro and their associates go home, the United Nations discussions may take a better turn'. As for the Congo itself, Lord Home – speaking with a frankness that, sixty years on, is striking –

'raised the question of why we are not getting rid of Lumumba at the present time', and 'stressed' that, with Lumumba now holed up in his official residence following a coup, the time to act was now (a week earlier, British diplomats had told the Americans that they were rather proud of the fact that they had been 'cultivating Colonel Mobutu for some time'). According to Herter, Hammarskjöld had told him that 'the United Nations would interpose no objection to the arrest of Lumumba if it were done by legal means'.\* The whole issue was, though, highly emotive – it was reported that, in conversations with both the British and the Americans, Nehru had spoken with great feeling about the 'wickedness' of Belgium for having 'left the Congo without having made any provision for its government'. The meeting ended with Eisenhower expressing his hopes that Nigeria, which was 'more populous and more advanced than the other countries', might be able to exercise real leadership in Africa. But as the meeting broke up, Lord Home provided a telling reminder that America's domestic difficulties over racial inequality, including in what some historians have come to call the 'Jim Crow North', were never far away. The First Secretary of the Nigerian delegation had approached him, he explained, to 'say that he is finding it impossible to get a place to live in New York because of his color'. Herter noted that 'this problem is a terribly difficult one', while Eisenhower advised that 'it should be taken up with Mayor Wagner and Police Commissioner Kennedy at once'.[2] This was, though, just one of a series of high-profile incidents of racial discrimination affecting delegates to the Fifteenth General

---

\* Lumumba left Léopoldville on 27 November, in an effort to rally support in his stronghold of Stanleyville, in the north-east of the country. He was captured by Mobutu's troops, with the active connivance of US and Belgian forces, on 1 December. After being humiliated in public and beaten mercilessly while in custody, he was executed by firing squad on 17 January 1961, in the presence of Tshombe, the Katangese leader. Lumumba's body was then dismembered before being dissolved in acid. To date, no one has been held accountable for this heinous crime.

Assembly, which ultimately prompted the NAACP to offer the UN Secretary General its help in resolving the situation.[3] The incidents included complaints from African officials about 'slow' service or 'condescending treatment' in hotels and restaurants; Fonmin Dejain of the Central African Republic reported that a newsboy had thrown a newspaper at him; and a Cameroonian diplomat accused the NYPD of having 'manhandled' him as he approached the UN headquarters.[4]

Eschewing his fellow leaders' fondness for limousines and motorcades (the city, noted one Soviet newspaper report, was 'echoing almost continuously to the wild, not to say hysterical, wail of sirens'), Macmillan, accompanied by a solitary detective, made the short walk to the United Nations General Assembly Building, where Nasser provided the day's main draw.[5] The British prime minister, who as chancellor of the exchequer had been one of the cabinet's most enthusiastic hawks during the Suez Crisis, must have had mixed feelings about Britain's old foe. But, the previous day, during a lull in proceedings at the General Assembly, Macmillan had made a point of walking over to the UAR delegation, so that he could shake hands with the Arab leader. The two men, it was reported, had 'wished each other a good day and exchanged other pleasantries'.[6]

'Almost unknown five years ago', noted Foster Hailey of the *New York Times*, today Nasser was 'a spokesman to whom world leaders listened closely'.[7] The UAR president began by welcoming the nations who had recently joined the United Nations, having 'struggled for their political independence' and making 'great sacrifices to achieve it', before urging member states to rally in defence of the UN Charter and ensure that the organization could pursue 'peaceful development and achieve its high ideals'. 'The work of safeguarding peace' at a time of heightened Cold War tensions was, he declared, 'not only a vital necessity' but 'a moral duty'.

After adding his voice to those calling for the admission of the People's Republic of China to the UN, Nasser turned his attention to 'imperialism'. Whereas 'the aggression of Suez was the end of unmasked imperialism and its graveyard', the UAR president warned that 'today we find the Congo presenting us with masked imperialism'. 'All who believe in freedom and in the United Nations' should, he said, stand united in defence of the people of the Congo.

Calling for the 'restoration of the full rights of the people of Palestine' (who had, he declared, not just been deprived of their homes but been 'robbed of their very lives') and reiterating his support for 'the right of the Algerian people to self-determination', Nasser celebrated the fact that 'the remnants of imperialism' were 'retreating everywhere before the march of the peoples'. But he captured the headlines with his call for Eisenhower and Khrushchev – these two 'great leaders' whom 'our peoples hold in high respect and esteem' – to meet 'either by themselves or with whoever may be selected among those who are present here in order for them to set up, under the aegis of the United Nations, guiding rules for a new attempt toward disarmament'. After all, he warned, in an age of nuclear weapons 'a miscalculation by any party' could 'in minutes destroy the greatest and most beautiful achievements of mankind throughout its long and glorious struggle'.[8]

The speech, which lasted for an hour and twenty minutes, was warmly received in the hall: Khrushchev, as was to be expected, was especially demonstrative – interspersing his clapping with 'gestures toward the United States delegation' – but, as the *New York Times* reported, 'even delegates from two of the Western countries whose policies he attacked – Britain and the United States', joined in the applause as Nasser stepped from the podium. Thronged by leaders from Asia, Africa and the Arab world, it took the UAR president fifteen minutes to make his way to the delegates' lounge, where he spent a further half an hour 'signing autographs and receiving congratulations'.[9] Praised by many Western commentators (according to the *Guardian*'s James Morris, the address was 'as sensible as any we have heard in this Assembly'[10]), Nasser's speech also received top billing – and 'eulogistic' commentary – in Cuba. *Revolución*, for instance, praised his 'impassioned' defence of 'all the peoples of the world who have risen up against the slavery imposed by imperialism'.[11]

For Fidel Castro, who had paid a final visit to the General Assembly in order to hear Nasser, the next stop was the Ghanaian mission, at 144 East 44th Street, and a meeting with Kwame Nkrumah, the country's president and renowned Pan-African revolutionary.

A Christian, a Marxist and a Pan-Africanist who remained captivated by Marcus Garvey's vision of a proud, unified Africa freed from European colonialism, Nkrumah – born in a small village in the south-west of the country in 1909 – had initially been disparaged by the British as 'our local little Hitler'. But, by demanding 'Self-government Now!' and launching a campaign of nonviolent civil disobedience in January 1950, he had wrested the initiative away from an older generation of more moderate nationalists and forced the colonial authorities, and the government in London, to recognize both his personal popularity and his legitimacy. Becoming the colony's prime minister in 1952, he led Ghana to independence from the British in March 1957 (three years later, it voted overwhelmingly to become a republic). Ghanaian independence – the first surrender of colonial power in sub-Saharan Africa – was a transformative moment in the history of European empire, energizing nationalist movements across Africa and the Caribbean. For a time, this signal achievement made Nkrumah one of Africa's most inspiring and admired leaders, and it was a striking sign of the respect in which he was held that Fidel decided to pay homage in person.[12]

Nkrumah had flown out of Accra, aboard a specially chartered Pan-Am aeroplane – the 'Jet Clipper Osagyefo'* – on the morning of Wednesday 21 September (the occasion of his fifty-first birthday), seen off in typically understated fashion by an honour guard, a twenty-one-gun salute and thousands of cheering, waving supporters.[13] The following afternoon, he met with Eisenhower at the Waldorf; he had, he explained, been keen to see the US president prior to any talks with Khrushchev. The discussions went well: Nkrumah thanked the Americans for their financial support for the ambitious Volta River hydroelectric power project – construction of the dam would begin the following year – and congratulated Eisenhower on his speech at the UN earlier that day (Nkrumah was, he said, 'most enthusiastic of all' about the proposals to send aid to Africa for education). Moreover, when it came to the ongoing crisis in the Congo, there appeared to be a strong consensus: the United Nations, they agreed, had to take the lead in resolving the situation, and both leaders held Dag Hammarskjöld in high esteem.[14]

The following morning, Friday 23 September, Nkrumah – 'dressed in traditional robes of gold and orange kente cloth', and with an elegant cane hanging from his left wrist – took to the podium in the General Assembly.[15] Celebrating 'the momentous impact of Africa's awakening upon the world' and welcoming the 'dawn of a new era', the African leader requested permanent seats on the Security Council for representatives of Africa, Asia and the Middle East; attacked Portuguese colonialism and South African apartheid; called for a negotiated settlement to the war in Algeria; and demanded that the Cold War be kept out of Africa. No African state, he said, should enter into a military alliance with 'any outside Power'. The bulk of his speech, though, focused on the Congo. Criticizing the record of Belgium and denouncing

* Nkrumah had taken the title Osagyefo, which means 'redeemer' in the Akan language.

[ 180 ]

continuing colonialist intrigue, Nkrumah declared that this was 'an acute African problem which can be solved by Africans only'. In remarks that drew 'enthusiastic applause', he suggested that the UN command in the Congo should be restricted to Africans and tasked with supporting the 'legitimate' government of Patrice Lumumba.[16] Fidel had been the first to his feet and when Khrushchev noticed the African delegates joining in the ovation, he too stood and gestured to his comrades to join him. As the Ghanaian president returned to his seat the Soviet leader, who was scheduled to speak next, made sure to grasp his hands and offer him warm – and very public – congratulations.[17]

One person who was not cheering was Christian Herter. Speaking to members of the Foreign Press Association a few hours later, the American Secretary of State (who, he freely admitted, had not even listened to the whole speech) declared that Nkrumah 'sounded to me as though he were definitely making a bid for the leadership of what you would call a left-wing group of African States [. . .] I think he has marked himself as very definitely leaning toward the Soviet bloc.'[18] Later, in a private meeting with the Israeli foreign minister, Golda Meir, Herter explained that 'he was frankly upset' by the speech because 'Nkrumah had talked entirely differently the day before . . .' He had, he confessed, also been 'disturbed that Nkrumah felt it desirable to make a great show of shaking hands with Khrushchev and comporting himself generally like a satellite'.[19]

Herter's outburst did the United States no favours. Naturally, it went down very badly in Ghana itself. The *Ghanaian Times* declared that Africans were 'sick and tired' of the 'vanity of the self-appointed mentors and spokesmen of the world', while the *Daily Record* noted that Nkrumah's uncompromising stance on how best to deal with Africa's problems was 'bound to frighten those world leaders' who sought to 'continue to dictate the course of world events and "keep the African in his place"'.[20] Nkrumah himself was diplomatic, though firm: Herter was, he said, 'the last person from whom I would have expected such a remark. I thought that [he] understood the African viewpoint . . .'[21] In the United States, the *Washington Post* decried Herter's 'gaffe', while a *New York Times* editorial lamented how the Secretary of State had permitted himself to fall into a trap of equating Nkrumah with the communists, simply because, on some questions, he took a similar position to that of the Soviet Union. 'The deep desire of many of the less-developed nations, especially in Asia and Africa, to remain outside of the power struggle between the United States and the Soviet Union' was, they explained, 'not fully appreciated in this country'.[22] In remarks to Malcolm MacDonald, Britain's outgoing High Commissioner to India, Nehru lamented Herter's lack of tact, pointing out that the issuing of 'such a public, as well as mis-placed, reproof could only do damage among America's would-be friends'. Notably, even some of Washington's staunchest allies were irritated.[23] On the afternoon of 27 September, the Canadian prime minister John Diefenbaker told Herter directly that he had 'never considered Nkrumah a Communist' and pointed out that 'the publicity concerning the Secretary's comment had discour-aged Nkrumah whereas a few kind words might have brought him back into line.'[24]

It was a damaging episode, and one that augured a deterior-ation in US–Ghanaian relations in the months ahead.[25] But the spat with Nkrumah was also indicative of how, in its attempts to win over the newly independent states of Africa, Washington was too often on the back foot. When it came to the crunch, Eisen-hower was unwilling to risk damaging relations with key allies in Europe by, for example, publicly criticizing their continued pres-ence on the African continent. And, eager not to reward countries that 'played both sides in the Cold War', the administration was also deeply suspicious of 'neutralism' (John Foster Dulles, who had served as Ike's influential Secretary of State until April 1959, had viewed it as merely a 'transitional stage to communism').[26] During a meeting with Jordan's King Hussein, on 7 October, for instance, Eisenhower 'said he was sometimes puzzled regarding the attitudes of some countries. He quite understands that they might say that they will be neutral as between the two power blocs. He does not understand how any nation can be neutral as between being free and not being free, or between right and wrong.'[27] It was a blinkered view of the emerging Global South that severely limited America's flexibility and succeeded only in handing the initiative to her enemies in Moscow and Beijing.

In contrast with Khrushchev, who launched something of a 'charm offensive' while in New York – eagerly pressing the flesh, and attending every reception going – Eisenhower was reluctant to expend too much energy on courting the new African leaders.[28] He did meet – briefly – with the leaders of fifteen African countries (including Cameroon, Nigeria and Ivory Coast) in the White House on 14 October, but as he told his cabinet, 'he couldn't have a lunch or a dinner for each of them – it takes too much out of the day'.[29] It was a stance that evidently caused some frustration among State Department officials, who understood the importance of getting off to a 'good start' with the delegates from the new African nations: 'in our judgment', stated an internal memorandum, '[the] first few weeks at UNGA may determine patterns of relationships that could have long-lasting influence on [the] outlook [of] these new delegations.'[30] When Eisenhower did engage directly with African leaders, though, it could do more harm than good. On the morning of 23 September, for instance, the president met with Sylvanus Olympio, leader of the Togolese Republic. Eisenhower found his African counterpart to be 'most impressive', and particularly admired his 'wonderful sense of humor' – which was, he later wrote, 'an unusual trait in the leaders of some of the newer nations'. But, as one historian has pointed out, Olympio, a proud and educated man (he had degrees from three European universities), was likely 'infuriated' by Eisenhower's 'insensitive and condescending' comments after he raised the subject of why Togo had to share an ambassador with faraway Cameroon. After Herter had mentioned budgetary constraints, Eisenhower, apparently unaware that 'civilization' had reached Togo's capital, Lomé, followed up with a suggestion that 'there would be no harm in a few of these Ambassadors living in tents. It would have a salutary effect if our Ambassadors would, in some of these regions, live in simple surroundings.'[31]

Even more damaging was the American decision – following a personal plea from Harold Macmillan – to abstain in a General Assembly vote on resolution 1514. Debated on 14 December, the measure, which had been proposed by delegates from the Afro-Asian bloc, declared that 'the process of liberation is irresistible and irreversible' and called for 'a speedy and unconditional end [to] colonialism in all its forms and manifestations'. The United States was one of only nine countries who failed to support the measure (Australia, Belgium, the Dominican Republic, France, Portugal, Spain, South Africa and the UK also abstained), and the decision prompted 'an audible gasp of surprise' in the Assembly Hall. Later, the head of the Nigerian delegation asked if Washington was 'trying to commit political suicide'.[32]

The Eisenhower administration might have been wittingly – or unwittingly – antagonizing the leaders of the newly independent nations, but Cuba's young leader was eager to show his support for the heroes of the anticolonial struggle. It was, then, in a mood of some excitement that Fidel arrived at the Ghanaian mission late on the afternoon of Tuesday 27 September, where, amid the throng of rush-hour commuters, he was loudly booed and hissed at by many of the hundreds of pedestrians who were passing by. He endured a twenty-minute wait until Nkrumah's 'gleaming Rolls-Royce Silver Wraith' – with the flag of Ghana and the president's personal emblem flying from the front bumper – finally drew up outside. After embracing warmly, the two leaders then chatted for about forty minutes, and Fidel presented the Osagyefo with a gift: a wooden box of Cuban cigars.[33] While the Cuban prime minister was delighted to meet with Nkrumah, the Ghanaian leader likely had rather more mixed feelings about the encounter. Carlos Moore, Fidel's eighteen-year-old translator, later noted that, in moving to Harlem, the Cuban leader had 'psychologically outflanked Africa's most politically radical leaders on their own terrain'.[34] And for Ghana's president, this was personal. When, during the course of their discussions, Fidel sought to steer the conversation on to the 'embarrassment of racial discrimination in the United States', Nkrumah's response was telling:

> Doctor Castro, you may not know that when I was young,
> I lived here. One day, I wandered the streets, entered a cafe
> and asked for water. I can never forget the white waiter's
> response: 'If you want me to give you water, you have to
> drink it in the spittoon that is on the floor.'[35]

In fact, for ten years from 1935, while a student at Lincoln University, Pennsylvania (where he studied theology, politics and philosophy), Nkrumah had spent his summers in Harlem, working a series of odd jobs – including stints in a soap factory and peddling fish from a wooden cart – and immersing himself in the neighbourhood's rich cultural life. He had browsed the shelves of Lewis Michaux's bookstore, attended revivalist church services and participated in meetings of the Blyden Society, which was dedicated to the study of African history. In July 1958, as prime minister of the newly independent Ghana, he had received a rapturous welcome on returning to Harlem, as ten thousand locals lined the parade route along Seventh Avenue, and a similar number packed into the 369th Anti-Aircraft Group Armory for an emotional 'homecoming' rally.[36] A week and a half after Fidel's departure from New York, the Osegyefo made a last-minute decision to go to Harlem himself. Standing outside the Theresa on the evening of 7 October, he addressed a 1,500-strong rally and, to cries of 'Long Live Nkrumah!' proclaimed that 'Africa is on the march', called on skilled African Americans to travel to Africa and 'help your brothers', and celebrated the 'solid bond we feel between the people of Africa and the Afro-Americans in this country'.[37] But, as Carlos Moore observed, Fidel's earlier 'theatrics' had stolen much of his thunder.[38]

After taking tea with Nkrumah, Castro headed back to the Theresa for a date with Jawaharlal Nehru, who had made the pilgrimage up to Harlem. 'I wanted to meet you for many reasons,' the Indian statesman told Castro, 'above all, because you are a very brave man.' 'If you had not come, I would have come to you,' Fidel replied. Speaking in a mix of broken English and Spanish (which he reverted to when the correct word or phrase evaded him), the Cuban leader told Nehru that 'you are a man of peace', and 'you are doing the work of all of us'. In the relaxed, informal and slightly chaotic setting of Fidel's suite, Nehru began by recalling how, when he was a young boy, his tutor's brother had regaled him with stories about the Cuban War of Independence (1895–8). He had, he explained, subsequently taken a keen interest in the Cuban Revolution. Fidel, who was clearly delighted by all this, then moved the conversation on to the current world situation before focusing on the question of land reform and the economic challenges facing Cuba. Reporting live from the Theresa, the influential radio commentator – and Fidel supporter – José Pardo Llada described how, having discussed these topics at some length, Fidel then:

> presented Nehru with a complete collection of the INRA [National Agrarian Reform Institute] magazine. Nehru put on his glasses and scanned the magazines carefully. He was especially interested in the Cuban system of house-building,

the cooperatives, and the land reform. Then Nehru asked
Fidel about the events that led to the Cuban revolution
and listened with interest while Fidel explained them to
him. Mr. Nehru was also interested in the conditions under
which the nationalization policy has been carried out.

Apologizing for his hoarse voice, Fidel explained that the New
York climate 'did not agree with him', though he was quick to
clarify that he had been talking about the weather rather than the
politics: 'they boo me in the middle-class areas,' he explained (the
hostile reaction of the bystanders near the Ghanaian mission still
fresh in his mind), but 'here in Harlem, where the poor live, they
cheer me.' As Nehru prepared to depart, Fidel handed him a gilded
bust of José Martí, as well as an alligator-skin handbag for his
daughter, Indira Gandhi, who was planning a visit to Cuba.[39] His
decision to meet with Castro had, Nehru later learned, 'incensed'
the Americans. But, he said, it would have been 'impossible for
him not to see Castro' when he was 'making a point of meeting
everyone else of importance'.[40]

Later that evening, Fidel was one of only fifty guests at a party
hosted by Nehru in the Victorian Suite, on the second floor of
the Carlyle Hotel, on Madison Avenue and 76th Street, as part
of an attempt by the Indian leader to ease Cold War tensions
and encourage meaningful disarmament. Over a buffet dinner of
lobster, Dover sole, chicken curry and roasted saddle of lamb, the
guests, who represented countries from across NATO (although
no British or American representative attended'), the Warsaw
Pact, Israel and the Arab world, and South America, chatted infor-
mally. The Soviet leader, Nikita Khrushchev – whose favourite

* Christian Herter later apologized to Nehru: the significance of the event
had, he claimed, not been made clear to him and, having already made dinner
plans, he had 'regretfully declined your kind invitation'. But, he said, he
'felt very badly about this misunderstanding on my part and hope you will
understand the circumstances'.

dish was known to be a Cossack stew made of millet and pork fat – 'sent guests into peals of laughter when, pointing to his girth, he resolved that he was henceforth going to live on cabbages. But he was, he said, also going to make up for it by a hearty meal now.'[41] It was a jocular display that contrasted starkly with his behaviour at the UN General Assembly. Just two days later, for instance, the Soviet leader appeared to take great offence at Harold Macmillan's speech (in which the British prime minister praised the 'energy' and 'integrity' of the UN Secretary General, and, turning to disarmament, called for a system of international inspection and control). Glowering, gesticulating and banging on his desk, Khrushchev eventually leaped to his feet and began shouting (in Russian). The prime minister paused, looked up from his notes and, in an effective put-down that prompted ripples of laughter throughout the chamber, simply said, 'I'd like that translated, if I may.'[42] Most famously of all, on 12 October, when a Filipino diplomat attacked Soviet 'colonialism' in Eastern Europe, Khrushchev, his face flushed red, suddenly leaped to his feet and began pounding on his desk with his right shoe (a brown loafer, it was said). Although some have questioned whether this extraordinary incident ever actually took place, it was later used against Khrushchev when he was removed from power in the autumn of 1964: evidence, his rivals said, of his increasingly erratic behaviour.[43]

In the course of just seventy-two hours, Fidel had enjoyed high-profile meetings with three men – Nasser, Nehru and Nkrumah – who were icons of the global struggle against colonialism, and leading lights among the non-aligned nations. It had been, if nothing else, a public relations triumph for Latin America's young firebrand. But some observers wondered whether the revolutionary government in Havana might be preparing, after all, to plot a middle course: accepting financial, economic and technical support from all who were willing to provide it, while refusing to slavishly take sides in the Cold War. Maybe. But, within hours, Cuba's increasing reliance on Moscow would be on public display once again.

Before heading home, Fidel made time for one final press conference outside
the Hotel Theresa.

Photograph by Bettman via Getty Images

# 12

# WEDNESDAY 28 SEPTEMBER

Castro, Go Home!
*NEW YORK CITIZEN-CALL*

After ten frenetic days in New York, it was finally time for Fidel to head home. For the New York *Daily News*, the Cuban's departure was a cause for celebration: 'Hurricane Fidel will roar homeward', they exclaimed, 'providing the rare but delightful meteorological spectacle of a big Caribbean wind going in a reverse, southward direction.'[1] But even among those who had been sympathetic to Fidel, there was a feeling that the Cuban premier now risked outstaying his welcome. 'Castro, Go Home!' proclaimed the front page of the *New York Citizen-Call*. Under pressure, it was said, from advertisers, the paper – which had earlier commented favourably on the Cuban 'invasion' of Harlem – now argued that Fidel had already 'proven his point'. By the 'simple act' of moving to Harlem, he had succeeded in shaping 'a most powerful propaganda image for the African nations, for all dark peoples of the world to see' and had focused international attention on black Americans' second-class citizenship. But, the paper now declared, the continued presence of Fidel's face 'bent forward from the window of the Theresa' was 'not going to solve anything for us'.[2] Standing outside his beloved hotel, Love B. Woods told the press that his Cuban guests 'didn't give me any trouble while they were here'. The party had paid in full and left their rooms in 'very good condition'. But, pressed repeatedly on whether he would be happy to 'take Castro back', Woods replied, 'Voluntarily, no. Compulsory, yes. This is the greatest country in the world,' he explained, and 'I don't agree with any guest, be he an American or foreigner who will lambast my country.'[3]

Having welcomed Cyrus Eaton to the Theresa for a thirty-minute meeting (the Cuban leader was, declared the industrialist, 'a man with great energy and ambition and devoted to helping his people'), Fidel motored to the UAR mission, on Park Avenue, for a courtesy call on President Nasser. Finally, at 1.40 p.m., the Cuban leader left the Theresa for the last time (ever the businessman, Woods had threatened to charge the Cubans for every hour that they stayed beyond the agreed 2 p.m. checkout time). Declaring that he was 'completely satisfied' with his UN performance, Fidel also thanked the NYPD for taking 'such good security measures', a comment that left James B. Leggett, Chief of Detectives, 'visibly startled'. Then, waving to the crowds, he bade them 'Good-bye and good luck' and '*buena cabeza*' ('don't do anything stupid'). Seconds later, his twenty-car motorcade – transporting Fidel as well as a large part of his delegation – was heading east, along 125th Street and over the Triborough Bridge, bound for the Grand Central Parkway, and then the Van Wyck Expressway that would take them to New York's international airport.[4]

Within hours of their departure, anti-Castro Cuban exiles had swooped in, staging a 'fiesta-like street "clean-up" for what they called an unwelcome guest, complete with rhumba music and sweep-up equipment'.[5] But not everyone was pleased to see Fidel go. Although some local store owners had suffered as a result of the heavy police barricades and tight security, the nightly pro-Castro crowds had, it was estimated, brought as much as half a million dollars in extra business to Harlem.[6] Julian Mayfield noted that 'the Baby Grand and every nearby bar did a thriving business, along with the pick-pockets and the sellers of "liberated" goods (records, clothing, home appliances), and they all must have shed a tear when Fidel finally went home.'[7]

On arriving at Idlewild Field, amid heavy security (some 300 police officers and detectives were on hand), Fidel was escorted to Hangar 17, where there was – naturally – time for one last press conference. Americans were, he declared, 'good people' who were 'not guilty' of all of the lies that were being told about his country and its revolution. Similarly, US reporters were 'wonderful', though 'not the bosses of the papers, they belong to the monopoly'. Asked 'if he wasn't afraid of being swallowed by the loveable Russian bear', Fidel responded by claiming that 'never before have the Cuban people felt so free as now'. As for whether he was a communist, the Maximum Leader declared, 'I am the same man, doing in Cuba what we promised to do in Cuba. This revolution is the revolution of humble people and for humble people – something like Lincoln said.' Pressed again, he responded, 'Wait for history, history will tell who we are.' In any case, he said, in his trademark broken English, the Americans were confused: 'When you are nationalistic here they say you are Communistic [. . .] You don't know what you call Communist. You call that of everyone.'[8]

In the end, the manner of Fidel's departure – forced to fly home in an Ilyushin Il-18, loaned by the Soviets, after his own plane had been impounded by American creditors – was telling. Not only did it encapsulate the chaotic and unpredictable nature of his stay in New York, as the US authorities attempted to thwart him one final time, but it also foreshadowed his country's growing reliance on Moscow for economic and military support.

The drama had unfolded shortly after 1 p.m. when, with fifteen members of the Cuban delegation already on board the Cubana Airways Bristol Britannia, Joseph Slavin, a Brooklyn attorney representing a US owner of stock in the newly nationalized company, suddenly appeared in Hangar 17. Holding a court order declaring that the aircraft was now the property of receivers – and backed up by two security guards as well as officers from the Port Authority Police Department – Slavin insisted that the plane, which bore the inscription 'Cuban Delegation to the UN' as well as the coat of arms of the Republic of Cuba, could not be moved. On hearing the news, Raúl Roa, who was leading the UN delegation in Fidel's absence, raced to Idlewild to remonstrate in person. When warned that 'any person who boards [the plane] will be arrested', he called their bluff, and spent an hour inside the aircraft, before heading to a nearby office to lobby the State Department for its release. In a classic case of bureaucratic incompetence, local officials had impounded the Cuban plane even though the State Department regarded it as a 'public aircraft immune from the jurisdiction of our courts'. Senior officials did eventually intervene: Thomas C. Mann, Assistant Secretary of State for Inter-American Affairs, issued a formal request that 'the appropriate United States attorney be instructed to suggest to the court hearing this matter . . . that the Department of State recognizes the immunity of the aircraft from the exercise of jurisdiction by the court'. But, with no judge immediately on hand, the hearing at Brooklyn Supreme Court had to wait until 8 a.m. the following day (whereupon the aeroplane was promptly released). In the meantime, with the Soviet aircraft accommodating only thirty-three passengers, thirty-one members of the Cuban delegation were left stranded – several of them camped aboard the impounded jet, wrapped in blankets to ward off the chilly night air; others, 'tough campaigners all, bivouacked in Cubana Airlines' offices . . . sleeping on benches'.[9]

This final drama of Fidel's trip provided a striking illustration of the deteriorating relationship between the United States and Cuba. But it also offered the revolutionaries one further opportunity to attack their hosts: the seizure of the plane, in violation of all accepted international norms, was, they declared, 'a new attempt by the American authorities to provoke a serious incident'. A cartoon in *Revolución*, meanwhile, showed the figure of Uncle Sam, wearing a bandit mask and with an aeroplane tucked under his arm, running away from a Cuban, who was shouting 'STOP!'[10]

On board the replacement Soviet aeroplane were several purchases that Fidel had made during his stay in New York. The idiosyncratic haul included a new refrigerator, two cages of white mice and a 'goodly supply of new checked, striped, and plaid sports jackets', as well as an oil painting of the Cuban leader, carrying a naked woman on his shoulder before hundreds of cheering admirers. The painting, entitled *Castro and the Victory of the People*, had been presented to him by the artist, Sarah Beach, a sixty-three-year-old Brooklyn dressmaker. His brand-new Oldsmobile, though, would have to be shipped back to Havana later.[11]

As he boarded the aircraft, Fidel declared: 'the Soviets are our friends. Here you took our planes – the authorities robbed our planes. Soviets gave us plane.' The friendship was, it seemed, reciprocated. Interviewed for Cuban radio, Nikita Khrushchev announced that 'Not only today, but throughout the course of your struggle for independence, we shall be with you.'[12] At 3.14 p.m., Fidel's aircraft, piloted by its Russian captain, Ivan Grouba, roared down the runway and soared into the clouds.

The opening session of the General Assembly did not, of course, come to an end with Fidel's departure. The following evening, for instance, in an effort to kick-start talks between Washington and Moscow, Harold Macmillan met with Khrushchev at the Soviet mission for almost two hours. The British prime minister turned on the charm, praising Khrushchev as a wise statesman and complimenting him on the quality of his oratory, before turning to the vexed issues of disarmament and the future of Berlin.[13] Although the exchanges were perfectly friendly it was, explained Macmillan, 'evident to both of us that in view of all that had happened no serious negotiation could take place during this late stage in Eisenhower's presidency'.[14] A treaty banning the testing of nuclear weapons in the atmosphere, under water and in outer space was eventually concluded in the summer of 1963, but serious progress on disarmament would have to wait until the 1970s.[15] As for Berlin, the crisis was resolved, in a manner of speaking, by the construction of the Berlin Wall (or, as the GDR authorities had it, the 'anti-fascist protection rampart') in August 1961, which left the city permanently divided until the end of the Cold War, almost thirty years later.

Although he had threatened to stay until Christmas, Khrushchev eventually left New York on 13 October. His 'boorish' behaviour in the General Assembly appears to have played rather poorly among the new African members, and his demand for Dag Hammarskjöld's resignation went unheeded. But Khrushchev had grounds to feel pleased, nonetheless. His 'barbs' against Hammarskjöld 'helped consolidate the opinions of several neutralist leaders' who came to believe that the UN mission in the Congo had been afflicted by a pro-Western bias. And, though he viewed Khrushchev's idea of a 'troika' as 'wholly impractical', Nehru did raise with Eisenhower the possibility of appointing three Assistant Secretaries General, to help 'deal with all the African developments', or undertaking some other reorganization to give the Soviets 'rather more apparent influence' (the suggestion was politely rebuffed). More broadly, the Soviet Union's call for an immediate end to colonialism helped inspire the tabling of Resolution 1514 by a number of Afro-Asian nations.[16] Declaring that 'the subjection of peoples to alien subjugation, domination and exploitation' constituted a 'denial of fundamental human rights', and proclaiming the right of 'all peoples' to 'self-determination', the resolution called for 'immediate steps' in 'Trust and Non-Self-Governing Territories or all other territories which have not yet attained independence, to transfer all powers to the peoples of those territories, without any conditions or reservations, in accordance with their freely expressed will and desire, without any distinction as to race, creed or colour, in order to enable them to enjoy complete independence and freedom.'[17] Passed in mid-December (in a vote in which France, the United Kingdom and the United States were prominent abstainers), the resolution was, according to the historian

Mark Mazower, 'the most powerful call yet from the UN against a continuation of European empires'.[18] And, of course, Khrushchev had worked hard, both in public and in private, to cement the alliance with a man whom, on his return to Moscow, he lauded as 'the heroic son of the Cuban people' – Fidel Castro.[19]

At Rancho-Boyeros airport, thousands of ordinary Cubans – as well as senior government officials and the Soviet and Czechoslovakian ambassadors – had gathered to welcome Fidel home. *Revolución* described how a giant banner, declaring 'Fidel, we feel proud of you', had been hoisted from the airport terrace by the Federation of Cuban Women, and 'hundreds of multi-coloured parasols, caps, [and] banners glittered in the blue, pink, mauve twilight'. In sentimental mode, they declared that 'it was as if Mother Nature had also done her bit in the people's homage to the leader who was returning, triumphant, once more'. Suddenly, the cry went up, 'Fidel has arrived', and 'hundreds of men and women rushed to the airport's runway, and thousands of tricolour flags fluttered, on which a star shone, a single star, pure and solitary'. At 6.46 p.m., Fidel 'emerged from the plane door, smiling', his military cap flapping 'in the darkness of the twilight, which was already drifting away', to be greeted by a rapturous ovation. After the playing of the national anthem and the 26 July Movement song, the Maximum Leader descended the aircraft steps and was met by President Osvaldo Dorticós, Che Guevara and Raúl Castro, who ceremonially presented him with his pistol and ammunition belt. After 'warm hand-shakes and embraces' – and, we are told, 'a knot in the throat of the humble women and men' who were there to witness these scenes – it was time to head into Havana.[20]

A convoy of several hundred cars, with Fidel standing in an open-top jeep, now made its way along streets 'lined with militia, well-wishers and the curious', to the Presidential Palace, where people had been gathering since the early evening. The scenes along the highway were, *Revolución* gushed, evidence of 'the most enthusiastic demonstrations of affection, the most emotional proof of the faith and confidence of his people'. The 'flowers thrown from the hands of Cuban women, the chanting of revolutionary slogans, handshakes from men of the people' and the raucous cheers all served to show Fidel that 'his people had understood precisely the significance of his speech to the UN, and what it will mean in the future of the world'. The American ambassador, Philip Bonsal, his wife, Margaret, and several guests were settling down to watch the live television feed, following dinner in the embassy residence (in retaliation for the security measures in New York, Bonsal had been restricted to the Vedado district, site of his residence and the US embassy, for the duration of Fidel's trip). He reported that, while the crowds in the public square waited for Fidel to appear, their enthusiasm 'was maintained with chanting of slogans, singing and presentation of dignitaries'. He was also struck by how 'the militia were a dominating component' at the rally. At 8.30 p.m., the crew of the Soviet aircraft that had carried Fidel back to Cuba were presented; five minutes later, Fidel himself appeared on the balcony of the palace – prompting wild cheers, and the singing of both the Cuban national anthem and that of the 26 July Movement.[21]

Just before 9 p.m., Violeta Casals – the revolutionary and radio announcer (she had, famously, broadcast for Radio Rebelde from the Sierra Maestra) – introduced Osvaldo Dorticós. The Cuban president declared that, in New York, Fidel had spoken 'not only for Cuba but also for the peoples of Latin America and all under-developed areas of the world'. His speech before the General Assembly had, he said, won the 'respect, admiration and support' of the world. To applause, Dorticós proclaimed that 'today, today we all have, over anything else, nurtured in our chests an uncontainable feeling that swells inside of us. It is the powerful and legitimate feeling of our patriotic pride, and of having seen raised on the highest flag-pole, just a few hours ago, our flag, placed there by Fidel.' Speaking in the name of the people of Cuba, Latin America and all the underdeveloped nations, Dorticós declared, simply, '*Gracias, Fidel!*'[22]

Fidel, who according to some reports appeared rather 'more tense and nervous' than normal, took to the stage at 9.05 p.m., to a thunderous ovation that lasted some ten minutes. According to the UPI news agency the crowds, who were waving banners proclaiming '*Viva Russia*' and 'Down with the Yankees', now numbered around 150,000. The start of Fidel's speech was marred by a technical glitch (the microphones did not work), prompting the Cuban premier to quip that they had been sabotaged by the imperialists.[23] But, soon, he was into his stride.

His recent experience 'inside the empire' had, he explained, only increased his pride at what they were building in Cuba – 'we are no longer a colony' but 'a nation, truly sovereign and free'. Fidel attacked the 'cold and hostile' United States – a so-called 'super-free . . . super-democratic . . . and super-civilized country' – as a place where 'the nightstick' and 'the truncheon' were 'an institution of terror'. He paid special tribute to Harlem, noting that 'from the time our delegation began travelling through Harlem, from the instant a Negro saw us, he began to wave to us in greeting'. There were warm words, too, for the members of the Fair Play for Cuba Committee, who 'have had the courage to express publicly their sympathy for the Cuban Revolution'.[24]

As Fidel lauded the 'honor and hospitality and generous conduct and decency among the humble Negroes', the sound of a small explosion rang out – a firecracker, or perhaps a bomb (there had been a series of clashes with anti-Castro forces over the previous few weeks). Cries of '*Paredón!*' ('To the wall!') broke out, and Casals led the crowds in a chant of '*Cuba Sí, Yanqui No!*' Resuming his speech after a brief pause during which music was played to quieten the crowd, Fidel exclaimed, 'We all know who is responsible for that little bomb! Imperialism!' He counselled, 'Let us be calm. But how naïve. When 500 lb bombs made in USA, napalm bombs, rockets and cannons could not defeat us in Sierra Maestra, how do they think throwing little bombs like this will deter us. These are mistakes of imperialism and cowardice.' Fidel was defiant. 'For every bomb', he declared, 'we shall build five hundred houses, construct three rural cooperatives, nationalize one Yankee property, refine hundreds of thousands of barrels of oil, convert a barracks into a school, arm and equip at least a thousand militiamen.'[25]

Fired up, the Maximum Leader declared that Cuba now found itself 'on the frontline' in the battle against 'Yankee imperialism' (a 'barbarous', aggressive force, led by 'men with fangs'). But, he continued, they would 'defend ourselves with the fierceness of slaves who have rebelled'. This was a battle not only for the liberation of Cuba but for 'all the other exploited nations of the world', and the Cuban people needed to 'redouble their efforts' and 'be aware of the great role we are playing in the world'.[26]

Rallying the crowds after a second small explosion was heard, Fidel finished by expressing 'thanks for the two little bombs', which had:

demonstrated the mettle of our people, the courage of our people [Applause] for not a single woman budged from her place [Applause] not a single man budged [Applause] nor will anyone budge from his post in face of any danger, any attack. We are soldiers of the country. We do not belong to ourselves: We belong to our country. [Applause] It does not matter if any one of us falls; what matters is that this flag shall remain high, the Idea shall go forward, our country shall live. [Applause].[27]

Later that evening, Fidel made an impromptu appearance on a television talk show, where, among other things, he derided Richard

Nixon and his Democratic opponent, John F. Kennedy, as 'young, beardless men. They are ignorant, illiterate, and cowards' who 'look like toys of the great vested interests'. Cuba might not, Fidel conceded, have 'swallowed the shark [the USA] in the United Nations', but, he declared, 'we certainly gave him a good bite.'[28]

Reporting back to Washington, Philip Bonsal acknowledged that, even allowing for its staged nature, the reception and rally at the Presidential Palace had clearly demonstrated the depth of Castro's popularity among the lower classes. And, although the speech had, in many ways, been 'in much the same vein as previous demagogic harangues', the ambassador drew attention to two aspects: Fidel's 'new bitterness against the United States, stemming from his experience with the security measures taken in New York, and his treatment at the hands of the United States press', and 'a deeper intoxication with the illusion that the Cuban Revolution is a great historic event with world-wide implications arising, no doubt, from the attention paid him by world figures at the UN and his four and a half hour speech at the General Assembly.'[29] Britain's 'man in Havana', Sir Herbert Marchant (a former Bletchley Park codebreaker), agreed: 'in his reference to the role of the Cuban revolution in the world', he explained, ominously, Castro 'was more megalomaniac than ever'.[30]

# 13

# '¡VIVA LA REVOLUCIÓN!'

Dr. Castro . . . and the senior members of his government
. . . act and speak like men confident that they have a future
– and I do not think that they are whistling in the dark.
BRITISH AMBASSADOR, HAVANA, 12 OCTOBER 1960

We cannot have the present government there go on.
PRESIDENT EISENHOWER TO PRESIDENT-ELECT
KENNEDY, 19 JANUARY 1961

Two weeks after Fidel's departure, another famous politician with
bags of charisma and a winning smile headed to the Hotel Theresa, eager to win over the locals. Towards the end of a hectic day
of campaigning in New York, John F. Kennedy – the Democratic
Party's presidential nominee – addressed an enthusiastic crowd of
more than 5,000 African Americans on the boulevard outside the
hotel. Standing close to the spot where Fidel and Khrushchev had
shared their historic embrace, the Junior Senator from Massachusetts declared, to loud applause, that he was 'happy to come to this
hotel' and 'delighted to come to Harlem'. 'I think the whole world
should come here', Kennedy explained, 'the whole world should
recognize that we all live right next to each other, whether here in
Harlem or on the other side of the globe.'

Turning directly to recent events, Kennedy claimed that 'behind
the fact of Castro coming to this hotel, Khrushchev coming to
Castro, there is another great traveler in the world, and that is the
travel of a world revolution, a world in turmoil'. He continued:

We should not fear the twentieth century, for this
worldwide revolution which we see all around us is part of

the original American Revolution. When the Indonesians revolted after the end of World War II, they scrawled on the walls, 'Give me liberty or give me death.' They scrawled on the walls 'All men are created equal.' Not Russian slogans but American slogans.

'There are', Kennedy claimed, 'children in Africa called George Washington. There are children in Africa called Thomas Jefferson. There are none called Lenin or Trotsky or Stalin in the Congo, or,' he quipped, 'Nixon.'

This last remark – a dig at his Republican opponent – drew laughter. But Kennedy had a serious message. If America was to seize back the initiative in the Cold War, she had to live up to the ideals embodied in the Constitution and the Declaration of Independence. 'We have to prove that we mean it,' he declared, 'not last year, not 10 years ago . . . but today, 1960, the years after . . .' By moving forward 'until the United States achieves this great goal of practicing what it preaches' and 'associat[ing] ourselves with the great fight for equality', Americans, Kennedy argued, would be able to demonstrate before the world that they truly believed in freedom and independence, fire the imagination of the peoples of the newly independent nations of Africa and Asia, and show that it was the United States, rather than Nikita Khrushchev's Soviet Union – or, for that matter, Fidel Castro's Cuba – that truly embodied a 'great revolutionary' tradition.[1]

Kennedy was far from unsympathetic when it came to Third World nationalism. In July 1957, during a speech on the Algerian crisis, he had proclaimed that 'the most powerful single force in the world today' was 'man's eternal desire to be free and independent'. If the United States wished to 'secure the friendship of the Arab, the African, and the Asian', Kennedy explained, then it could not rely solely on 'billion-dollar foreign aid programs', military alliances and warnings about the 'perils of communism'. 'No', he

declared, 'the strength of our appeal to these key populations –
and it is rightfully our appeal, and not that of the Communists
– lies in our traditional and deeply felt philosophy of freedom
and independence for all peoples everywhere.'² The following
year, as chairman of the African Affairs Subcommittee of the
Senate Foreign Relations Committee, Kennedy – motivated
both by idealism and a fear of ceding the initiative to the Soviet
Union – repeatedly urged the Eisenhower administration to work
constructively with anticolonial nationalists. The idea that 'it is no
longer necessary to remain in bondage' was, he noted, 'spreading
like wildfire in nearly a thousand dialects and languages' right
across the African continent, and it was high time for the United
States to give its support to those who sought freedom from the
old colonial powers.³ He also warned against the illusion that 'the
voice of Moscow' was, inevitably, behind every anti-American
voice in Latin America.⁴ When it came to Cuba, Kennedy had
acknowledged both the strength and the legitimacy of anti-Batista
feeling: the United States, he observed, had too often given the
impression that it had been more 'interested in the money we
took out of Cuba than . . . in seeing Cuba raise its standard of
living for its people'.⁵ When Fidel took power in January 1959,
JFK advocated patience. But, as the Cuban government moved
to nationalize property, postponed elections and bore down on
opponents and the free press, he soon came to talk of a revolution
that had been betrayed.⁶

While he had been appalled by Castro's antics in New York in
September 1960, Kennedy had sensed an opportunity to gain an
advantage against his Republican opponent, Richard Nixon. On
15 September, just days before Castro's arrival in New York, he
had noted acerbically that 'in 1952 the Republicans ran on a program of rolling back the Iron Curtain in Eastern Europe. Today
the Iron Curtain is 90 miles off the coast of the United States.'⁷
Now, with some senior party activists urging that he 'blast away

on the administration's record here in the western hemisphere', he decided to raise the stakes even further.[8]

On 20 October, the eve of the fourth – and final – presidential debate, the Kennedy campaign trashed the Eisenhower administration's record on Cuba as an 'incredible history of blunder, inaction, retreat and failure'. JFK also declared that the incoming administration should 'strengthen the non-Batista democratic anti-Castro forces in exile, and in Cuba itself, who offer eventual hope of overthrowing Castro'. 'Thus far', Kennedy noted, 'these fighters for freedom have had virtually no support from our Government.'[9]

The statement (which JFK's speech-writer Richard Goodwin later claimed was the only campaign statement that Kennedy had not seen prior to its release) bordered on the reckless: the *Washington Post* accused Kennedy of 'shooting from the hip', while a British Foreign Office official noted, with characteristic understatement, that JFK had 'stuck his neck remarkably far out, even if one makes allowances for the customary gap between pre-election expressions of intent and post-victory actions'.[10] Nixon, meanwhile, was incandescent. 'For the first and only time in the campaign', he explained, 'I got mad at Kennedy – personally.' And 'my rage was greater because I could do nothing about it.' Nixon knew – or, at least, very strongly suspected – that Kennedy had been briefed by Allen Dulles on the Eisenhower administration's covert programme against Cuba. He therefore viewed Kennedy's statement as 'jeopardizing the security of a United States foreign policy operation'. Nixon, though, could hardly now come out in support of the policy (let alone explain that such a course of action was already being pursued); even hinting that Washington might be prepared to support rebel forces inside, and outside, of Cuba risked exposing the operation. The vice president decided, then, to 'go to the other extreme': Kennedy's proposals were, he declared publicly, 'probably the most dangerously irresponsible recommendations that he's made during the course of this campaign'. Were the United States to follow this course of action, Nixon explained, 'we would lose all our friends in Latin America' and provide Khrushchev with 'an open invitation' to come into the region.[11]

On 8 November, Kennedy won the White House in one of the closest elections in American history, defeating Nixon by just 49.72 to 49.55 per cent in the popular vote, and with narrow wins in Illinois, New Jersey and Texas proving decisive when it came to the electoral college (which he took by 303 to 219). He had been helped over the winning line by a late surge in African American support. Along with his high-profile pledge to outlaw discrimination in federally subsidized housing, and his rhetorical support for African independence, Kennedy's appeal among black voters owed much to his deft response to the arrest of Martin Luther King, Jr, during an Atlanta sit-in at the end of October. While Nixon, who in fact had a fairly strong civil rights record, dithered, Kennedy telephoned King's pregnant wife, Coretta, to offer his support, while his brother and campaign manager Robert worked behind the scenes to secure King's release.[12]

The charm, sophistication, idealism and energy that – on the surface at least – characterized Kennedy's short presidency would help to make him, like Fidel, an icon of the 1960s.[13] And, like Castro, JFK would inspire (if only briefly) a generation of student activists. In his speech outside the Hotel Theresa, Kennedy had offered assurances that the United States sought to 'hold out our hand in friendship' and be a 'good neighbor to Latin America'.[14] But, when it came to Cuba, the die had already been cast.

In the weeks following Fidel's sojourn in Harlem, the CIA's 'Program of Covert Action Against the Castro Regime', which Eisenhower had approved back in March, underwent a dramatic metamorphosis. As Richard M. Bissell, Jr, the Agency's Deputy Director for Plans, explained, the early efforts to establish an effective guerrilla force in Cuba had failed – undermined by Fidel's increasingly sophisticated intelligence operation and his militia's effectiveness in rooting out and destroying local resistance groups. Meanwhile, hopes of marshalling the opposition forces in Miami into a 'unified, cooperative coalition' had foundered amid factional rivalry, ideological conflict and competing egos. Faced with these problems, the emphasis now shifted instead onto the invasion force that was being assembled and trained in Guatemala. Troubled by Fidel's tightening grip on Cuba, his growing closeness to the Soviet Union and his enthusiasm for exporting revolution, Eisenhower pushed the CIA to move more forcefully, telling Bissell and Dulles, 'Boys, if you don't intend to go through with this, let's stop talking about it.' At the end of November, during a top-secret meeting at the White House, the president asked his senior advisers, 'Are we being sufficiently imaginative and bold, subject to not letting our hand appear?' 'We should', he said, 'be prepared to take more chances.' Soon, Bissell was talking of an invasion force that would number not a few hundred, but 1,500.[15]

When JFK assumed the presidency, on 20 January 1961, he inherited a burgeoning crisis over Cuba. Three months earlier, in response to the nationalization of oil refineries, the US had placed a trade embargo on exports to the island (food and medicine were exempt). Then, on 3 January, after Fidel ordered Washington to cut its embassy staff to just eleven, the US had severed diplomatic relations with Havana. Cuba had been at the top of the agenda when Kennedy met with Eisenhower on 6 December for an informal one-on-one to discuss the presidential transition. They met for a second time, on the morning of 19 January, for talks that lasted almost three hours. When JFK asked whether the United States should 'support guerrilla operations in Cuba', Ike replied yes, 'to the utmost', emphasizing that it would soon fall to Kennedy to 'do whatever is necessary'. 'We cannot', Eisenhower declared, 'have the present government there go on.'[16]

Early on the morning of 17 April 1961 a brigade of 1,400 Cuban exiles landed at the Bahía de Cochinos (Bay of Pigs), on Cuba's southern shore. Less than forty-eight hours before, eight American B-52 bombers, painted in Cuban colours and piloted by CIA-trained Cubans, had carried out a preliminary (and ineffective) air strike on Cuban air bases. (A second strike was cancelled when journalists started to ask awkward questions about the real identity of the B-52s.) Throughout the final planning for what would become 'Operation Bumpy Road', President Kennedy had been insistent that there could be no overt American support. Dulles had believed that, in the end, 'any request required for success would be authorized' if the alternative was to 'permit the enterprise to fail'. He was wrong. Despite coming under intense pressure from both the CIA and the Joint Chiefs of Staff to authorize air or naval support, Kennedy remained firm, declaring, 'I don't want the United States involved in this.' In the event, the invasion – which was intended to establish a beach-head, spark a popular uprising and lead to the installation of an alternative government – was a disaster. With its ships picked off by the Cuban Air Force and the rebel forces soon surrounded by 20,000 heavily armed Cuban soldiers, artillery and Soviet-built T-34 tanks (under the personal command of Fidel Castro), the invading army, despite putting up stout resistance, was routed. By the evening of 19 April, it was all over: 140 exiles were killed and almost 1,200 captured. As for the hoped-for popular uprising, it never stood a chance, killed off by a combination of genuine support for Fidel, poor coordination with opposition groups on the island, and the Cuban government's quick decision to round up as many as 100,000 known or suspected dissidents, just in case.[17]

Although Fidel revelled in his victory it soon became clear that, far from being chastened by the defeat, JFK remained determined to do away with his regime. Convinced that 'there can be no long-term living with Castro as a neighbor', the Kennedy administration launched what one historian has characterized as 'a multi-track program of covert, economic, diplomatic, and prop-agandistic elements'.[18] The economic blockade was tightened; the CIA built a large facility in Miami for the recruitment and train-ing of Cuban exiles and launched 'Operation Mongoose', with its myriad hit-and-run raids, sabotage operations and ever more outrageous plots to assassinate Fidel; and the president warned, gravely, that 'our restraint is not inexhaustible.'[19] Fearing an Amer-ican invasion, it is little wonder that the government in Havana turned to the Soviet Union for additional military assistance. And Khrushchev proved all too willing to provide it. In the spring of 1962, the Soviet leader decided to send thirty-six medium-range rockets, armed with nuclear warheads with a destructive power of 200–700 kilotons (ten to thirty-five times the power of the bomb dropped on Hiroshima), and twenty-four intermediate-range bal-listic missiles, with warheads of 200–800 kilotons, together with launchers, mobile support bases, IL-28 bombers, tanks, helicopters and around 40,000 Soviet military personnel, to Cuba. It was an extraordinarily reckless decision, which Khrushchev later claimed had been intended to 'restrain the United States from precipitous military action against Castro's government'. (He understood that, even if Washington knocked out most of the missiles, 'we could still hit New York, and there wouldn't be much of New York left.') The move would also, Khrushchev hoped, strengthen the Soviet Union's wider strategic position in the Cold War, and demonstrate – to the Chinese in particular – that Moscow had not 'gone soft' when it came to supporting communists in the Global South.[20] In the event, of course, the discovery of medium-range ballistic mis-siles by a U-2 overflight, on 14 October 1962, sparked a crisis that took the world to the very brink of nuclear annihilation.[21]

If the public embrace outside the Hotel Theresa, in Septem-ber 1960, signalled the start of the Cuban honeymoon with the Soviet Union, then the missiles of October – which did so much to crystallize wider public fears about the threat of nuclear war – marked the moment it turned sour. Fidel was livid with the Soviets not only for failing to consult with him throughout the thirteen-day standoff, but for keeping Havana in the dark when it came to the major decisions. At the height of the crisis, the Cuban leader had written to Khrushchev stating that if, as he feared, the Americans invaded, Moscow should under no circumstances allow the imperialists to launch the first strike. No matter how 'harsh and terrible' a solution this might be, Fidel insisted that there was no other option. Khrushchev – who was shocked by what he read as a call to launch an immediate first strike against the United States – eventually agreed to withdraw the missiles in exchange for a public pledge by the Americans not to invade Cuba, and a private undertaking that the US would remove its own Jupiter missiles from Turkey.[22]

Fidel, who did not learn about this second concession until the spring of 1963, was further incensed when, under pressure from Washington, at the end of November 1962, Moscow agreed to withdraw its Ilyushin Il-28 bombers from Cuba, too. Berating Khrushchev in private as a 'son of a bitch . . . bastard . . . asshole', a 'maricón' (a 'fag') who lacked cojones, Fidel ensured that Anastas Mikoyan, who had been despatched to Havana to soothe relations, received a frosty welcome.[23] As Fidel later put it, 'we were irritated for a long time [. . .] This incident, in a certain way, damaged the existing relations between Cubans and Soviets for a number of years.'[24]

For a time, the streets of Havana buzzed with rumours that 'Fidel's head is with Moscow but his heart is with Beijing'. But although China's enthusiasm for guerrilla warfare and the 'export' of revolution offered ideological sustenance, the Soviet Union's continued willingness to act as a powerful industrial and economic patron won out. Fidel travelled to the Soviet Union, at Khrushchev's invitation, in the spring of 1963, spending more than a month 'roaming from far northern Murmansk to Central Asia'. There was an official welcome in Red Square, a mammoth rally in a sports stadium (where Fidel was presented with the Gold Star of Lenin and the medal of Hero of the Soviet Union), endless banquets and receptions, a wild boar hunt, and new promises of economic and military assistance.[25]

While the tour was a triumph, the Cuban–Soviet romance had definitely cooled. In the USSR, the official excitement surrounding Cuba waned, and – as the historian Anne E. Gorsuch has pointed out – the language of 'passionate enthusiasm was downgraded to the cooler, safer, and more familiar relationship of "friendship"'. As for Cuba, US intelligence experts noted that Fidel had 'no intention of subordinating himself to Soviet discipline and direction'; in March 1965, the Cuban leader declared, 'We're no one's satellite and never will be.' Throughout the 1960s, in fact, Fidel was willing to challenge Moscow publicly: he rejected the 1963 Nuclear Test Ban Treaty, attacked the USSR for trading with Latin American countries that opposed his regime, and criticized Moscow's stinginess when it came to aid for Third World countries and support for liberation movements. Moscow, for its part, viewed Havana's adventurism in Latin America as a serious irritant when it came to its own relations with Washington, and other governments in the hemisphere.[26] Despite the public criticisms, disagreements over policy and higher-than-anticipated economic costs, Moscow's support for Cuba nevertheless held firm. After all, the cost of breaking with this beacon of socialism in the New World would have been too high, delivering a grievous blow to the Soviet Union's international standing and reputation.[27]

Assessing the significance of Fidel's trip to the United Nations at the end of September 1960, Ambassador Philip Bonsal noted the Cuban premier's 'conviction that Cuban revolution is [a] historic example and he [a] historic leader of peoples not only of L[atin]

A[merica] but of all underdeveloped countries toward their liberation'. Fidel's recent experiences at the UN General Assembly had, Bonsal declared, 'undoubtedly strengthened that conviction, and whetted his appetite to indulge in world politics'.[28]

It was an astute observation. Fidel had returned from New York with his reputation as a hero for the oppressed peoples of the world strengthened immeasurably.[29] In the coming years, Havana would host a series of international conferences, designed, as one historian has put it (referring to the 1955 conference of the Afro-Asian bloc), to position Cuba 'as the torch bearer of the post-Bandung world'. Perhaps the most famous of these gatherings was the First Solidarity Conference of the Peoples of Africa, Asia and Latin America, more commonly known as the Tricontinental Conference. Convened in January 1966, it saw almost 500 delegates representing some eighty nations, including Salvador Allende (Chile), Amílcar Cabral (Guinea–Bissau), Carlos Marighella (Brazil), Nguyen Van Tien (of South Vietnam's NLF) and the French philosopher-cum-guerrilla fighter Régis Debray, gather in the Cuban capital to coordinate support for national liberation struggles, advance the cause of Third World solidarity, affirm 'the right of the peoples to meet imperialist violence with revolutionary violence', and denounce US imperialism (which, it was claimed, underpinned a 'worldwide system of exploitation').[30]

In the decade that followed Fidel's trip to New York, Havana – motivated by both self-interest (if 'all of Latin America is in flames', Fidel declared, then the United States would 'not be able to hurt us') and a genuine sense of revolutionary mission and anti-imperialist sentiment – offered both ideological and practical support to a host of liberation movements across Latin America and Africa. It provided 'political indoctrination' and 'guerrilla warfare training' to at least 2,000 Latin Americans between 1961 and 1964; encouraged leftist revolution in Bolivia, Colombia, Guatemala,

Venezuela and elsewhere; funnelled weapons to the Front de Libération Nationale (FLN) in Algeria; sent soldiers to support rebels in
Zaire (formerly Congo-Léopoldville) and military instructors to
Angola and Guinea–Bissau; and despatched a column of troops
to the Republic of the Congo (Congo-Brazzaville) to support the
leftist government of Alphonse Massamba-Débat.[31]

Cuba enjoyed some success; for instance, Fidel's soldiers
thwarted the 1966 coup in Congo-Brazzaville, and Cuban military
instructors and medics remained in Guinea–Bissau until independence from the Portuguese was secured in 1974. But Havana's
'revolutionary offensive' in Latin America failed – coming to a
symbolic end in the rainforests of Bolivia in October 1967, with
the capture and subsequent squalid execution of Che Guevara.[32]

As Havana retreated from the politics of revolution in Latin
America and grappled with serious economic difficulties at home,
it drew closer to the Soviet Union – accepting Moscow's leadership
of the socialist camp and refraining from public criticism. During
the Prague Spring of August 1968, Fidel even delivered a televised
speech to the Cuban people in which, while acknowledging that
'some of the things we are about to say are in some cases in conflict
with the emotions of many', he accepted the 'bitter necessity' of
sending Warsaw Pact forces into Czechoslovakia; an invasion that
crushed Alexander Dubček's efforts to promote 'Socialism with a
human face'.[33]

Fidel's support for the Soviet-led invasion of Czechoslovakia came
as a disappointment to a generation of Sixties radicals.[34] They had
been attracted by the Cuban leader's charisma, machismo and
audacity; by the 'hip' and 'beatnik' style of the *Fidelistas*; and by
Havana's uncompromising support for anticolonialism and
anti-racism. And they had been inspired by what they saw as Fidel's
attempt to 'direct human history, to take hold of one's environment
and shape it, to institutionalize better human values'.[35] Todd Gitlin,

who served as president of the American Students for a Democratic Society (SDS) in 1963–4, recalled seeing:

> the black-and-white footage of bearded Cubans wearing fatigues, smoking big cigars, grinning big grins to the cheers of throngs deliriously happy at the news that Batista had fled; and we cheered too. The overthrow of a brutal dictator, yes. But more, on the face of the striding barbudos surrounded by adoring crowds we read redemption – a revolt of young people, underdogs, who might just cleanse one scrap of earth of the bloodletting and misery we had heard about all our lives. From a living room in the Bronx we saluted our unruly champions.[36]

In the Cuba of Fidel Castro, young leftists like Gitlin saw an alternative to capitalism, imperialism and racism; one that was neither constrained by the rigid doctrinal disputes of the 'Old Left', nor tainted by the mass murders, human rights violations and other terrible crimes that had been committed under Soviet communism.[37]

That the reality on the ground in Cuba might not always live up to the ideals was something that the black freedom fighter Robert F. Williams had learned some years earlier. Williams, along with his wife, Mabel, and their two children, had fled to Cuba in the autumn of 1961, to escape trumped-up kidnapping charges that had been levelled after they had taken a white couple into their home to protect them from an angry crowd of black protesters during civil rights disturbances in Monroe, North Carolina. From exile in Havana, he continued to support the black freedom struggle in the United States, publishing his *Crusader* newsletter, and broadcasting 'Radio Free Dixie' – a mix of music (including jazz, soul and rock 'n' roll), news about the civil rights struggle, and Williams's own powerful political commentary – to the South. But, despite his personal friendship with Fidel, he soon ran into difficulties (money failed to arrive, promised support never materialized and he was pressured to alter the content of his broadcasts). Williams's forceful personality did not help. On touring the Foreign Ministry and noticing its all-white staff, Mabel recalled how 'Rob told them it looks like Mississippi in here'. ('I thought', she said, 'they would shoot him for sure.') But there were serious political disagreements too: following the official communist line, the Cubans insisted that class trumped race. Black nationalism, it was said, would alienate the white working class – who were the 'primary revolutionary force'. Unwilling to become what he termed a 'socialist Uncle Tom', Williams left Cuba for Beijing in 1965. Writing to Fidel the following year, Williams declared that he would 'always be a friend of the Cuban Revolution', but he deplored the fact that 'while in Cuba all of my work for the Afro-American struggle was sabotaged.'[38]

Such disillusionment would not, though, significantly diminish Cuba's hold over American and Western European radicals. A new generation of French leftists, for instance, developed a deep sympathy for the Cuban Revolution over their shared support for Algeria's FLN, to whom Fidel sent arms, troops and, later, medical support.[39] The Cuban government's steadfast support for the Vietnamese struggle for national liberation (Fidel declared 1967 to be the 'Year of Heroic Vietnam'), meanwhile, earned the approval of much of the global anti-war movement.[40] In February 1968, at the height of Sixties activism, it was the German student leader Rudi Dutschke who ensured that Che Guevara's famous slogan, 'The Duty of a Revolutionary is to Make the Revolution' ('*Die Pflicht des Revolutionärs ist es, Revolution zu machen*'), appeared on a giant banner that stretched around the lecture hall at West Berlin's Free University during the International Vietnam Congress.[41]

In the United States, both Stokely Carmichael and Angela Davis were profoundly affected by the trips that they made to

Cuba in the late 1960s. Carmichael, the former leader of the Student Nonviolent Coordinating Committee (which was at the sharp edge of civil rights activism during the first half of the 1960s) and popularizer of the 'Black Power' slogan, visited Havana in August 1967. He was there for the First Conference of the Latin American Organization of Solidarity – the latest in a series of gatherings that sought to generate a united front against US-led imperialism and foment revolution across the Global South.[42] He described the experience as 'mind blowing. I mean, here were brothers and sisters from around the whole world, Jack, especially the "third world", who were struggling to liberate humanity from colonialism [and] economic exploitation.'[43] It was in Cuba that, for Carmichael, 'the international struggle became tangible, a human reality, names, faces, stories, no longer an abstraction, and our struggle in Mississippi or Harlem was part and parcel of this great international and historical motion'.[44]

Addressing the conference, Carmichael declared that 'we share with you a common struggle' and face 'a common enemy' – 'white Western imperialist society'. 'Our struggle', he proclaimed, 'is to overthrow the system that feeds itself and expands itself through the economic and cultural exploitation of non-white, non-Western peoples – of the Third World.' Arguing that 'black communities in America are the victims of white imperialism and colonial exploitation', Carmichael told the Latin American representatives that 'we are moving to control our African-American communities as you are moving to wrest control of your countries . . . from the hands of foreign imperialist powers.' And, in this struggle, he declared, 'we look upon Cuba as a shining example of hope in our hemisphere.'[45] Fidel, for his part, lauded Carmichael as a friend for whom Cuba 'will always be his home' and called on revolutionaries across the world to offer him their support and protection.[46] Carmichael, whose status as an 'observer' had been upgraded to 'delegate of honor', met with Fidel, who gave him a brief tour of the Sierra Maestra, pointing out the battle sites and explaining how the rebels had won their unlikely victory. The African American firebrand, who had moved to Harlem from his native Trinidad in 1952, aged eleven, took the opportunity to ask him about a rumour that was still doing the rounds. During a meeting with black nationalists at the Theresa, it was said, 'the brothers' had talked at length about their ambitious plans to 'wage armed struggle in the belly of the beast', right there in New York. After listening patiently Fidel had apparently stood up, walked over to the window and peered out. Finally, after several minutes of silence, they had asked the Cuban leader what he was looking for. In a subtle dismissal of their somewhat naïve plans for armed insurrection, Fidel is supposed to have replied: 'the Sierra Maestra, the mountains. I don't see any mountains out there.' Rather than confirming or denying the truth of the story, the Cuban prime minister simply roared with laughter. '*Verdad*,' he said, 'there were no mountains to be seen.'[47]

Angela Davis, the UCLA philosophy professor, political activist and Black Power icon, visited Cuba in the summer of 1969 as part of a delegation from the Communist Party of the United States of America. Joining a nationwide effort to gather in the sugar and coffee harvest, she described 'buses, vans, trucks and automobiles' packed with 'young and old, proudly dressed in work clothes, singing as they made their way to the country'. 'It seemed', she said, 'as if every able-bodied resident of Havana was rushing to the fields as though in a joyous carnival.' Watching the people cutting the sugar cane, and intoxicated by the 'palpable' sense of 'human dignity' that she encountered everywhere on the island, Davis reflected on how the Cubans were 'finished with the politics of class and race, done with the acid bile of outdoing one's neighbor for the sake of materially rising above them'. This was a socialist society made thrillingly real.[48] The trip, she later said, marked 'a great climax in my life. Politically I felt infinitely more mature, and it seemed like the Cubans' limitless revolutionary enthusiasm had left a permanent mark on my existence.'[49]

Carmichael and Davis were not alone. Black Panthers, members of SDS, opponents of the Vietnam War, and activists in the women's liberation, Puerto Rican and Chicano movements were among those who, inspired by the Cuban Revolution's achievements in education, healthcare and housing, its championing of liberation struggles (including its support for the Vietnamese) and its willingness to face down the superpower to the north, continued to look to Havana during the 1960s and beyond.[50]

The Cubans' sojourn at the Theresa produced a series of iconic images – a smiling Fidel and Malcolm, perched on the edge of the bed in the prime minister's suite; a beaming Khrushchev, enveloped in an enthusiastic hug; Foreign Minister Raúl Roa eating a hot dog at the nearby Chock Full o'Nuts lunch counter – and folk tales (the chicken feathers, the visits by 'women of the night') that have lived long in popular memory. The beatnik-revolutionary aesthetic of their stay in Harlem also came to the silver screen, thanks to Alfred Hitchcock's 1969 spy thriller, *Topaz*.[51] Set on the eve of the Cuban Missile Crisis, the movie, which was based on the best-selling novel by Leon Uris, sees a Western intelligence agent infiltrate the Cuban delegation to the United Nations (which, in a show of solidarity with the black community, is staying at the Hotel Theresa). The film was released by Universal Pictures at the end of the year to mixed reviews. Writing in the *New York Times*, Vincent Canby praised this 'quirky, episodic espionage tale', with its 'beautifully composed sequences, full of surface tensions, ironies [and] absurdities', as a 'huge success'. Indeed, he was so impressed that he selected it as one of his ten best films of the year, placing it in such august company as Arthur Penn's *Alice's Restaurant*, John Schlesinger's *Midnight Cowboy*, François Truffaut's *Stolen Kisses* and Sam Peckinpah's *The Wild Bunch*.[52]

But others, disappointed by the movie's lack of 'star power', were less convinced.[53]

Whether they rated it or not, the critics were agreed that one of the best things in the movie was the 'superb' sequence set in Harlem (the *Los Angeles Times*' Kevin Thomas claimed it was among the best work that the legendary English director had ever produced).[54] Filmed on location at the Theresa, the sequence included hotel corridors crammed with nervous police and security personnel, journalists desperate for a scoop, and swaggering, bearded revolutionaries (some with slightly dishevelled women on their arm). At one point, a top-secret document, now stained by grease underneath a half-eaten hamburger, is discovered on top of a desk, and the overall atmosphere is one of barely controlled anarchy.[55] Later in the movie, the French agent André Devereaux (played by Frederick Stafford) is questioned by Rico Parra (John Vernon) – the leader of the Cuban delegation to the UN, and a figure clearly inspired by Fidel Castro. While Devereaux denies any involvement in espionage, he does admit to having been outside the Hotel Theresa on the night when a secret Russian–Cuban aide-mémoire was photographed. 'I did go up to Harlem to see the show you were putting on,' explains Devereaux. 'And . . . it was a very good show.'[56]

Compelling, unpredictable, at times scarcely believable, and riotously entertaining, the week and a half that Fidel spent in New York constituted a story that, the *New Yorker* declared, 'no sensible playwright would dare to compose' and which 'even the most dogged critic would have a hard time recapitulating'.[57] Reflecting on the trip from a distance of some thirty years, Fidel appeared to agree: 'those days . . . were rough. It was madness . . . we were a little younger then. In fact, we didn't know much about politics.' But, while the Cuban leader and his fellow *barbudos* may have lacked experience, they 'had a rebel spirit, a spirit of struggle'. 'We were', Fidel explained, 'convinced of our cause.'[58]

Fidel's visit to New York in September of 1960 was, in the words of one historian, a 'Cold War watershed'.[59] The trip put the Cuban leader firmly on the world stage, confirming his international standing and strengthening his own commitment to lead the global struggle against imperialism. For the Americans, his antics, as well as the contents of his speech before the General Assembly, confirmed their belief that he had to go: a week or so after Fidel's departure, *Time* magazine predicted (correctly) that a 'showdown' with the United States was now 'much closer'.[60] The excellent personal chemistry with Nikita Khrushchev served to cement a critically important alliance with the Soviet Union and, in the process, offered a powerful illustration of how the Cold War's focus was shifting, inexorably, from Europe to the Global South. Meanwhile, Fidel's move to Harlem placed a global spotlight on America's 'race problem', inspired adulation from an emergent New Left and helped to usher in a new decade of political, social and cultural tumult in an appropriately irreverent, rebellious and anarchic manner.

They were ten days, then, that launched the Sixties, and changed the world.

# ACKNOWLEDGEMENTS

This book was initially conceived, and a good portion of the research for it undertaken, while I was Head of the School of History at the University of Leeds. It is fitting, then, that I begin by thanking colleagues there, particularly Rachel Utley and Andrea Major, who, as (successive) Deputy Heads of School, offered sage advice as well as invaluable support, and held the fort when I was away; Frank Finlay, Dean of the Faculty, for his backing and friendship; my fellow Heads of School for their camaraderie; and Sarah Foster, Esther Burton and Addi Manolopoulou for their administrative skill and (almost) endless reserves of patience. I am also grateful to Simon Ball, Manuel Barcia (several times over), Adam Cathcart, Ingo Cornils, Gina Denton, Kate Dossett, Claire Eldridge, William Gould, Rafe Hallett, Rob Hornsby and Andy Stafford, for pointing me in the direction of useful materials or otherwise offering encouragement.

Daniel Geary, Todd Gitlin, Piero Gleijeses, Van Gosse, Lillian Guerra, Rosemari Mealy, Roger Lipsey, Dan Matlin, Besenia Rodriguez, Tim Tyson, Javier Trevino and James West all responded helpfully to various queries, while Benjamin Young generously sent me a copy of his terrific PhD dissertation on North Korea's relations with the Third World. Lauren Mottle copied materials for me while undertaking her own research at the Wisconsin Historical Society, and Nat Andrews translated Cuban newspaper reports with skill and efficiency. Say Burgin, Sean Fear, Nick Grant and Elisabeth Leake deserve a big shout out for taking the trouble to read drafts of the manuscript, and for offering incisive and thoughtful suggestions for how I might improve it.

[ 225 ]

I am pleased to acknowledge the financial support offered by the Roosevelt Institute for American Studies in Middelburg, Netherlands (who awarded me a Marilyn Blatt Young Research Grant), the Eisenhower Foundation in Abilene, Kansas, and my own department. Leeds also granted me a full year of sabbatical leave in 2018–19 for which I am enormously grateful.

Over the past few years I have benefited greatly from the expertise, patience and generosity of administrators, academics, archivists and librarians at numerous institutions, including the National Archives at Kew; RIAS (Leontien Joosse, Ceese Herre, Dario Fazzi, Damian Pargas and Giles Scott-Smith offered a warm welcome); the Dwight David Eisenhower Presidential Library (Mary Burtzloff fielded numerous enquiries and went out of her way to ensure that my visit ran smoothly); the Library of Congress; the National Archives at College Park (I owe a particular debt to David Langbart); the New York Public Library (both the main branch on Fifth Avenue and the Schomburg Center for Research in Black Culture); the Rare Book & Manuscript Library, Columbia University; the Gelman Library, George Washington University; the Tamiment Library, New York University; the John F. Kennedy Presidential Library in Boston; and the Brotherton Library at the University of Leeds (where Tim Wright was especially helpful when it came to tracking down materials via inter-library loan).

I would also like to pay tribute to the brilliant Sally Holloway, at Felicity Bryan Associates, for all her support and hard work in making this project fly, and to thank George Lucas at Inkwell Management in New York, for his advice and enthusiasm. It is my tremendous good fortune to be published by Faber, and so it gives me particular pleasure to thank Julian Loose, who offered vital early encouragement, Laura Hassan, who gave the project the thumbs up and then brought it to a successful conclusion, and Rowan Cope, who offered helpful editorial interventions and advice along the way. Meanwhile, Eleanor Rees copy-edited the manuscript with her customary care and skill, and Josephine Salverda guided the book expertly through to production.

I count myself lucky indeed to have had Patrick Michelson as a friend these past twenty years. As well as furnishing me with relevant portions of the *Foreign Broadcast Information Service, Daily Report, Foreign Radio Broadcasts,* and other materials, he – along with Martha and Peter – offered generous hospitality, in their modest mountain home, during a much-needed vacation in Fraser, Colorado in the summer of 2018. Similarly, Jordi Getman and Frances Mejia went above and beyond in putting us up in New York a few months later, during a week that saw time spent in the NYPL nicely offset by visits to RuPaul's Drag Con and the Flaming Saddles Saloon. In Baltimore and Amsterdam, respectively, François Furstenberg and Moritz Föllmer offered a welcome respite from boxes of documents and microfilm reels. Back home, the friendship of Thomas Booth, Dean Clayton, Shane Doyle, Stuart Lewis, Stephan Petzold, Matthew Treherne and Richard Watts – among others – has been greatly appreciated.

Finally, I would like to acknowledge the love and support of my family, particularly my parents, Brian and Marilyn, as well as Emma, Ian, Matilda and Barney (who arrived just in time to make it into the acknowledgements). When it comes to János, words are – as ever – simply not up to the job. But I dedicate this book to him, anyway: igaz szeretettel.

# SELECT BIBLIOGRAPHY

PRIMARY SOURCES

Netherlands

Roosevelt Institute for American Studies, Middelburg
    President Dwight D. Eisenhower's Office Files, 1953–61 (Parts 1 & 2)
    The Diaries of Dwight D. Eisenhower, 1953–61
    The Dwight D. Eisenhower National Security Files: Subject Files, 1953–61
    Minutes and Documents of the Cabinet Meetings of President
        Eisenhower, 1953–61
    CIA Research Reports: Latin America, 1946–76
    Records of the US Information Agency Part 1: Cold War Era Special
        Reports Series A: 1953–63
    Records of the US Information Agency Part 3: Cold War Era Research
        Reports Series A: 1960–63
    The John F. Kennedy 1960 Campaign (Parts I & II)

United Kingdom

Brotherton Library, University of Leeds
    Robert F. Williams Papers
    The Claude A. Barnett Papers: The Associated Negro Press, 1918–67, Part
        1, Associated Negro Press News Releases 1928–64, Series C 1956–64
    Papers of the Revolutionary Action Movement, 1962–96, Malcolm X
        Symposium

National Archives, Kew
    FO 371: Foreign Office: Political Departments: General Correspondence
        1906–66 – Foreign Office Files for Cuba (1959–60); 15th Session of UN
        General Assembly (1960).

United States of America

Rare Book & Manuscript Library, Columbia University
    Andrew Wellington Cordier Papers, 1918–75

Allen Ginsberg Papers, 1943–91 [Bulk Dates: 1945–76] – Series I, Correspondence, 1943–82

Malcolm X Project Records, Series VI: Primary Source Research – Government Surveillance Files, 1953–2008; Series IX: Biography Research Files

Barry Miles Papers, 1958–90 [Series IV: *Ginsberg: A Biography* Materials, 1943–2000]

Dwight David Eisenhower Presidential Library, Abilene, KS

Eisenhower Dwight D.: Papers as President (Ann Whitman File):

Ann Whitman Diary Series

Cabinet Series

DDE Diary Series

Dulles-Herter Series

International File

Name Series

NSC Series

Presidential Transition Series

Administration series

Eisenhower, Dwight D.: Papers as President (White House Central Files), Official File

Eisenhower, Dwight D.: Papers as President (White House Central Files), General File

Alphabetical File; Confidential File

Eisenhower, Dwight D.: Post-Presidential Papers, 1961–9, Augusta-Walter Reed Series

Herter, Christian: Papers, 1957–61

White House Office, Office of the Special Assistant for National Security Affairs: Records, 1952–61, NSC Series, Briefing Notes Subseries

White House Office, Office of the Special Assistant for National Security Affairs: Records, 1952–61, NSC Series, Subject Subseries

US National Security Council Presidential Records, Intelligence Files: 1953–61

OCB Series, Subject Subseries

Special Assistant Series, Chronological Subseries

White House Office, Office of the Staff Secretary: Records, 1952–61, International Series

White House Office, Office of the Staff Secretary: Records, 1952–61, Subject Series

Republican National Committee: News Clippings and Publications, 1932–65, Box 257 (Cuba – Crisis of Sept. 1960 #5); Box 628 – United Nations Assembly: Castro

Oral History Transcripts:
    Bissell, Richard M., Jr (OH 168 & OH 382)
    Burke, Arleigh A. #3(LA), #4
    Dillon, C. Douglas #1 (LA)
    Eisenhower, Milton S. (OH-292) #1 (LA), #2
    Goodpaster, Andrew (OH 37, OH 378, OH 477)
    Gray, Gordon (OH 73, OH 342)
    Mann, Thomas C. (OH 57, OH 353)
    Rubottom, Roy (OH 268)

Gelman Library, George Washington University
    Richard T. Gibson Papers

Library of Congress
    Philip W. Bonsal Papers
    NAACP Records, Part III: Administrative File, 1909–69
    *Bohemia* (Cuba)
    *Daily Graphic* (Ghana)
    *Ghanaian Times*
    *The Progressive*
    *Revolución* (Cuba)

National Archives, College Park, Maryland
    033.3711 – Visits of Cuban officials to the United States
    304.37 – Permanent delegation of Cuba to the UN
    320 – United Nations General Assembly
    611.37 – Political relations between the US and Cuba
    RG 59 Entry A1-1609: Executive Secretariat: Minutes and Notes of the
        Secretary's Staff Meetings, 1952–61
    RG 59 Entry A1-1566: Executive Secretariat: Secretary's and Under
        Secretary's Memorandums of Conversation, 1953–64
    RG 59 entry A1-5036: Executive Secretariat: Presidential Correspondence,
        1953–60
    RG 59 Bureau of Inter-American Affairs: Office of the Coordinator of
        Cuban Affairs, Subject Files, 1960–63; Office of the Special Assistant
        on Communism; Subject Files of the Assistant Secretary, 1959–62

New York Public Library
    *Fair Play*
    *New York Daily News*

Schomburg Center for Research in Black Culture
　John Henrik Clarke Papers
　Julian Mayfield Papers
　*New York Citizen-Call*

Other Newspapers and Magazines consulted
　*Baltimore Afro-American*
　*Chicago Defender*
　*Dissent*
　*The Guardian*
　*Harper's*
　*The Nation*
　*National Guardian (New York)*
　*The New Republic*
　*New York Amsterdam News*
　*New York Times*
　*The New Yorker*
　*The Observer*
　*Pittsburgh Courier*
　*Studies on the Left*
　*The Times*
　*The Times of India*
　*Time*
　*The Worker*

PUBLISHED PRIMARY SOURCES

*Confidential US State Department Central Files, Cuba, 1960–January 1963 For-
eign Affairs, Decimal Numbers 637 and 611.37* (LexisNexis 2004)
*Confidential US State Department Central Files, Cuba, 1960–January 1963 Inter-
nal Affairs, Decimal Numbers 737, 837 and 937* (LexisNexis 2003)
*Department of State Bulletin, July–December 26, 1960*
*Foreign Broadcast Information Service: Daily Report, Foreign Radio Broadcasts*
　(September & October 1960)
*Foreign Relations of the United States, 1958–1960, United Nations and General
International Matters, Volume II*
*Foreign Relations of the United States, 1958–1960, Cuba, Volume VI*
*Public Papers of the Presidents of the United State*s (Dwight D. Eisenhower and
　John F. Kennedy – available at https://www.presidency.ucsb.edu/presidents)
*Khrushchev in New York: A Documentary Record of Nikita S. Khrushchev's trip
to New York, September 19th to October 13th, 1960, including all his speeches
and proposals to the United Nations and major addresses and news conferences*
　(New York: Crosscurrents Press, 1960)

Maya Angelou, *The Heart of a Woman* (London: Virago Press, 2008)

Richard M. Bissell. Jr., *Reflections of a Cold Warrior: From Yalta to the Bay of Pigs* (New Haven: Yale University Press, 1996)

Philip B. Bonsal, *Cuba, Castro, and the United States* (Pittsburgh: University of Pittsburgh Press, 1971)

Herb Boyd, ed., *The Harlem Reader* (New York: Three Rivers Press, 2003)

Stokely Carmichael with Ekwueme Michael Thelwell, *Ready for Revolution: The Life and Struggles of Stokely Carmichael (Kwame Ture)* (New York: Scribner, 2003)

Clayborne Carson, ed., *Malcolm X: The FBI File* (New York: Carroll & Graf, 1991)

Teresa Casuso, *Cuba and Castro* (New York: Random House, 1961)

Peter Catterall, ed., *The Macmillan Diaries, Volume II: The Premiership 1957–1966* (London: Macmillan, 2014)

Angela Davis, *Angela Davis: An Autobiography* (London: Arrow Books, 1976)

David Deutschmann and Deborah Shnookal, eds, *Fidel Castro Reader* (Melbourne: Ocean Press, 2007)

Dwight David Eisenhower, *The White House Years: Waging Peace, 1956–1961* (London: Heinemann, 1966)

Carlos Franqui, *Family Portrait with Fidel: A Memoir* (New York: Random House, 1984)

Mohamed Heikal, *The Cairo Documents: The Inside History of Nasser and His Relationship with World Leaders, Rebels, and Statesmen* (New York: Doubleday & Company, 1973)

LeRoi Jones, *Home: social essays* (London: Macgibbon & Kee, 1968)

*Memoirs of Nikita Khrushchev, Volume 3: Statesman [1953–1964]*, edited by Sergei Khrushchev (Philadelphia: University of Pennsylvania Press, 2007)

Peter Kornbluh, ed., *Bay of Pigs Declassified: The Secret CIA Report on the Invasion of Cuba* (New York: The New Press, 1998)

Harold Macmillan, *Pointing The Way, 1959–1961* (London: Macmillan, 1972)

Manning Marable and Garrett Felber, eds, *The Portable Malcolm X Reader* (London: Penguin, 2013)

Rosemari Mealy, *Fidel and Malcolm X: Memories of a Meeting* (Baltimore: Black Classic Press, 2013)

Bill Morgan, ed., *Allen Ginsberg: Deliberate Prose. Selected Essays 1952–1995* (London: Penguin Books, 2000)

Bill Morgan, ed., *An Accidental Autobiography: The Selected Letters of Gregory Corso* (New York: New Directions Publishing, 2003)

Richard M. Nixon, *Six Crises* (Garden City, New York: Doubleday & Company, Inc., 1962)

Antonio Núñez Jiménez, *En Marcha con Fidel 1960* (Havana: Editorial de Ciencas Sociales, 2003)

Kathleen Tynan, *Kenneth Tynan Letters* (London: Weidenfeld and Nicolson, 1994)

Kenneth Tynan, *Tynan Right & Left* (London: Longmans, 1967)

*Full details of all secondary works cited can be found in the endnotes.*

# NOTES

## PROLOGUE

1. Carlos Franqui, *Family Portrait with Fidel: A Memoir* (New York: Random House, 1984), 82.
2. Bonsal to Secretary of State, 6 September 1960, 320/9-660, College Park; Department of State, For the Press, no. 49, 21 January 1959, Nomination of Philip Wilson Bonsal to be Ambassador to Cuba', in DDE Office Files, Part 2, Reel 5, Cuba (2), RIAS.
3. 'Castro Plans U.N. Trip, Reports in Havana Say', *New York Times*, 12 September 1960, 3; R. Hart Phillips, 'Castro to Attend Assembly Session', *NYT*, 14 September 1960, 1.

## 1. THE STAGE IS SET

1. Thomas J. Hamilton, 'Leaders at the U.N.', *NYT*, 2 October 1960, E11.
2. UN Charter at http://www.un.org/en/charter-united-nations/.
3. Mark Mazower, *No Enchanted Palace: The End of Empire and the Ideological Origins of the United Nations* (Princeton: Princeton University Press, 2009), 6–9, 16, 17, 196; Sunil Amrith and Glenda Sluga, 'New Histories of the United Nations', *Journal of World History*, vol. 19, no. 3 (September 2008). For a history of the UN see also Paul Kennedy, *The Parliament of Man: The Past, Present and Future of the United Nations* (London: Penguin, 2007); for a recent study of America's support for the creation of the UN see Stephen Wertheim, 'Instrumental Internationalism: The American Origins of the United Nations, 1940–3', *Journal of Contemporary History*, published online 20 February 2019.
4. Mazower, *No Enchanted Palace*, 152. For a thoughtful discussion of how anticolonial nationalists were able to transform the General Assembly 'into a platform for the international politics of decolonization' see Adom Getachew, *Worldmaking After Empire: The Rise and Fall of Self-Determination* (Princeton: Princeton University Press, 2019), chapter 3: 'From Principle to Right: The Anticolonial Reinvention of Self-Determination', 71–106.
5. For a discussion of this see Mazower, *No Enchanted Palace*, 149–89 ; Lorna Lloyd, '"A Most Auspicious Beginning": The 1946 United Nations General Assembly and the Question of the Treatment of Indians in South Africa', *Review of International Studies*, vol. 16, no. 2 (April 1990), 131–53; Saul Dubow, *Apartheid, 1948–1994* (Oxford: Oxford University Press, 2014), 47–9; and Nico Slate, *Colored Cosmopolitanism: The Shared Struggle for Freedom in the United States and India* (Cambridge, MA: Harvard University Press, 2012), 179, 181–2.
6. http://www.un.org/en/sections/member-states/growth-united-nations-membership-1945-present/index.html#footnote30; Mazower, *No Enchanted Palace*, 185.
7. Mazower, *No Enchanted Palace*, 188. For an interesting discussion of the UN's role in the decolonization process see Eva-Maria Muschik, 'Managing the world: the United Nations, decolonization, and the strange triumph of state sovereignty in the 1950s and 1960s', *Journal of Global History*, vol. 13 (2018), 121–44.
8. Getachew, *Worldmaking After Empire*, 71, 73–4.

9. Getachew, *Worldmaking After Empire*, 73.
10. Odd Arne Westad, *The Cold War: A World History* (London: Allen Lane, 2017), 292–3; William Taubman, *Khrushchev: The Man, His Era* (London: The Free Press, 2005), 467, 482–3; Lawrence Freedman, *Kennedy's Wars: Berlin, Cuba, Laos, and Vietnam* (New York: Oxford University Press, 2000), 58–60; 'Memorandum of Discussion at the 460th Meeting of the National Security Council', 21 September 1960, *Foreign Relations of the United States, 1958–1960, Berlin Crisis, 1958–1960; Germany; Austria, Volume IX*, document 214; 'Memorandum of Discussion at the 460th Meeting of the National Security Council', 7 September 1960, p. 11, in DDE Papers as President, 1953–61 (Ann Whitman File), NSC Series, Box 13, 458th Meeting of NSC, 7 September 1960, DDE.
11. 'Memorandum of Conversation: Possible Discussion of Germany and Berlin at Forthcoming Session of United Nations General Assembly', 9 September 1960, 320/9-960, College Park.
12. Odd Arne Westad, *The Global Cold War* (Cambridge: Cambridge University Press, 2007), 136–7; Westad, *The Cold War: A World History*, 282; Aleksandr Fursenko and Timothy Naftali, *Khrushchev's Cold War: The Inside Story of an American Adversary* (New York: W. W. Norton, 2006), 297–9, 307; Roger Lipsey, *Hammarskjöld: A Life* (Ann Arbor: The University of Michigan Press, 2013), 298; 387–95; Patrice Lumumba, 'Speech at the Ceremony of the Proclamation of the Congo's Independence', 30 June 1960, available at https://www.marxists.org/subject/africa/lumumba/1960/06/independence.htm.
13. Westad, *The Global Cold War*, 138–9; Fursenko and Naftali, *Khrushchev's Cold War*, 307–18; Lipsey, *Hammarskjöld*, 396–405, 410–11; Miles Larmer and Erik Kennes, 'Rethinking the Katangese Secession', *The Journal of Imperial and Commonwealth History*, vol. 42, no. 4 (2014), 741–61.
14. Westad, *The Global Cold War*, 138–9; Fursenko and Naftali, *Khrushchev's Cold War*, 307–18; Lipsey, *Hammarskjöld*, 396–405, 410–11.
15. Christopher Andrew and Vasili Mitrokhin, *The KGB and the World: The Mitrokhin Archive II* (London: Penguin, 2006), 5.
16. Andrew and Mitrokhin, *The KGB and the World*, 5; Andreas Hilger, 'Communism, Decolonization and the Third World' in Norman Naimark, Silvio Pons and Sophie Quinn-Judge, eds, *The Cambridge History of Communism, Volume II, The Socialist Camp and World Power 1941–1960s* (Cambridge: Cambridge University Press, 2017), 322–5.
17. Fursenko and Naftali, *Khrushchev's Cold War*, 57.
18. Sara Lorenzini, 'The Socialist Camp and the Challenge of Economic Modernization in the Third World' in Naimark et al., eds, *The Cambridge History of Communism, Volume II*, 344; Taubman, *Khrushchev*, 354.
19. Andrew and Mitrokhin, *The KGB and the World*, 6.
20. Westad, *The Global Cold War*, 138–9; Fursenko and Naftali, *Khrushchev's Cold War*, 307–18; Lipsey, *Hammarskjöld*, 396–405, 410–11.
21. Robert Cook, *Sweet Land of Liberty? The African-American Struggle for Civil Rights in the Twentieth Century* (London: Routledge, 2013), 113–15; https://kinginstitute.stanford.edu/encyclopedia/sit-ins; Claude Sitton, 'Negro Sitdowns Stir Fear of Wider Unrest in South' and David Halberstam, 'A Good City Gone Ugly' in *Reporting Civil Rights, Part One, American Journalism 1941–1963* (New York: The Library of America, 2003), 433–46.
22. Devyn Spence Benson, *Antiracism in Cuba: The Unfinished Revolution* (Chapel Hill: The University of North Carolina Press, 2016), 161. On the Cuban–African American connection see also Manning Marable, 'Race and Revolution in Cuba: African American Perspectives', *Souls*, Spring 1999, 6–17 and Lisa Brock and Digna

Casteñeda Fuertes, eds, *Between Race and Empire: African Americans and Cubans before the Cuban Revolution* (Philadelphia: Temple University Press, 1998).

23. Cook, *Sweet Land of Liberty?*, 113–21.

24. Howard Zinn, *The Zinn Reader: Writings on Disobedience and Democracy* (New York: Seven Stories Press, 1997), 56–7.

25. Carl Nolte, '"Black Friday," birth of U.S. Protest Movement', 13 May 2010 at https://www.sfgate.com/news/article/Black-Friday-birth-of-U-S-protest-move- ment-3188770.php and 'May 14, 1960: Firehoses Confront Free Speech in S.F. City Hall', Zinn Education Project – https://www.zinnedproject.org/news/tdih/ firehoses-confront-free-speech/; Todd Gitlin, *The Sixties: Years of Hope, Days of Rage* (New York: Bantam, 1993), 82–3.

26. On the heart attack see, for instance, Robert E. Gilbert, 'Eisenhower's 1955 Heart Attack: Medical Treatment, Political Effects, and the "Behind the Scenes" Lead- ership Style', *Politics and the Life Sciences*, vol. 27, no. 1 (March 2008), 2–21 and Richard Nixon, *Six Crises* (New York: Doubleday & Company, Inc., 1962), 131–81. On Nixon's role within the Eisenhower administration see Irwin F. Gellman, *The President and the Apprentice: Eisenhower and Nixon, 1952–1961* (New Haven: Yale University Press, 2015).

27. Richard M. Nixon, Acceptance Address, 1960 Republican National Convention, Chicago, 28 July 1960, available at https://www.americanrhetoric.com/speeches/ richardnixon1960rnc.htm.

28. John F. Kennedy, Acceptance Speech, Los Angeles, 15 July 1960, available at https:// www.jfklibrary.org/learn/about-jfk/historic-speeches/acceptance-of-democrat- ic-nomination-for-president.

29. Tony Perrottet, *Cuba Libre! Che, Fidel, and the Improbable Revolution* (New York: Blue Rider Press, 2019), 33–4; Tad Szulc, *Fidel: A Critical Portrait* (London: Coro- net Books, 1989), 91, 99.

30. Perrottet, *Cuba Libre!*, 34; Szulc, *Fidel*, 94–5.

31. Perrottet, *Cuba Libre!*, 24–6, 34–6, 37–41; Szulc, *Fidel*, 85, 98, 104, 111–12, 116, 135, 202; Michael Collins, '"Pure Feelings, Noble Aspirations and Generous Ideas": The Martí–Dana Friendship and the Cuban War of Independence', *Radical Americas*, vol. 1, no. 1 (2016), 1–24 and Lillian Guerra, 'Re-evaluating the Influence of José Martí', *New West Indian Guide*, vol. 75, no. 1–2 (2001), 89–96. For more on Martí see Lillian Guerra, *The Myth of José Martí: Conflicting Nationalisms in Early Twentieth-Century Cuba* (Chapel Hill: The University of North Carolina Press, 2005).

32. Simon Hall, *1956: The World in Revolt* (London: Faber & Faber, 2016), 363–9. On the legal practice see, for instance, Leycester Coltman, *The Real Fidel Castro* (New Haven: Yale University Press, 2003), 51–2. Fidel's eventual victory owed a great deal to the urban-based opposition and tacit alliances with the trades unions, the Church and the middle classes, as well as the flaws of his enemy (Batista's repres- sive tactics proved counterproductive) and misjudgements of his rivals. See, for instance, Steve Cushion, *A Hidden History of the Cuban Revolution: How the Work- ing Class Shaped the Guerrillas' Victory* (New York: Monthly Review Press, 2016) and Julia E. Sweig, *Inside the Cuban Revolution: Fidel Castro and the Urban Underground* (Cambridge, MA: Harvard University Press, 2002). On the naming of the yacht see Perrottet, *Cuba Libre!*, 13, 76.

33. Szulc, *Fidel*, 536–43; Robert E. Quirk, *Fidel Castro* (New York: W. W. Norton & Co., 1993), 236–43; Coltman, *The Real Fidel Castro*, 155–8; Lindesay Parrott, 'Castro Defends Election Delay', *NYT*, 23 April 1959, 1, 2.

34. Szulc, *Fidel*, 575.

35. Juan Arcocha, 'Fidel at the UN' ('Fidel en la ONU'), *Revolución*, 15 September 1960, 2. On the Bandung Conference see, for example, Antonia Finnane and Derek

McDougall, eds, *Bandung 1955: Little Histories* (Caulfield: Monash University Press, 2010); See Seng Tang and Amitav Acharya, eds, *Bandung Revisited: The Legacy of the 1955 Asian-African Conference for International Order* (Singapore: NUS Press, 2008); Su Lin Lewis and Carolien Stolte, 'Other Bandungs: Afro-Asian Internationalisms in the Early Cold War', *Journal of World History*, vol. 30, no. 1–2 (June 2019), 1–19; Thomas Borstelmann, *The Cold War and the Color Line: American Race Relations in the Global Era* (Cambridge, MA: Harvard University Press, 2001), 95–7.

## 2. INTO THE BELLY OF THE BEAST

1. Quirk, *Fidel Castro*, 334; 'La Voz de la Revolución' ('The Voice of the Revolution'), *Bohemia*, 25 September 1960, 44; *Revolución*, 19 September 1960, 12.
2. Franqui, *Family Portrait*, 84.
3. Quirk, *Fidel Castro*, 27–8; Coltman, *The Real Fidel Castro*, 47–8.
4. See Alan McPherson, 'The Limits of Populist Diplomacy: Fidel Castro's April 1959 Trip to North America', *Diplomacy & Statecraft*, 18.1 (2007), 237–68; Perrottet, *Cuba Libre!*, 331.
5. Aviva Chomsky, *A History of the Cuban Revolution* (Oxford: Wiley-Blackwell, 2011), 71; Louis A. Peréz, Jr, *Cuba: Between Reform and Revolution* (New York: Oxford University Press, 2006), 243; Lillian Guerra, *Visions of Power in Cuba: Revolution, Redemption, and Resistance, 1959–1971* (Chapel Hill: The University of North Carolina Press, 2012), 58.
6. Timeline of events, WHO – Office of Special Assistant NSA, NSC Series, Briefing Notes Subseries, Box 6, DDE; 'Cuba: Annual Review for 1960', FO371/151637; Quirk, *Fidel Castro*, 317; Alejandro de la Fuente, *A Nation for All: Race, Inequality and Politics in Twentieth-century Cuba* (Chapel Hill: University of North Carolina Press, 2001), 271; Guerra, *Visions of Power in Cuba*, 57, 61, 135.
7. Hall, *1956*, 361.
8. Braddock to Secretary of State, 5 January 1960, 611.37/1-560 and W. H. Benson to Secretary of State, 611.37/2-660, *Confidential State Department Files, Decimal 637*, reel 3.
9. Department of State, for the Press, 6 June 1960, *Confidential State Department Files, Decimal 637*, reel 3. See also, 'Responsibility of the Cuban Government for Increased International Tensions in the Hemisphere', 73–8, Report to the Inter-American Peace Committee 1 August 1960, White House Office, Office of the Staff Secy: Records, 1952–61, International Series, Box 4, Cuba (5), DDE.
10. Brooks Hamilton to James Hagerty, 30 June 1960, WHCF General File, Box 805, Cuba (5), DDE.
11. 'Progress Report on Cuba', 17 May 1960, p. 2, WHO – Office of Special Assistant NSA, NSC Series, Subject Series, Box 4, 'Cuba (May 1959–September 1960) (2), DDE; 'Responsibility of the Cuban Government for Increased International Tensions in the Hemisphere', 37–46, Report to the Inter-American Peace Committee, 1 August 1960, White House Office, Office of the Staff Secretary: Records, 1952–61, International Series, Box 4, Cuba (5), DDE; 'Cuba: Annual Review for 1960', 6, FO371/151637, Kew. On the nationalization of the press see, for instance, Guerra, *Visions of Power in Cuba*, chapter 3 ('War of Words'), 107–34.
12. 'Cuba: Annual Review for 1960', 6, FO371/151637, Kew; Guerra, *Visions of Power in Cuba*, 143–4.
13. Lloyd A. Free, 'The Cuban Situation', 1, 13 April 1960, Whitman-International, Cuba (1), Box 8, DDE.
14. 'Czechoslovakia-Cuba Relations and the Cuban Missile Crisis, 1959–1962: Evidence

from the Prague Archives', *Cold War International History Project Bulletin*, Issue 17/18, 349–74.

15. Havana to State, 17 June 1960, 637.60/1-760, *Confidential State Department Files, Decimal 637*, reel 1 and 'Progress Report on Cuba, June 7, 1960', 'Cuba (May 1959–September 1960' (3), WHO-Office of Special Assistant NSA, NSC Series, Subject Series, Box 4, DDE. See also AK10338/5, 24 June 1960, FO371/148211.

16. Chomsky, History of the Cuban Revolution, 77; Quirk, Fidel Castro, 295–6.

17. Quirk, Fidel Castro, 320. On the pressure from the US government see Bonsal to Rubottom, 2 August 1960, 011/37/8-260, Confidential State Department Files, Decimal 637, reel 4; 'Memorandum of Conversation re: Petroleum Situation', 8 June 1960 (meeting participants included Roy Rubottom and the Chairman of Sinclair Oil', Bureau of Inter-American Affairs, Subject Files of the Assistant Secretary, 1959–62, Box 1, College Park; and British Ambassador, Havana to Foreign Office, London, AK1531/11, 6 June 1960, FO371/148293.

18. Quirk, Fidel Castro, 321; Lisa Reynolds Wolfe, 'Cold War Havana: Prelude to American Sanctions', 13 December 2010 at https://coldwarstudies.com/2010/12/13/cold-war-havana-prelude-to-american-sanctions/.

19. Eugenio Suárez Pérez, 'Cuba Nationalizes U.S. Companies', *Granma*, 10 August 2015 at http://en.granma.cu/cuba/2015-08-10/cuba-nationalizes-us-companies.

20. Hall, *1956*, 361; Alex von Tunzelmann, *Red Heat: Conspiracy, Murder and the Cold War in the Caribbean* (London: Simon & Schuster, 2011), 12–13.

21. See, for instance, Fidel Castro's televised speech on the evening of 20 January 1960, Philip Bonsal to Christian Herter, 21 January 1960, 611.37/1-2160, *Confidential State Department Files, Decimal 637*, reel 3.

22. Quirk, *Fidel Castro*, 297–9; Bonsal to Herter, 26 January 1960, 611.37/1-2660, *Confidential State Department Files, Decimal 637*, reel 3.

23. Westad, *The Cold War*, 345–7; von Tunzelmann, *Red Heat*, 56–9.

24. Quirk, *Fidel Castro*, 297–9; Bonsal to Herter, 26 January 1960, 611.37/1-2660, *Confidential State Department Files, Decimal 637*, reel 3.

25. AK1015/21 – 9 March 1960, FO371/148180, Kew; Quirk, *Fidel Castro*, 301–2; Franqui, *Family Portrait*, 69–70; 'Cuban-U.S. Relations: Talking Points for Informal Discussions Abroad', *Confidential State Department Files, Decimal 637*, reel 3.

26. Quirk, *Fidel Castro*, 302.

27. Bureau of Inter-American Affairs, Subject Files of the Assistant Sec, 1959–62, Box 1, College Park.

28. Bureau of Inter-American Affairs, Office of Coordinator Cuban Affairs, Box 8: script of Juan Sintierra, 'Bearing Witness to the Truth', broadcast on Radio Mambi, 26 March 1960 at 23.30 GMT–E, College Park.

29. 'Havana Will Lose its Baseball Club', *NYT*, 8 July 1960, 24; Joseph O. Haff, 'Ex-Sugar Kings Get a Noisy Welcome in New Home', *NYT*, 16 July 1960, 11; Travis Waldron, 'Havana's Forgotten Baseball Team Played a Key Role in US-Cuba Relations', *Huffington Post*, 19 March 2016; Stephen Kinzer, *The Brothers: John Foster Dulles, Allen Dulles, and Their Secret World War* (New York: Times Books, 2013), 290–1.

30. 'Cuban-U.S. Relations: Talking Points for Informal Discussions Abroad', *Confidential State Department Files, Decimal 637*, reel 3.

31. On the OAS see, for instance, https://www.britannica.com/topic/Organization-of-American-States and Bertram D. Hulen, 'Marshall Urges Latins to Put Need of Our Help After ERP', *NYT*, 2 April 1948, 1, 12.

32. 'Declaration of San José', in 'Cuba (May 1959–September 1960) (6), WHO – Office of Special Assistant NSA, NSC Series, Subject Series, Box 4, DDE. See also Quirk, *Fidel Castro*, 328–31.

33. Bonsal to Herter, 2 September 1960, 737.00/9-260, and 3 September, 737.00/9-360, *Confidential State Department Files, Decimal 737*, reel 6; Quirk, *Fidel Castro*, 331–2; text of the First Declaration of Havana available at http://www.walterlippmann.com/fc-09-02-1960.html. See also Guerra, *Visions of Power in Cuba*, 38.

34. 'La Voz de la Revolución' ('The Voice of the Revolution'), *Bohemia*, 25 September 1960, 52.

35. Mae Mallory, 'Fidel Castro in New York', *The Crusader*, 8 October 1960, 5; Robert McCarthy and Jack Smee, 'Mob Serenades Fidel with Cheers & Jeers', *Daily News*, 19 September 1960, 3, 6; Max Frankel, 'Castro Arrives in Subdued Mood', *NYT*, 19 September 1960, 1; 'Castro Jeered, Cheered on New York Arrival', *Washington Star* (AP report), 19 September 1960; *Revolución*, 19 September 1960, 12.

36. Mallory, 'Fidel Castro in New York', *The Crusader*, 8 October 1960.

37. Frankel, 'Castro Arrives in Subdued Mood', *NYT*, 19 September 1960, 1.

38. Frankel, 'Castro Arrives in Subdued Mood', *NYT*, 19 September 1960, 1.

39. Max Frankel, 'Cuban in Harlem', *NYT*, 20 September 1960, 1, 16; McCarthy and Smee, 'Mob Serenades Fidel with Cheers & Jeers', *Daily News*, 19 September 1960, 3, 6.

40. McCarthy and Smee, 'Mob Serenades Fidel With Cheers & Jeers', *Daily News*, 19 September 1960, 3, 6; 'La Voz de la Revolución' ('The Voice of the Revolution'), *Bohemia*, 25 September 1960, 54; Bonsal to Secretary of State, 14 September 1960, 320/9-1460, College Park.

41. Coverage in *Revolución*, Bonsal to Secretary of State, 19 September 1960, 737.13/9-1960, *Confidential State Department Files, Decimal 737, 837, 937*, reel 25; Frankel, 'Cuban in Harlem', *NYT*, 20 September 1960, 1, 16; *Revolución*, 19 September 1960, 1, 12.

42. *Revolución*, 19 September 1960, 12.

43. Department of State to US UN Delegation, NY and US Embassy, Havana, 14 September 1960 (outgoing telegram and aide-memoire), 033.3711/9-1450, College Park and 'Notes on Telephone Conversation, 4.45 p.m., Wednesday 14 September 1960, 033.3711, College Park; Perrottet, *Cuba Libre!*, 332–3.

44. Frankel, 'Castro Arrives in Subdued Mood', *NYT*, 19 September 1960, 1.

45. Mallory, 'Fidel Castro in New York', *The Crusader*, 8 October 1960; Frankel, 'Castro Arrives in Subdued Mood', *NYT*, 19 September 1960, 1.

46. 'La Voz de la Revolución' ('The Voice of the Revolution'), *Bohemia*, 25 September 1960, 54.

47. Frankel, 'Castro Arrives in Subdued Mood', *NYT*, 19 September 1960, 1; McCarthy and Smee, 'Mob Serenades Fidel with Cheers & Jeers', *Daily News*, 19 September 1960, 3, 6; 'La Voz de la Revolución' ('The Voice of the Revolution), *Bohemia*, 25 September 1960, 55.

48. Max Frankel, 'Castro Can't Find Lodging Here; One Hotel Cancels Reservation', *NYT*, 16 September 1960, 1.

49. 'The Secretary's Staff Meeting, 16 September 1960, p. 2, Minutes & Notes of the Secretary's Staff Meetings, 1952–1961', College Park; Telegram, Office of International Conferences, Department of State to Edward Spatz, 17 September 1960, 320/9-1760, College Park; Frankel, 'Cuban in Harlem', *NYT*, 20 September 1960, 1, 16; Kennett Love, 'Castro Walkout Termed a Stunt', *NYT*, 21 September 1960.

50. 'Cuba Restricts U.S. Ambassador', *NYT*, 17 September 1960, 1, 11; Michael Frayn, 'Miscellany', *The Guardian*, 23 September 1960, 11.

51. Victor Rabinowitz, *Unrepentant Leftist: A Lawyer's Memoir* (Urban & Chicago: University of Illinois Press, 1996), 205.

## 3. MONDAY 19 SEPTEMBER

1. Anthony Marino and Henry Lee, 'K and His Pals Meet at Park Av. Kremlin', *New York Daily News*, 20 September 1960, 3, 30; Edward A. Morrow, 'Premier Watches Pickets in Harbor', *NYT*, 20 September 1960, 1, 15; *Memoirs of Nikita Khrushchev, Volume 3: Statesman [1953–1964]*, edited by Sergei Khrushchev (Philadelphia: University of Pennsylvania Press, 2007), 264; Noel E. Parmentel, Jr, 'East River Showboat . . .', *The Nation*, 1 October 1960, 193–5. For a detailed and entertaining account of Khrushchev's earlier trip to New York see Peter Carlson, *K Blows Top* (London: Old Street Publishing, 2009), 108–43.
2. The best biography of Khrushchev is William Taubman's Pulitzer Prize-winning *Khrushchev* (London: The Free Press, 2005); Hall, *1956*, 49–56.
3. 'Khrushchev – A Personality Sketch', 2-3, CIA Research Reports – Soviet Union, 1946–1976, Reel 3, RIAS.
4. Hall, *1956*, 50–1, 58.
5. Hall, *1956*, 65, 345. On reform under Khrushchev see, for instance, Miriam Dobson, *Khrushchev's Cold Summer: Gulag Returnees, Crime, and the Fate of Reform Under Stalin* (Ithaca, NY: Cornell University Press, 2009).
6. For a comprehensive account of this trip see Carlson, *K Blows Top*.
7. Carlson, *K Blows Top*, 253–60, 263; Taubman, *Khrushchev*, 445–60, 460–8.
8. Carlson, *K Blows Top*, 266; Taubman, *Khrushchev*, 472; *Memoirs of Nikita Khrushchev, Volume 3*, 258–9.
9. Lord Hood to Lord Home, 31 October 1960, AU2291/5, FO371/148649; Carlson, *K Blows Top*, 268.
10. Nixon to Thompson quoted in Jenny Thompson and Sherry Thompson, *The Kremlinologist: Llewellyn E. Thompson, America's Man in Cold War Moscow* (Baltimore: John Hopkins University Press, 2018), 226. On the Soviet dogs in space see Elizabeth Dohrer, 'Laika the Dog and the First Animals in Space' at https://www.space.com/17764-laika-first-animals-in-space.html. On the 'kitchen debate' see, for example, Nixon, *Six Crises*, 252–60 and Gellman, *The President and the Apprentice*, 522–4.
11. Christian A. Herter to President Eisenhower, 2 September 1960, *Foreign Relations of the United States, 1958–1960, Volume II, United Nations and General International Matters* (Washington, DC: United States Government Printing Office, 1991), document 151, p. 305.
12. See, for instance, letter from William Macomber, Jr, to Paul G. Rogers, 16 September 1960 – 320/9-960, College Park.
13. Taubman, *Khrushchev*, 472–3; Carlson, *K Blows Top*, 266–8; *Memoirs of Nikita Khrushchev, Volume 3*, 260–2.
14. *Memoirs of Nikita Khrushchev, Volume 3*, 264.
15. William Federici and Robert McCarthy, 'K Visits and the Skies Weep', *New York Daily News*, 20 September 1960, 4; Harrison E. Salisbury, 'Russian Bids Eisenhower Join in New Summit Here', *NYT*, 20 September 1960, 14.
16. Federici and McCarthy, 'K Visits and the Skies Weep', *New York Daily News*, 20 September 1960, 4.
17. Anthony Marino and Henry Lee, 'K and His Pals Meet at Park Av. Kremlin', *New York Daily News*, 20 September 1960, 30.
18. Salisbury, 'Russian Bids Eisenhower Join in New Summit Here', *NYT*, 20 September 1960, 14. See also Taubman, *Khrushchev*, 474 and Carlson, *K Blows Top*, 269–70.
19. Nikita Khrushchev, 'Statement at the Pier', 19 September 1960, in *Khrushchev in New York: A Documentary Record of Nikita S. Khrushchev's trip to New York, September 19th to October 13th, 1960, including all his speeches and proposals to the United Nations and major addresses and news conferences* (New York: Crosscurrents Press, 1960), 7–10.

20. Vladislav M. Zubok, *A Failed Empire: The Soviet Union in the Cold War from Stalin to Gorbachev* (Chapel Hill: The University of North Carolina Press, 2007), 127, 129, 134.

21. Salisbury, 'Russian Bids Eisenhower Join in New Summit Here', *NYT*, 20 September 1960, 14.

22. Federici and McCarthy, 'K Visits and the Skies Weep', *New York Daily News*, 20 September 1960, 4.

23. Marino and Lee, 'K and His Pals Meet at Park Av. Kremlin', *New York Daily News*, 20 September 1960, 30.

24. http://www.bigapplesecrets.com/2014/01/russians-on-park-avenue-vyshinskiy-and. html; https://en.wikipedia.org/wiki/McKim,_Mead_%26_White#New_York_City.

25. Sidney Kline, 'Fidel Quits His Hotel And Moves to Harlem', New York *Daily News*, 20 September 1960, 2, 6; 'Castro Moves Out of Hotel . . .', *Washington Post*, 20 September 1960; Mary McGrory, 'Harlem Gives Home to Volatile Castro', *Washington Star*, 20 September 1960, 1, 6; 'Castro Bitter Over Suite, Shuffles Off to Harlem', *Washington News*, 20 September 1960; Frankel, 'Cuban in Harlem', *NYT*, 20 September 1960, 1, 16; 'Hotel Asks Cash, Castro Storms Out to the U.N.', *New York Herald Tribune*, 20 September 1960. See also Quirk, *Fidel Castro*, 335.

26. Frankel, 'Cuban in Harlem', *NYT*, 20 September 1960, 1.

27. 'La Voz de la Revolución' ('The Voice of the Revolution'), *Bohemia*, 25 September 1960, 68–9.

28. Frankel, 'Cuban in Harlem', *NYT*, 20 September 1960, 16.

29. Brian Urquhart, *Hammarskjold* (New York: W. W. Norton, 1994), 7, 9, 16.

30. Urquhart, *Hammarskjold*, 15.

31. Urquhart, *Hammarskjold*, 12.

32. Lipsey, *Hammarskjöld*, 67.

33. Lipsey, *Hammarskjöld*, 114; Andrew Gilmour, 'Dag Hammarskjold: Statesman of the Century', *The Nation*, 9 September 2013 at https://www.thenation.com/article/dag-hammarskjold-statesman-century/.

34. Gilmour, 'Dag Hammarskjold: Statesman of the Century'; Lipsey, *Hammarskjöld*, 358, 422; Urquart, *Hammarskjold*, 13, 251, 256.

35. Urquhart, *Hammarskjold*, 256.

36. Urquhart, *Hammarskjold*, 457–8; Emery Kelen, *Hammarskjöld* (New York: G. P. Putnam's Sons, 1966), 201–2.

37. Lipsey, *Hammarskjöld*, xi.

38. Kline, 'Fidel Quits His Hotel and Moves to Harlem', New York *Daily News*, 20 September 1960, 6; Frankel, 'Cuban in Harlem', *NYT*, 20 September 1960, 16; 'Mr. Khrushchev in Harlem', *The Times*, 21 September 1960, 12; William B. Macomber, Jr, Assistant Secretary, to Senator Harry F. Byrd, 30 September 1960 – 320/9-2360, College Park; 'Intolerable Insolences and Insults', *Revolución*, 20 September 1960, 3.

39. Teresa Casuso, *Cuba and Castro* (New York: Random House, 1961), 240–1.

40. 'The Rucksack', *Revolución*, 19 September 1960, 12.

41. Christopher Gray, 'Streetscapes: The Hotel Theresa – Fidel Castro Slept Here', *NYT*, 30 April 2009 at https://archive.nytimes.com/www.nytimes.com/2009/05/03/realestate/03scapes.html.

42. Philip Benjamin, 'Theresa Hotel on 125th St. Is Unruffled by Its Cuban Guests', *NYT*, 21 September 1960, 16.

43. For a history of the Hotel Theresa see Sondra Kathryn Wilson, *Meet Me at the Theresa: The Story of Harlem's Most Famous Hotel* (New York: Atria Books, 2004); 'Hotel Theresa', Landmarks Preservation Commission, 13 July 1993 at http://s-media.nyc. gov/agencies/lpc/lp/1843.pdf; Marcia Mayne, 'Historic Harlem – The Hotel Theresa', 5 August 2011 at https://insidejourneys.com/historic-harlem-hotel-theresa/.

44. 'A New Kind of Crowd', *New York Citizen-Call*, 24 September 1960, 28.

45. Maya Angelou, *The Heart of a Woman* (London: Virago Press, 2008), 119–20; Rosemari Mealy, *Fidel and Malcolm X: Memories of a Meeting* (Baltimore: Black Classic Press, 2013), 21–2.

46. 'Solidarity and Support for the Cuban Revolution', *Revolución*, 20 September 1960, 14.

47. Julian Mayfield, 'Autobiographical Writings – Chapter Ten: To Monroe and Back', 207, in Julian Mayfield Papers, Box 15, Folder 9, Schomburg.

48. Carolyn Dixon, 'Sidelights', *New York Citizen-Call*, 24 September 1960, 27.

49. Bonsal to Secretary of State, 22 September 1960: 611.37/9-2260, *Confidential State Department Files, Decimal 637*, reel 4; 'Joint WEEKA No. 38, 24 September 1960, 737.00(W)/9-2460, *Confidential State Department Files, Decimal 737*, reel 23; 'Castro Bitter over Suite, Shuffles Off to Harlem', *Washington News*, 20 September 1960; Bonsal to Secretary of State, 20 September 1960, 737.13/9-2060, *Confidential State Department Files, Decimal 737*, reel 25; 'The Future is Ours' ('El Futuro es Nuestro'), *Bohemia*, 25 September 1960, 69, 73.

50. AK10345/154 (memo from Marchant, Havana), 22 September 1960, FO371/148219; Bonsal to State, 20 September 737.13/9-2060. Description of Raúl taken from 'Leading Personalities in Cuba', 7 (AK1012/1), FO371/139397 and AK1015/60, Havana to London, 1 (6 August 1960), FO371/148182. On the organization of the rally (movie theatre reference) see Bonsal to Secretary of State, 17 October 1960, 737.00/10-1760, *Confidential State Department Files, Decimal 737*, reel 6.

51. See, for instance, *The Autobiography of Malcolm X*, with the assistance of Alex Haley (London: Penguin Books, 1968); Manning Marable, *Malcolm X: A Life of Reinvention* (London: Allen Lane, 2011).

52. For the NoI see, for instance, C. Eric Lincoln, *The Black Muslims in America* (Boston: Beacon Press, 1961); Marable, *Malcolm X*, 77–90; and Garrett Felber, *Those Who Don't Know Say: The Nation of Islam, the Black Freedom Movement, and the Carceral State* (Chapel Hill: The University of North Carolina Press, 2020).

53. Manning Marable and Garrett Felber, eds, *The Portable Malcolm X Reader* (London: Penguin, 2013), 150; Marable, *Malcolm X*, 174.

54. Marable and Felber, eds, *The Portable Malcolm X Reader*, 154.

55. 'Comments by Malcolm Little at New York, New York', NY105-8999, 12-16, Malcolm X Project Records 1960–2008 (2001–2008), MS#1735, Series VII: Primary Source Research, Box 37, Columbia University.

56. Marable and Felber, eds, *The Portable Malcolm X Reader*, 172; Karl Evanzz, *The Judas Factor: The Plot to Kill Malcolm X* (New York: New Wave Books, 2011), Marable, *Malcolm X*, 127–9.

57. Marable, *Malcolm X*, 172.

58. Ralph Matthews, 'Up in Fidel's Room', *New York Citizen-Call*, 24 September 1960, 5, 16; Jimmy Booker recollection in Mealy, *Fidel and Malcolm X*, 46–7. See also Elombe Brath, 'I Remember Malcolm (a narrative)' in Klytus Smith and Abiola Sinclair, eds, *The Harlem Cultural/Political Movements 1960–1970* (Gumbs & Thomas: New York, 1995), 13.

59. Matthews, 'Up in Fidel's Room', *New York Citizen-Call*, 24 September 1960, 16. On the lack of furniture see Nancy Stout, *One Day in December: Celia Sánchez and the Cuban Revolution* (New York: Monthly Review Press, 2013), 363.

60. Matthews, 'Up in Fidel's Room', *New York Citizen-Call*, 24 September 1960, 16; Jimmy Booker, 'Castro Talks', *New York Amsterdam News*, 24 September 1960, 1, 34.

61. Clayborne Carson, ed., *Malcolm X: The FBI File* (New York: Carroll & Graf, 1991), 198.

62. Matthews, 'Up in Fidel's Room', *New York Citizen-Call*, 24 September 1960, 16;

Booker, 'Castro Talks', *New York Amsterdam News*, 24 September 1960, 34.

63. Malcolm quoted in Evanzz, *The Judas Factor*, chapter 7, 'Castro Comes to Harlem'.

64. 'Malcolm X Explains Wee-Hour Visit to Castro at Theresa', *Pittsburgh Courier*, 1 October 1960, 3.

65. Claude Andrew Clegg, III, *The Life and Times of Elijah Muhammad* (Chapel Hill: The University of North Carolina Press, 1997), 156, chapter 5; Dennis D. Wainstock, *Malcolm X, African American Revolutionary* (London: McFarland & Company, Inc., 2009), 54; Marable, *Malcolm X*, 109, 133–4, 173.

66. Karl Evanzz, *The Messenger: The Rise and Fall of Elijah Muhammad* (New York: Vintage, 2001), 222–3.

67. 'Roundtable – Manning Marable, *Malcolm X: A Life of Reinvention*', *Journal of American Studies*, vol. 47, no. 1 (February 2013), 39; 'Fidel Castro in Harlem', in Marable and Felber, eds, *The Portable Malcolm X Reader*, 167; Malcolm X, 'Speech on the Founding of the OAAU, June 28, 1964 at http://www.thinkingtogether.org/rcream/archive/Old/S2006/comp/OAAU.pdf.

68. Mealy, *Fidel and Malcolm X*, 58.

69. McGrory, 'Harlem Gives Home to Volatile Castro', *Washington Star*, 20 September 1960, A-6.

4. TUESDAY 20 SEPTEMBER

1. Harrison E. Salisbury, 'Russian Goes to Harlem, Then Hugs Cuban at UN', *NYT*, 21 September 1960, 16; William Frederici and Henry Lee, 'Komrade Kop Fights Finest At Castro HQ', *Daily News*, 21 September 1960, 32; *Memoirs of Nikita Khrushchev, Volume 3*, 271.

2. Szulc, *Fidel*, 580; Taubman, *Khrushchev*, 487.

3. *Khrushchev Remembers: The Last Testament*, trans. and ed. by Strobe Talbott (Boston: Little Brown, and Co., 1974), 477–9.

4. Edward J. Silberfarb, 'When Castro Left, So Did Hotel Head – for Hospital', *New York Herald Tribune*, 21 September 1960.

5. Frederici and Lee, 'Komrade Kop Fights Finest At Castro HQ', *Daily News*, 21 September 1960, 2, 32; Nikolai Zakharov, 'How Khrushchev Subdued America', in *Memoirs of Nikita Khrushchev, Volume 3*, 891; 'Diplomacy: Flight to Harlem', *Time*, 3 October 1960.

6. *Memoirs of Nikita Khrushchev, Volume 3*, 272; Quirk, *Fidel Castro*, 337–8.

7. *Memoirs of Nikita Khrushchev, Volume 3*, 271–2.

8. Nikolai Karev and Nikolai Polyanov, 'Handshake in Harlem', *The Current Digest of the Soviet Press*, vol. XII, no. 38, 5. See also 'Record of Conversation Between N. S. Khrushchev and Prime Minister of Cuba Fidel Castro', 20 September 1960, available at https://digitalarchive.wilsoncenter.org/document/208455.

9. 'Rebel Zone: Khrushchev Goes to Meet Fidel' ('Zona Rebelde: Khrushchev Va al Encuentro de Fidel'), *Revolución*, 21 September 1960, 4.

10. 'Cuba's Stature Proved by Castro Visit', Havana, Radio Mambi (21 September 1960), *El Mundo* Editorial, in *Foreign Broadcast Information Service, Daily Report, Foreign Radio Broadcasts, No. 185* (22 September 1960), g2–g3.

11. 'Rebel Zone: Khrushchev Goes to Meet Fidel' ('Zona Rebelde: Khrushchev Va al Encuentro de Fidel'), *Revolución*, 21 September 1960, 4.

12. G. H. Summ to Department of State, 'Opposition Growing in Oriente Province', 23 September 1960, 2, in *Confidential State Department Files, Decimal 737*, reel 6.

13. Letter, John Robertson (Colonel USAF, Maxwell Air Force Base, Alabama) to Roy Rubottom, 2 September 1960, 320/9-260, College Park.

14. Salisbury, 'Russian Goes to Harlem, Then Hugs Cuban at UN', *NYT*, 21 September 1960, 1.
15. *Memoirs of Nikita Khrushchev, Volume 3*, 271.
16. Karev and Polyanov, 'Handshake in Harlem', *The Current Digest of the Soviet Press*, vol. XII, no. 38, 5.
17. Silberfarb, 'When Castro Left, So Did Hotel Head – for Hospital', *New York Herald Tribune*, 21 September 1960; Edward J. Silberfarb, 'Castro Stays in Room; Well Liked at Hotel', *New York Herald Tribune*, September 22, 1960.
18. Salisbury, 'Russian Goes to Harlem, Then Hugs Cuban at UN', *NYT*, 21 September 1960, 16; Georgie Anne Geyer, *Guerrilla Prince: The Untold Story of Fidel Castro* (Boston: Little, Brown, 1991), 263; Coltman, *The Real Fidel Castro*, 175. For the details of the formal opening, and election of the General Assembly president, see *Foreign Relations of the United States, 1958–1960, United Nations and General International Matters, Volume II*, document 177 – editorial note.
19. 'Record of a meeting in Mr Merchant's suite at the Waldorf at 3 p.m. on Tuesday 20 September 1960 – AK1015/74, FO371/148183.
20. Macmillan to Eisenhower, 25 July 1960, AK10345/138, FO371/148218. On British policy towards Cuba during this period see Christopher Hull, 'Parallel spheres: Anglo-American cooperation over Cuba, 1959–61', *Cold War History*, vol. 12, no. 1 (February 2012), 51–68.
21. Jeffrey J. Safford, 'The Nixon-Castro Meeting of 19 April 1959', *Diplomatic History*, vol. 4, no. 4 (October 1980), 431. For the location of the meeting, see Szulc, *Fidel*, 537. On the wider question of Washington's response to the emergence of Castro see, for instance, Alan H. Luxenberg, 'Did Eisenhower Push Castro into the Arms of the Soviets?', *Journal of Interamerican Studies and World Affairs*, vol. 30, no. 1 (Spring 1988), 37–71 and Vanni Pettinà, 'The shadows of Cold War over Latin America: the US reaction to Fidel Castro's nationalism, 1956–59', *Cold War History*, vol. 11, no. 3 (August 2011), 317–39.
22. Special Group Meeting, 13 January 1960, 1, NSC, Presidential Records, Intelligence Files, Box 1, DDE.
23. 'Synopsis of State and Intelligence material reported to the President', 13–20 February 1960, WHO Office of Staff Secretary, Subject Series, Alphabetical Subseries, Intelligence Briefing Notes, vol. II (1), Box 14, DDE.
24. 'Covert Action Operations Against Fidel Castro', 17 February 1960 – 'Country Files/INT Subject Files (6) [Cuba], US National Security Council Presidential Records, Intelligence Files: 1953–61, Box 2, DDE.
25. Memorandum of meeting – Andy Goodpaster and Dwight David Eisenhower, 17 February 1960, 3 p.m., WHO – Office of Special Assistant NSA, Special Assistant Series, Presidential Subseries, Box 4, Folder, '1960 – Meetings with President – Volume 1 (6)'; Oral History – Gordon Gray (OH-#342), 27, DDE; Chester J. Pach, Jr, and Elmo Richardson, eds, *The Presidency of Dwight D. Eisenhower* (Lawrence: University Press of Kansas, 1991), 223; Dwight David Eisenhower, *The White House Years: Waging Peace, 1956–1961* (London: Heinemann, 1966), 524.
26. 'A Program of Covert Action Against the Castro Regime', 16 March 1960, 'CIA Policy Paper re Cuba [17 March 1960], White House Office, Office of the Staff Secretary: Records, 1952–61, International Series, Box 4, DDE. On the evolution of covert operations against Cuba under Eisenhower see Richard M. Bissell, Jr., *Reflections of a Cold Warrior* (New Haven: Yale University Press, 1996), 152–63; Stephen G. Rabe, *Eisenhower and Latin America: The Foreign Policy of Anticommunism* (Chapel Hill: University of North Carolina Press, 1988), 126–33, 162–73; Howard Jones, *The Bay of Pigs* (Oxford: Oxford University Press, 2008), 9–44; Peter

Kornbluh, ed., *Bay of Pigs Declassified: The Secret CIA Report on the Invasion of Cuba* (New York: The New Press, 1998); Jim Rasenberger, *The Brilliant Disaster: JFK, Castro, and America's Doomed Invasion of Cuba's Bay of Pigs* (New York: Scribner, 2011), 39–109; Don Bohning, *The Castro Obsession: U.S. Covert Operations Against Cuba, 1959–1965* (Washington, DC: Potomac Books, Inc., 2005), 10–30. 2018 costs calculated using https://www.measuringworth.com/calculators/ppowerus/.

5. WEDNESDAY 21 SEPTEMBER

1. 'Liberty's Torch Now Atop Hotel Theresa', Havana, Radio Mambi (21 September 1960), *Foreign Broadcast Information Service, Daily Report, Foreign Radio Broadcasts, No. 186* (23 September 1960), g4–g5.
2. Les Matthews, 'Love B. Woods to Pass By Hotels', *New York Amsterdam News*, 3 June 1967, 1–30; Wilson, *Meet Me at the Theresa*, 63, 160; 'Love Woods Dies; Ran the Theresa', *NYT*, 30 May 1967, 19; Alvin White, 'Historic Theresa in the News Again', *Baltimore Afro-American*, 1 October 1960, 8.
3. Benjamin, 'Theresa Hotel on 125th St. Is Unruffled by Its Cuban Guests', *NYT*, 21 September 1960, 16; 'Diplomacy: Flight to Harlem', *Time*, 3 October 1960; 'Love B. Woods and the Summit Set', *New York Citizen-Call*, 1 October 1960, 3, 29; McGrory, 'Harlem Gives Home to Volatile Castro', *Washington Star*, 20 September 1960, 1; Love B. Woods to President Eisenhower, 31 October 1960, *Confidential State Department Files, Decimal 637*, 611.37/10-3160, reel 4; 'Figura Estelar de Harlem' ('Stellar Figure of Harlem'), *Bohemia*, 2 October 1960, 49. One of the more outlandish articles was Phil Santora, 'Tale of a Little Red Hen in the Castro Coop', New York *Daily News*, 26 September 1960, 26.
4. 'Cuban Hotel Now the "Theresa"', *NYT*, 21 September 1960, 17; 'They Rename St. John's Hotel the "Theresa"' ('Denominan "Theresa" al Hotel St. John's'), *Revolución*, 22 September 1960.
5. 'Harlemites Cry "Cuba Si, Yanquis No"', Radio Garcia Serra (21 September 1960), *Foreign Broadcast Information Service, Daily Report, Foreign Radio Broadcasts, No. 184* (21 September 1960), g2.
6. William Worthy, '20-Story Hotel in Cuba is now Habana Theresa', *Baltimore Afro-American*, 1 October 1960, 1.
7. Alvin White, 'Fidel calls Harlem "an Oasis in Desert"', *Baltimore Afro-American*, 1 October 1960, 2.
8. 'Liberty's Torch Now Atop Hotel Theresa', Havana, Radio Mambi (21 September 1960), *Foreign Broadcast Information Service, Daily Report, Foreign Radio Broadcasts, No. 186* (23 September 1960), g4–g5.
9. Margaret Randall, *To Change The World: My Years in Cuba* (New Brunswick, NJ: Rutgers University Press, 2009), 1.
10. 'Police Break Up Harlem Crowd as Groups Mingle', *NYT*, 22 September 1960, 14; Marable, *Malcolm X*, 172.
11. Chomsky, *History of the Cuban Revolution*, 134–6; Benson, *Antiracism in Cuba*, 1–3; Guerra, *Visions of Power in Cuba*, 54–6.
12. The most famous revisionist critique of Castro's Cuba and race is Carlos Moore, *Castro, the Blacks, and Africa* (Los Angeles: Center for Afro-American Studies, University of California, 1988). See also Guerra, *Visions of Power in Cuba*, 265–78. For a concise summary of the historiographical debate, see Benson, *Antiracism in Cuba*, 18–21.
13. Marable, 'Race and Revolution in Cuba', 13.
14. Timothy B. Tyson, *Radio Free Dixie: Robert F. Williams and the Roots of Black Power* (Chapel Hill: University of North Carolina Press, 1999), 221; Van Gosse, *Where the*

*Boys Are: Cuba, Cold War America and the Making of a New Left* (New York: Verso, 1993), 120–1; Adam Clayton Powell, Jr, *Adam By Adam: The Autobiography of Adam Clayton Powell, Jr.* (New York: Kensington Publishing, 1994), 189–94.

15. Gosse, *Where the Boys Are*, 122. On the wider history of Cuba and Afro-America see, for instance, Marable, 'Race and Revolution in Cuba', 6–17; Brock and Castañeda Fuertes, eds, *Between Race and Empire* – which contains 'The African-American Press Greets the Cuban Revolution' by Van Gosse (pp. 266–80); John A. Gronbeck-Tedesco, *Cuba, the United States, and Cultures of the Transnational Left, 1930–1975* (Cambridge: Cambridge University Press, 2015), 198–234; Besenia Rodriguez, '"De la Esclavitud Yanqui a la Libertad Cubana": U.S. Black Radicals, the Cuban Revolution, and the Formation of a Tricontinental Ideology', *Radical History Review*, 92 (Spring 2005), 62–87; Cynthia A. Young, *Soul Power: Culture, Radicalism, and the Making of a U.S. Third World Left* (Durham: Duke University Press, 2006), esp. 18–53; Cynthia Young, 'Havana Up in Harlem: LeRoi Jones, Harold Cruse and the Making of a Cultural Revolution', *Science & Society* vol. 65, no. 1 (Spring 2001), 12–38; and H. Timothy Lovelace, Jr, 'William Worthy's Passport: Travel Restrictions and the Cold War Struggle for Civil and Human Rights', *Journal of American History* (June 2016), 107–31.

16. Thomas Sugrue, *Sweet Land of Liberty: The Forgotten Struggle for Civil Rights in the North* (New York: Random House, 2009), xv; Matthew D. Lassiter, 'De Jure/De Facto Segregation: The Long Shadow of a National Myth' in Matthew D. Lassiter and Joseph Crespino, eds, *The Myth of Southern Exceptionalism* (New York: Oxford University Press, 2009), 25–48; Chin Jou, 'Neither Welcomed, Nor Refused: Race and Restaurants in Postwar New York City', *Journal of Urban History*, vol. 40, no. 2 (2014), 232–51; Brian Purnell, 'Desegregating the Jim Crow North: Racial Discrimination in the Postwar Bronx and the Fight to Integrate the Castle Hill Beach Club (1953–1973)', *Afro-Americans in New York Life and History*, vol. 33, no. 2 (July 2009), 47–78. See also Brian Purnell and Jeanne Theoharis, 'Introduction. Histories of Racism and Resistance, Seen and Unseen: How and Why to Think about the Jim Crow North' in Brian Purnell and Jeanne Theoharis, eds, *The Strange Careers of the Jim Crow North: Segregation and Struggle outside of the South* (New York: New York University Press, 2019), 1–42.

17. On the longer history of the African American-Cuban connection, see Brock and Castañeda Fuertes, eds, *Between Race and Empire*.

18. Rodriguez, '"De la Esclavitud Yanqui a la Libertad Cubana"', 70.

19. Pach and Richardson, *The Presidency of Dwight D. Eisenhower*, 137.

20. Hall, *1956*, 248–51, 386. There was, in fact, a long history of African Americans identifying with Cuba's struggles against racism. See, for instance, Lovelace, 'William Worthy's Passport', 112; Brock and Castañeda Fuertes, eds, *Between Race and Empire* and Frank Andre Guridy, *Forging Diaspora: Afro-Cubans and African Americans in a World of Empire and Jim Crow* (Chapel Hill: The University of North Carolina Press, 2010).

21. Tyson, *Radio Free Dixie*, esp. 149, 150–65; Robert F. Williams, 'The Streets of Cuba', *The Crusader*, 3 September 1960; Besenia Rodriguez, '"De la Esclavitud Yanqui a la Libertad Cubana"', 73–8.

22. Translation of interview with Robert F. Williams while in Cuba, published in *Revolución*, 14 July 1960, translation by Paul Joseph Lalli, 1 August 1960 in Fair Play for Cuba Committee, FBI file, 99-4196-91, p. 3.

23. Postcard to Irene Rose, sent 6 July 1960, Richard T. Gibson Papers, Box 12, Folder 11, Gelman Library, George Washington University.

24. Statement by John Henrik Clarke, July 1960, John Henrik Clarke Papers, Box 35, Folder 24, Schomburg; Lovelace, 'William Worthy's Passport', 113. Worthy travelled

to Cuba several times and was eventually convicted for violating the State Department's travel ban, a verdict that he overturned in the US Supreme Court.

25. Tyson, *Radio Free Dixie*, 222.

26. https://web.archive.org/web/20100212141227/http://gothamgazette.com/article//20080827/255/2635.

27. On the NAACP see Patricia Sullivan, *Lift Every Voice: The NAACP and the Making of the Civil Rights Movement* (New York: The New Press, 2009); on Garvey and the UNIA see Colin Grant, *Negro with a Hat: Marcus Garvey* (New York: Vintage, 2009) and E. David Cronon, *Black Moses: The Story of Marcus Garvey and the Universal Negro Improvement Association* (Madison: University of Wisconsin Press, 2006).

28. On the Harlem Renaissance see, for example, Nathan Irvin Huggins, *Harlem Renaissance* (Oxford: Oxford University Press, 1971); David Levering Lewis, *When Harlem Was in Vogue* (New York: Penguin, 1997) and Cheryl A. Wall, *The Harlem Renaissance: A Very Short Introduction* (New York: Oxford University Press, 2016).

29. 'Gospel Caravan New Show at Apollo Friday', *New York Amsterdam News*, 17 September 1960, 17; 'Finger Popping Time', *New York Amsterdam News*, 24 September 1960, 17; Sidney Poitier, 'Life in Black and White' in Herb Boyd, ed., *The Harlem Reader* (New York: Three Rivers Press, 2003), 158.

30. Marable, *Malcolm X*, 108, 127.

31. 'How Some People Live: $150 a Month . . .', *New York Amsterdam News*, 17 September 1960, 5.

32. On police brutality and corruption see Themis Chronopoulos, 'Police Misconduct, Community Opposition, and Urban Governance in New York City, 1945–1965', *Journal of Urban History*, vol. 44, no. 4 (2018), 643–68.

33. Marable, *Malcolm X*, 108, 127; James Baldwin, *Nobody Knows My Name: More Notes of a Native Son* (New York: Dell, 61–2). On police brutality and corruption see Chronopoulos, 'Police Misconduct, Community Opposition, and Urban Governance in New York City', 643–68: quotations from 654–5.

34. Michele Wallace, 'Memories of a Sixties Girlhood: The Harlem I Love' in Boyd, ed., *The Harlem Reader*, 244, 245.

35. LeRoi Jones/Amiri Baraka, 'City of Harlem', in LeRoi Jones, *Home: social essays* (London: Macgibbon & Kee, 1968), 93.

36. On Romare Bearden see https://beardenfoundation.org/romare-bearden/. For Faith Ringgold see, for instance, https://nmwa.org/exhibitions/american-people-black-light and https://nmwa.org/sites/default/files/shared/educator_guide-faith_rinngold.pdf.

37. On the Harlem Writers Guild see http://theharlemwritersguild.org/about.html.

38. Roger W. Stump, 'Place and Innovation in Popular Music: The Bebop Revolution in Jazz', *Journal of Cultural Geography*, vol. 18, no. 1 (1988), 11–34, esp. 22–7; Peter Rutkoff and William Scott, 'Bebop: Modern New York Jazz', *The Kenyon Review*, vol. 18, no. 2 (Spring 1996), 91–121; and Charles Waring, 'What is Bebop? Deconstructing Jazz Music's Most Influential Development', 13 April 2019 at https://www.udiscovermusic.com/stories/what-is-bebop-jazz/.

39. David H. Rosenthal, 'Jazz in the Ghetto: 1950–70', *Popular Music*, vol. 7, no. 1 (January 1988), 51–6.

40. 'Upstairs Room to Feature Jazz', *New York Amsterdam News*, 17 September 1960, 16. On Wells' see https://www.harlemworldmagazine.com/wells-restaurant-in-harlem-the-best-chicken-and-waffles-in-the-world-1938-1982/.

41. 'Guide to Harlem's Gay Spots', *New York Amsterdam News*, 17 September 1960, 16.

42. 'Guide to Harlem's Gay Spots', *New York Amsterdam News*, 17 September 1960, 16;

on the Baby Grand see https://www.harlemworldmagazine.com/the-baby-grand-harlem-1953/.

43. 'Bowling News', *New York Amsterdam News*, 17 September 1960, 26 and 'Opening September 30: Harlem Lanes', *New York Amsterdam News*, 24 September 1960, 27.

44. On the civil rights movement in New York City see, for example, Martha Biondi, *To Stand and Fight: The Struggle for Civil Rights in Postwar New York City* (Cambridge, MA: Harvard University Press, 2003); Clarence Taylor, ed., *Civil Rights in New York City: From World War II to the Giuliani Era* (New York: Fordham University Press, 2011); Brian Purnell, *Fighting Jim Crow in the County of Kings: The Congress of Racial Equality in Brooklyn* (Lexington: University Press of Kentucky, 2013).

45. Marable, *Malcolm X*, 108–9. On the New York demonstration see, for example, Brian Purnell, *Fighting Jim Crow in the County of Kings: The Congress of Racial Equality in Brooklyn* (Lexington: The University Press of Kentucky, 2013), 38.

46. 'Mr. Controversy', *New York Amsterdam News*, 17 September 1960, 16; 'Harlem Labor Union Gift', *New York Amsterdam News*, 17 September 1960, 35. For more on Ornette Coleman see https://www.britannica.com/biography/Ornette-Coleman.

47. Adina Back, 'Exposing the "Whole Segregation Myth": The Harlem Nine and New York City's School Desegregation Battles' in Jeanne Theoharis and Komozi Woodard, eds, *Freedom North: Black Freedom Struggles Outside the South, 1940–1980* (New York: Palgrave, 2003), 65–91: quotations from 74, 77; Kristopher Bryan Burrell, 'Black Women as Activist Intellectuals: Ella Baker and Mae Mallory Combat Northern Jim Crow in New York City's Public Schools during the 1950s' in Purnell and Theoharis, eds, *The Strange Careers of the Jim Crow North*, 89–112.

48. Chronopoulos, 'Police Misconduct, Community Opposition, and Urban Governance in New York City', 653–4.

49. John Henrik Clarke, 'The New Afro-American Nationalism', *Freedomways*, vol. 1, no. 3 (Fall 1961), 285–95; Marable, *Malcolm X*, 108–9; Tyson, *Radio Free Dixie*, 204; C. Gerald Fraser, 'Lewis Michaux, 92, Dies; Ran Bookstore in Harlem', *NYT*, 27 August 1976, 34; Thomas Morgan, 'Street-Corner Orator's Death Marks End of Era in Harlem', *NYT*, 15 March 1987, 37. See also Nab Eddie Bobo, 'Carlos Cooks: African Nationalism's Missing Link' and Abiola Sinclair, 'Harlem Street Speakers of the 1960s' in Smith and Sinclair, eds, *Harlem Cultural/Political Movements*, 21–6; 39–42. On post-war Harlem and black organizing see Peniel E. Joseph, 'Malcolm X's Harlem and Early Black Power Activism' in Peniel E. Joseph, ed., *Neighborhood Rebels: Black Power at the Local Level* (New York: Palgrave Macmillan, 2010), 21–43 (description of Michaux on p. 23). For a brief history of Lewis (or Louis) Michaux and the National Memorial African Bookstore see Abiola Sinclair, 'Louis H. Michaux: The Bookman', in Smith and Sinclair, eds, *Harlem Cultural/Political Movements*, 43–7.

50. James H. Meriwether, *Proudly We Can Be Africans: Black Americans and Africa, 1935–1961* (Chapel Hill: The University of North Carolina Press, 2002), 194.

51. Chuck Stone, 'Top Nigerian Tells Harlem Group "We Must Unite Around World"', *New York Citizen-Call*, 30 July 1960, 3, 28.

52. See, for example, 'Profiles of African Leaders: No. 2 – Patrice Lumumba', *New York Citizen-Call*, 13 August 1960, 13; 'Profiles of African Leaders – Sylvanus Olympio', *New York Citizen-Call*, 20 August 1960, 13; 'Profiles of African Leaders: No. 4 – Kenneth Kaunda', *New York Citizen-Call*, 27 August 1960, 13; 'Profiles of African Leaders: No. 5 – Julius K. Nyerere', *New York Citizen-Call*, 3 September 1960, 13.

53. Meriwether, *Proudly We Can Be Africans*, 197.

54. The historic association between the African American freedom struggle and the

wider struggle for decolonization has produced a rich historiography. Some of the most recent works include Nicholas Grant, *Winning Our Freedoms Together: African Americans and Apartheid, 1945–1960* (Chapel Hill: The University of North Carolina Press, 2017); Meriwether, *Proudly We Can Be Africans*; John Munro, *The Anticolonial Front: The African American Freedom Struggle and Global Decolonisation, 1945–1960* (Cambridge: Cambridge University Press, 2017); Brenda Gayle Plummer, *In Search of Power: African Americans in the Era of Decolonization, 1956–1974* (Cambridge: Cambridge University Press, 2013); Penny M. Von Eschen, *Race Against Empire: Black Americans and Anticolonialism, 1937–1957* (Ithaca, NY: Cornell University Press, 1997); Young, *Soul Power*.

55. Alfred Duckett, 'Why Castro Fled to Harlem', *Chicago Defender*, 1 October 1960, 1; 'Harlem Mood is Pro-Castro', *New York Citizen-Call*, 1 October 1960, 2; Max Frankel, 'Diplomats Study His Ties to Soviet', *NYT*, 22 September 1960, 14; Mallory, 'Fidel Castro in New York', *The Crusader*, 8 October 1960; 'Fidel at the UN – He Broke the Barrier of the Dollar' ('Fidel en la ONU – Rompió la Barrera del Dólar') *Bohemia*, 2 October 1960, 71.

56. Eslanda Robeson, 'K and C in Harlem', *Baltimore Afro-American*, 15 October 1960, 4.

57. Steve Duncan, 'Exclusive: Castro Interview', *Baltimore Afro-American*, 1 October 1960, 2.

58. Duncan, 'Exclusive: Castro Interview', *Baltimore Afro-American*, 1 October 1960, 2; Sherry Finer, 'Castro Has Shown the Way to Freedom', *Young Socialist*, November 1960, 6.

59. 'Brother!, the People Shouted to Almeida' ('Hermano! Gritó el Pueblo a Almeida'), *Revolución*, 22 September 1960, 1, 12; Perrottet, *Cuba Libre!*, 334.

60. 'Castro Toils on Speech', *Washington Post*, 22 September 1960, A6; Silberfarb, 'Castro Stays in Room', *New York Herald Tribune*, 22 September 1960; Frankel, 'Diplomats Study His Ties to Soviet', *NYT*, 22 September 1960, 14.

61. Simon Hall, *Peace and Freedom: The Civil Rights and Antiwar Movements in the 1960s* (Philadelphia: University of Pennsylvania Press, 2005), 94; Gerald Horne, *Black and Red: W. E. B. Du Bois and the Afro-American Response to the Cold War, 1944–1963* (Albany: State University of New York Press, 1986); Mary Dudziak, *Cold War Civil Rights: Race and the Image of American Democracy* (Princeton: Princeton University Press, 2000); Azza Salama Layton, *International Politics and Civil Rights Policies in the United States, 1941–1960* (Cambridge: Cambridge University Press, 2000); Carol Anderson, *Eyes off the Prize: The United Nations and the African American Struggle for Human Rights, 1944–1955* (Cambridge: Cambridge University Press, 2003); Von Eschen, *Race Against Empire*, 109–10; Manfred Berg, 'Black Civil Rights and Liberal Anticommunism: The NAACP in the Early Cold War', *Journal of American History* (June 2007), 75–96; Carol Anderson, 'Bleached Souls and Red Negroes: The NAACP and Black Communists in the Early Cold War, 1948–1952' in Brenda Gayle Plummer, ed., *Window on Freedom: Race, Civil Rights, and Foreign Affairs, 1945–1988* (Chapel Hill: University of North Carolina Press, 2003), 93–113; Sullivan, *Lift Every Voice*, 346–9, 369–70, 374–5.

62. Telegram, Gloster Current to multiple NY officials, 21 September 1960, in NAACP 1956–65, General Miscellany, 'Telegrams July–Dec, 1960'; Jesse H. Walker, 'Joe Overton, labor leader, was AmNews circulation director', *New York Amsterdam News*, 2 November 1991, 16.

63. https://munchies.vice.com/en_us/article/9kznep/harlem-whiskey-rebellion; NAACP Administration 1956–1965, General Office File, 'Liquor Salesmen Dispute, 1956–1961', NAACP Records Part III, LoC; NAACP Board of Directors Meeting, Minutes, 11 April 1960, 2, in NAACP Administration 1956–65, Board of Directors,

'Minutes, 1960'. On Overton's election see 'Committee for the Election of L. Joseph Overton: President New York Branch NAACP', *New York Amsterdam News*, 3 December 1958, 4; 'Mr Overton States Why He's Candidate', *New York Amsterdam News*, 3 December 1958, 4.

64. Frankel, 'Diplomats Study His Ties to Soviet', *NYT*, 22 September 1960, 14; White, 'Fidel Calls Harlem "an Oasis in Desert"', *Baltimore Afro-American*, 1 October 1960, 2.

65. 'Text of Wire Received at WLIB, December 20, 1960' in Records of the National Association for the Advancement of Colored People, Part III, Box C102.

66. Kevin K. Gaines, *African Americans in Ghana: Black Expatriates and the Civil Right Era* (Chapel Hill: The University of North Carolina Press, 2006), 181.

67. Duckett, 'Why Castro Fled to Harlem', *Chicago Defender*, 1 October 1960, 1.

68. Tyson, *Radio Free Dixie*, 234; Silberfarb, 'When Castro Left, So Did Hotel Head – For Hospital', *New York Herald Tribune*, 21 September 1960.

69. 'Harlem Mood is Pro-Castro', *New York Citizen-Call*, 1 October 1960, 2.

70. 'Kennedy, Nixon Both See Red Phantoms', Cadena Oriental (Havana), 23 September 1960, *Foreign Broadcast Information Service, Daily Report, Foreign Radio Broadcasts, No. 187* (26 September 1960), g3.

71. On Robert F. Wagner, Jr, see Clarence Taylor, 'Conservative and Liberal Opposition to the New York City School-Integration Program' in Taylor, ed., *Civil Rights in New York City*, 97–100.

72. White, 'Fidel Calls Harlem "an Oasis in Desert"', *Baltimore Afro-American*, 1 October 1960, 1.

73. Earl Brown, 'Visitors to Harlem', *New York Amsterdam News*, 1 October, 11.

74. James L. Hicks, 'Our Achilles Heel', *New York Amsterdam News*, 24 September 1960, 10, 35.

75. Drew Pearson, 'American Sold Castro on Overture to U.S. Negroes', *Easton Express*, 26 September 1960, in RFW Papers, Newspaper and Periodical Articles on Robert F. Williams 1 January 1959–31 December 1960.

76. 'The Other Side of the Picture . . .', Special to Associated Negro Press, 28 September 1960, 4, in Claude A. Barnett Papers, Part 1, Series C, 'Coverage of 1960 Olympics in Rome and other news from the Associated Negro Press'.

77. Duckett, 'Why Castro Fled to Harlem', *Chicago Defender*, 1 October 1960, 1.

78. 'Powell Blasts Fidel', *New York Citizen-Call*, 1 October 1960, 3; Powell, *Adam By Adam*, 194–8; Gosse, *Where The Boys Are*, 120–1, 134 n. 49; Steven Cohen, 'When Castro Came to Harlem', *The New Republic*, 21 March 2016 at https://newrepublic.com/article/131793/castro-came-harlem.

79. See, for instance, 'Picketing Groups Clash in Harlem', *NYT*, 26 September 1960, 16 and 'Police Swarm to Castro's Hotel; Alarm Follows a Day of Quiet', *NYT*, 27 September 1960, 21.

80. 'Girl Shot in Fray of Cubans is Dead', *NYT*, 23 September 1960, 17; 'Diplomacy: Flight to Harlem', *Time*, 3 October 1960; 'Innocent Girl Dies – Victim of Political Terrorist's Bullet', *Philadelphia Inquirer*, 23 September 1960; Eugene Spagnoli and Joseph McNamara, 'Girl, 9, and Man Shot In Castro Tavern Riot', New York *Daily News*, 22 September 1960, 2; 'War Criminals' ('Criminales de Guerra'), *Bohemia*, 2 October 1960, 51, 71; 'Monstruosa conjura contra cubanos planea el "State Department"' ('Monstrous Conspiracy Against Cubans Planned by the State Department'), *Revolución*, 23 September 1960, 1.

81. 'Diplomacy: Flight to Harlem', *Time*, 3 October 1960; 'Because Castro Is in Harlem, a Child Is Dead', *New Journal and Guide*, 24 September 1960.

6. THURSDAY 22 SEPTEMBER

1. Felix Blair, Jr, 'Eisenhower Busy, But He Enjoys It', *NYT*, 23 September 1960, 1; Whitman – Ann Whitman Diary Series, Box 11. Folder – '[ACW] Diary September 1960', 22 September, DDE; 'The President's Appointments, Thursday, September 22, 1960', DDE Diaries, Reel 27, Schedules (2) September 1960, RIAS.

2. Memorandum of Conversation, Eisenhower and Herter, 1 September 1960, re: President's Speech at UN General Assembly, 320/9-160, College Park. On Khrushchev as a 'murderer' see, for instance, Eisenhower phone call with Herter, 4 October 1960, 9.30, DDE Diaries, reel 27, Box 54 phone calls, RIAS; Eisenhower to John Diefenbaker, 30 September 1960, Meeting with Diefenbaker, 30 September 1960, 3, Whitman – DDE Diary Series, Box 53. Folder, 'Staff Notes – September 1960 (1), DDE.

3. Memo of conversation, 2 September 1960, Italian Ambassador Brosio and Kohler, Lewis – 320/9-260

4. Department of State circular to diplomatic posts, 2 September 1960, 320/9-260, College Park.

5. Paris (Houghton) to Secretary of State, 8 September 1960, 320/9-860, College Park.

6. Khrushchev wrote to various heads of state – including Nehru – in late August, encouraging heads of state/heads of government to attend the forthcoming UNGA to discuss important matters of disarmament and world peace. See New Delhi to Sec of State, 1 September 1960 – 320/9-160, College Park.

7. On the Non-Aligned Movement see, for example, Lorenz M. Lüthi, 'Non-Alignment, 1946–1965: Its Establishment and Struggle against Afro-Asianism', *Humanity*, vol. 7, no. 2 (2008), 201–3; Nataša Mišković et al., eds, *The Non-Aligned Movement and the Cold War: Delhi – Bandung – Belgrade* (London: Routledge, 2014); and Jürgen Dinkel, *The Non-Aligned Movement: Genesis, Organization and Politics (1927–1992)* (London: Brill, 2018).

8. Goodpaster to Herter, 8 September, 11.55 p.m., Herter Papers, Box 10, folder 'Presidential Telephone Calls' 7/1960-1/20/1960, DDE.

9. https://www.presidency.ucsb.edu/documents/the-presidents-news-conference-224.

10. Acting Sec. Dillon, discussion with Ambassador Beale (Australia), 20 September 1960, State to USUNNY and AmEmbassy, Canberra, 21 September – 320/9-2160, College Park.

11. Cabinet discussion quoted in Alessandro Iandolo, 'Beyond the Shoe: Rethinking Khrushchev at the Fifteenth Session of the United Nations General Assembly', *Diplomatic History*, vol. 41, no. 1 (2017), 134; Sir Patrick Dean to Foreign Office, 13 September 1960, FO371/153631 UN22812/30.

12. Dwight D. Eisenhower to Harold Macmillan, 20 September 1960, *FRUS – UN*, document 176; Macmillan to Eisenhower, 15 September 1960, in Presidential and Secretary of State Correspondence with Foreign Heads of State, 1953–1964, College Park.

13. Dwight D. Eisenhower to Harold Macmillan, 20 September 1960, *FRUS – UN*, document 176; Letter, Harold Macmillan to Dwight D. Eisenhower, 22 September 1960, DDE Office Files, Part 2, Reel 14 – GB(2), RIAS; Macmillan's diary entry for 22 September 1960 in Peter Catterall, ed., *The Macmillan Diaries, Volume II: Prime Minister and After, 1957–1966* (London: Macmillan, 2014), 328; Harold Macmillan, *Pointing the Way, 1959–1961* (London: Macmillan, 1972), 270.

14. State to London, Paris, Rome, Ottawa, 13 September 1960; 320/9-1360, College Park.

15. 'The President's Appointments, Thursday, September 22, 1960', DDE Diaries, Reel 27, Schedules (2) September 1960, RIAS; United Nations General Assem-

bly, Fifteenth Session, 22 September 1960, 43–4 at http://www.un.org/ga/search/
view_doc.asp?symbol=A/PV.868; 'The Voice of Brazil', *NYT*, 23 September 1960,
28; 'Telegram from the Department of State to the Mission at the United Nations',
18 September 1960, *FRUS – United Nations*, document 172; UNGA NY, Substan-
tive miscellaneous, vol. VI, CF-1772 – Frank Mewshaw and Andrew Cordier 'had
agreed the President should be at the public entrance at 10:50 am, and then proceed
to the entrance to the Podium offices, arriving behind the Podium at 10:55 am.
He goes on at 11:00 am. He [Mewshaw] wanted both of you [Krebs and Bane] to
have this information, saying that it supercedes the memo he sent you previously
on this subject.'; https://www.unmultimedia.org/s/photo/detail/761/0076195.html;
Ingeborg Glambek, 'The Council Chambers in the UN Building in New York',
*Scandinavian Journal of Design History*, vol. 15 (2005), 8–9.

16. 'Challenge to the Soviets', *NYT*, 23 September 1960, 28.
17. Dwight D. Eisenhower, 'Address Before the 15th General Assembly of the United
Nations', New York City, 22 September 1960, https://www.presidency.ucsb.edu/
documents/address-before-the-15th-general-assembly-the-united-nations-new-york-
city.
18. Max Frankel, 'Cuban Is Cautious on Issues at U.N.', *NYT*, 23 September 1960, 17.
19. James Morris, 'Eisenhower's Speech Falls Flat', *Guardian*, 23 September 1960, 1.
20. Houghton (Paris) to Secretary of State, 23 September 1960, 320/9-2360, College
Park; Moscow to Secretary of State, 24 September 1960 (no. 830), 320/9-2460, College Park.
21. Wadsworth to Secretary of State, 22 September 1960, 320/9-2260; Andrew Cordier to Blair Helman, 26 September 1960, Andrew W. Cordier Papers, Columbia
University; Wadsworth to Sec of State, 22 September 1960, 320/9-2260; Zellerbach
(Rome) to Secretary of State, 23 September 1960, 320/9-2360, College Park; Dwight
D. Eisenhower, *Waging Peace*, 579.
22. 'Call to Greatness', *The Times*, 23 September 1960, 15.
23. 'Reactions to the UN Issues: Near East and South Asia', 30 September 1960,
Records of the US Information Agency, Part 1, Series A, Reel 14 – S-18-60, RIAS;
James Reston, 'Eisenhower's Bold Political Strategy', *NYT*, 23 September 1960, 28.
24. Harrison E. Salisbury, 'Khrushchev Calls Speech by President Conciliatory', *NYT*,
23 September 1960, 1, 13.
25. 'The President's Appointments, Thursday, September 22, 1960', DDE Diaries, Reel
27, Schedules (2) September 1960, RIAS.
26. Dwight D. Eisenhower, 'Remarks at a Luncheon for Latin American Delegates to
the U.N. General Assembly, New York City', 22 September 1960, *PPPUS*.
27. Frankel, 'Cuban Is Cautious on Issues at U.N.', *NYT*, 23 September 1960, 17.
28. 'The Employees Satisfied' (Prensa Libre), *Revolución*, 23 September 1960, 15.
29. Bonsal to Secretary of State, 23 September 1960, 320/9-2360 – see also *Revolución*,
23 September 1960, 1.
30. 'Cuba "Honored" by Eisenhower Slight', Radio Mambi, 21 September 1960, *Foreign
Broadcast Information Service, Daily Report, Foreign Radio Broadcasts, No. 185* (22
September 1960), g1.
31. 'The President's Appointments, Thursday, September 22, 1960', 6, DDE Diaries,
Reel 27, Schedules (2) September 1960, RIAS; Eisenhower, *Waging Peace*, 524.
32. White, 'Fidel Calls Harlem "an Oasis in Desert"', *Baltimore Afro-American*, 1 October 1960, 1.
33. Gosse, *Where the Boys Are*, 151; Carlos Franqui, *Family Portrait*, 89–90; Quirk, *Fidel
Castro*, 339; Barry Miles, *Allen Ginsberg: Beat Poet* (London: Virgin Books, 2010),
272; Allen Ginsberg, 'Prose Contribution to the Cuban Revolution' in Bill Morgan,
ed., *Allen Ginsberg: Deliberate Prose. Selected Essays 1952–1995* (London: Penguin

Books, 2000), 142, 143–4; Todd F. Tietchen, 'The Cubalogues (and After): On the Beat Literary Movement and the Early Cuban Revolution', *Arizona Quarterly: A Journal of American Literature, Culture, and Theory*, vol. 63, no. 4 (Winter 2007), 141–3.

34. Gosse, *Where the Boys Are*, 151; Carlos Franqui, *Family Portrait*, 89–90; Quirk, *Fidel Castro*, 339; Miles, *Allen Ginsberg*, 272; Dominic Shellard, *Kenneth Tynan: A Life* (New Haven: Yale University Press, 2003), 236–8. On Tynan's appearance before the Senate subcommittee see Kenneth Tynan, 'Command Performance: A British Critic's Report on His Interrogation by a Senate Committee', *Harper's*, October 1960, 39–44 (quotation p. 43). The full-page advert in the *New York Times* was headed, 'What Is Really Happening in Cuba', and appeared on page 33 of the 6 April 1960 edition. For a discussion of the Beat poets and the Cuban Revolution see Tietchen, 'The Cubalogues (and After)', 119–52. On C. Wright Mills and the Cuban Revolution see Daniel Geary, '"Becoming International Again": C. Wright Mills and the Emergence of a Global New Left, 1956–1962', *Journal of American History*, vol. 95, no. 3 (December 2008), 726–36; A. Javier Treviño, *C. Wright Mills and the Cuban Revolution: An Exercise in the Art of Sociological Imagination* (Chapel Hill: University of North Carolina Press, 2017). On Carleton Beals see Gosse, *Where The Boys Are*, 17–19, 125–6, 140; 'Carleton Beals' Energetic Protest', *Revolución*, 19 September 1960, 12.

35. Nathan Kanter and Jack Smee, 'Cops Take Weapons from 3 at Fidel Fete', *New York Daily News*, 23 September 1960, 2, 6.

36. Julian Mayfield to 'Maga', 25 September 1960, in Julian Mayfield Papers, Box 7, Folder 2, Schomburg.

37. Kanter and Smee, 'Cops Take Weapons from 3 at Fidel Fete', *New York Daily News*, 23 September 1960, 2, 6; Michael Conant, 'Reception at the Theresa', Columbia *Owl*, 5 October 1960, 1, 4.

38. Theodore C. Achilles, 'Memorandum for the Files', 23 September 1960, in Executive Secretariat Conference Files, 1949–1963, CF1767-1773, College Park.

39. Julian Mayfield to 'Maga', 25 September 1960, in Julian Mayfield Papers, Box 7, Folder 2, Schomburg.

40. White, 'Fidel Calls Harlem "an Oasis in Desert"', *Baltimore Afro-American*, 1 October 1960, 2; Casuso, *Cuba and Castro*, 243.

41. Conant, 'Reception at the Theresa', Columbia *Owl*, 5 October 1960, 1, 4.

42. Caption, photograph, *Revolución*, 24 September 1960, 7 (bottom right).

43. Moore, Castro, The Blacks, and Africa, 82.

44. 'Fidel in Harlem', Fair Play, 7 October, 3; Julian Mayfield to 'Maga', 25 September 1960, in Julian Mayfield Papers, Box 7, Folder 2, Schomburg; 'Fidel at the UN – He Broke the Barrier of the Dollar' ('Fidel en la ONU – Rompió la Barrera del Dólar'), *Bohemia*, 2 October 1960, 44.

45. Julian Mayfield to 'Maga', 25 September 1960, in Julian Mayfield Papers, Box 7, Folder 2, Schomburg.

46. K. S. Karol, *Guerrillas in Power: The Course of the Cuban Revolution* (London: Jonathan Cape, 1971), 37.

47. Tom Wolfe, 'Radical Chic: That Party at Lenny's', *New York*, 8 June 1970, 27–56.

48. Arthur M. Schlesinger, Jr, *A Thousand Days: John F. Kennedy in the White House* (Boston: Houghton Mifflin, 1965), 220.

49. Eric Hobsbawm, 'The Cuban Revolution and Its Aftermath', in Leslie Bethell, ed., *Viva La Revolución: Eric Hobsbawm on Latin America* (London: Little, Brown, 2016), 262.

50. William Rowlandson, *Sartre in Cuba – Cuba in Sartre* (Cham, Switzerland: Palgrave Macmillan, 2018), 2.

51. Rowlandson, *Sartre in Cuba*, 4.

52. Rowlandson, *Sartre in Cuba*, 4–5, 59.

53. Rowlandson, *Sartre in Cuba*, 50–2; Jean-Paul Sartre, *Sartre on Cuba* (Westport, CT: Greenwood Press, 1974), 94, 98–9.

54. Rowlandson, *Sartre in Cuba*, 5; Sartre, *Sartre on Cuba*, 138–9.

55. Franqui, *Family Portrait*, 68.

56. Rowlandson, *Sartre in Cuba*, 4–5.

57. Eugene Wolters, 'Incredible Candid Photos of Jean-Paul Sartre and Simone de Beauvoir in Cuba', 20 June 2014 at http://www.critical-theory.com/incredible-candid-photos-of-jean-paul-sartre-and-simone-de-beauvoir-in-cuba/; Rowlandson, *Sartre in Cuba*, 97; Simone de Beauvoir, *Force of Circumstance*, trans. Richard Howard (London: Penguin, 1985), 503.

58. De Beauvoir, *Force of Circumstance*, 501.

59. Rowlandson, *Sartre in Cuba*, 30.

60. Rowlandson, *Sartre in Cuba*, 39.

61. Rowlandson, *Sartre in Cuba*, 53, 54, 55.

62. Rowlandson, *Sartre in Cuba*, 33; Sartre, *Sartre on Cuba*, 44

63. Sartre, *Sartre on Cuba*, 146.

64. LeRoi Jones, 'Cuba Libre', in Mealy, *Fidel and Malcolm X*, 62–78 (originally published in *Evergreen Review*, November/December 1960); Gosse, *Where the Boys Are*, 183–7.

65. Bill Morgan, ed., *An Accidental Autobiography: The Selected Letters of Gregory Corso* (New York: New Directions Publishing, 2003), 263–4; Miles, *Allen Ginsberg*, 272, 337–48, 349–51; Michael Schumacher, *Dharma Lion: A Critical Biography of Allen Ginsberg* (New York: St. Martin's Press, 1992), 419–28; Bill Morgan, *I Celebrate Myself: The Somewhat Private Life of Allen Ginsberg* (London: Penguin, 2006), 402–3; José Quiroga, *Cuban Palimpsests* (Minneapolis: University of Minnesota Press, 2005), 235 n. 28. On the Cuban government's sustained campaign against homosexuals see, for instance, Guerra, *Visions of Power in Cuba*, 227–9, 245–55.

66. Rowlandson, *Sartre in Cuba*, 88–9. The protest was triggered by the arrest and humiliation of the poet Heberto Padilla. See Guerra, *Visions of Power in Cuba*, 353–60.

## 7. FRIDAY 23 SEPTEMBER

1. Harrison E. Salisbury, 'Khrushchev Dinner Waits for Tardy Castro', *NYT*, 24 September 1960, 9.

2. Thomas J. Hamilton, 'Premier Is Harsh', *NYT*, 24 September 1960, 1, 9.

3. Nikita Khrushchev, Statement in the General Debate at the Fifteenth Session of the United Nations General Assembly, 23 September 1960, in *Khrushchev in New York: A documentary record . . .* (New York: Crosscurrents Press, 1960), 11–57 (esp. 15–17, 22, 24, 26, 39–41, 46, 53–4, 57).

4. Remarks by the Secretary of State, Waldorf-Astoria Hotel, New York, 23 September 1960, 3.30 p.m., *FRUS-UN*, doc. 184.

5. DDE Office Files, Part 2, Reel 17 (5), meeting with Nehru, 26 September, Waldorf, 3 p.m., RIAS.

6. DDE Diaries, reel 27, Phone Calls September 1960: Whitman memo, 24 September, RIAS; Benjamin Welles, 'New States Are Aroused by Khrushchev's Attack', *NYT*, 25 September 1960, 1, 36.

7. Whitman – Ann Whitman Diary Series, Box 11, Folder – '[ACW] Diary September 1960', 25 September, DDE Library.

8. NS1022/114 – 26 September, Moscow to London, FO371/151930; NS1014/8 – 11 October 1960, Moscow to London, FO371/151910.

9. James Morris, 'Week of Futility at UN', *Guardian*, 26 September 1960, 9.

10. 'Little New Seen in Premier's Talk', *NYT*, 26 September 1960, 14.

11. James Reston, 'The New Soviet Strategy: Boring Us to Death', *NYT*, 25 September 1960, E12.

12. See, for instance, Dillon to USUN, 24 September 1960, discussing world reaction to Khrushchev's speech, 320/9-2460; Rome to Secretary of State, 26 September 1960, 320/9-2660; 'Opinion of the Week: At Home and Abroad', *NYT*, 25 September 1960, E13.

13. Max Frankel, 'Castro Plays Fan to Soviet Premier', *NYT*, 24 September 1960, 3.

14. Bonsal to Secretary of State, 24 September 1960 (no. 1144), 320/9-2460.

15. Nikita Khrushchev, Statement in the General Debate at the Fifteenth Session of the United Nations General Assembly, 23 September 1960, in *Khrushchev in New York: A documentary record . . .* (New York: Crosscurrents Press, 1960), 18–19. On the coup in Guatemala see von Tunzelmann, *Red Heat*, 56–9 and Rabe, *Eisenhower and Latin America*, 42–63.

16. Taubman, *Khrushchev*, 532; *Memoirs of Nikita Khrushchev, Volume 3*, 315–16.

17. Piero Gleijeses, 'Cuba and the Cold War, 1959–1980' in Melvyn P. Leffler and Odd Arne Westad, eds, *The Cambridge History of the Cold War, Volume II: Crises and Détente* (Cambridge: Cambridge University Press, 2010), 328.

18. Piero Gleijeses, *Conflicting Missions: Havana, Washington, and Africa, 1959–1976* (Chapel Hill: The University of North Carolina Press, 2002), 14, 15–18.

19. Andrew and Mitrokhin, *The KGB and the World*, 35–6; Sergo Mikoyan, *The Soviet Cuban Missile Crisis* (Washington, DC: Woodrow Wilson Center Press, 2012), 41–2, 53–5.

20. Fursenko and Naftali, *Khrushchev's Cold War*, 295–7.

21. Gleijeses, *Conflicting Missions*, 17–18.

22. Mikoyan, *The Soviet Cuban Missile Crisis*, 3, 11–24.

23. Mikoyan, *The Soviet Cuban Missile Crisis*, 61–79; Andrew and Mitrokhin, *The KGB and the World*, 36.

24. 'Mikoyan Lauded at Cuban Meeting', *The Stanford Daily*, 8 February 1960, 1. On the assassination scare see Guerra, *Visions of Power in Cuba*, 113–14.

25. Mikoyan, *The Soviet Cuban Missile Crisis*, 82.

26. Mikoyan, *The Soviet Cuban Missile Crisis*, 74.

27. Mikoyan, *The Soviet Cuban Missile Crisis*, 82; Anne E. Gorsuch, '"Cuba, My Love": The Romance of Revolutionary Cuba in the Soviet Sixties', *American Historical Review*, April 2015, 497–526 (esp. 505).

28. Taubman, *Khrushchev*, 532–3.

29. Jonathan C. Brown, *Cuba's Revolutionary World* (Cambridge, MA: Harvard University Press, 2017), 80.

30. Bonsal to Secretary of State, 26 July 1960, 637.61/7-2660, *Confidential State Department Files, Decimal 637*, reel 1.

31. Fursenko and Naftali, *Khrushchev's Cold War*, 305; Brown, *Cuba's Revolutionary World*, 76–81.

32. Salisbury, 'Khrushchev Dinner Waits for Tardy Castro', *NYT*, 24 September 1960, 9; Quirk, *Fidel Castro*, 340.

33. Quirk, *Fidel Castro*, 340–1; Franqui, *Family Portrait*, 88–9; Salisbury, 'Khrushchev Dinner Waits for Tardy Castro', *NYT*, 24 September 1960, 9; 'Fidel at the UN – He Broke the Barrier of the Dollar' ('Fidel en la ONU – Rompió la Barrera del Dólar'), *Bohemia*, 2 October 1960, 52, 53, 71; 'Informal Dinner between Khrushchev and Fidel' ('Cena sin Protocolo de Jruschov a Fidel'), *Revolución*, 24 September 1960, 1, 16.

34. Franqui, *Family Portrait*, 89.

NOTES

## 8. SATURDAY 24 SEPTEMBER

1. Text of article, 'The U.S. Imperialists Reveal Their True Colors as Robbers More Nakedly', from *Rodong Sinmun*, 23 September 1960, *Foreign Broadcast Information Service, Daily Report, Foreign Radio Broadcasts, No. 186* (23 September 1960) JJJ1, JJJ3.
2. 'Insults to Castro Bare U.S. Hysteria', Peking, 22 September 1960, *Foreign Broadcast Information Service, Daily Report, Foreign Radio Broadcasts, No. 185* (22 September 1960), AAA6–AAA8.
3. The cabinet discussion was reported in 'Diplomacy: Flight to Harlem', *Time*, 3 October 1960 and 'Cuba Backs Khrushchev's Plans; Recognizes China, North Korea', *NYT*, 25 September 1960, 36. See also Szulc, *Fidel*, 583.
4. 'Cuba Woos Red China', *NYT*, 4 September 1960, 126.
5. Daniel M. Braddock to State Department, 17 June 1960, 637.60/1-760, *Confidential State Department Files, Decimal 637*, reel 1; Tad Szulc, 'Havana Reported Set to Recognize Regime in Peiping', *NYT*, 6 June 1960, 1, 3; 'Cuban Ends Visit to Peiping', *NYT*, 7 June 1960, 46; Brown, *Cuba's Revolutionary World*, 78.
6. Charles P. Cabell (deputy director CIA) to Gordon Gray, n.d. and 'Observations of Latin American CP Delegations to the 21ˢᵗ CPSU Congress and their Experiences with CP China in Peiping', 4, 16–18, 21, WHO – Office of Special Assistant NSA, NSC Series, Briefing Notes Subseries, Box 12, DDE Library; Communist Propaganda Activities in Latin America, 1960' (7 June 1961), iv–v, Records of the USIA, Part 3, Series A, Reel 4, RIAS; 'Responsibility of Cuban Government for Increased International Tensions in the Hemisphere', 54; Brown, *Cuba's Revolutionary World*, 77. See also Andrés Suárez, *Cuba: Castroism and Communism, 1959–1966* (Cambridge, MA: The MIT Press, 1967), 102–6.
7. Charles P. Cabell (deputy director CIA) to Gordon Gray, n.d. and 'Observations of Latin American CP Delegations to the 21ˢᵗ CPSU Congress and their Experiences with CP China in Peiping', 4, 21, WHO – Office of Special Assistant NSA, NSC Series, Briefing Notes Subseries, Box 12, DDE Library. On Mao's guerrilla tactics see Mao Tse-tung, *On Guerrilla Warfare* (Urbana-Champaign, IL: University of Illinois Press, 2000).
8. 'Responsibility of Cuban Government for Increased International Tensions in the Hemisphere', 47.
9. Brown, *Cuba's Revolutionary World*, 81.
10. 'Synopsis of State and Intelligence material reported to the President', 27 July 1960, 4, WHO Office of Staff Secretary, Subject Series, Alphabetical Subseries, 'Intelligence Briefing Notes, vol. II (4), box 14, DDE Library.
11. Fidel Castro speech before the National Congress of Cuban Women (August 1960), in Dillon to San José, 611.37/8-2460, *Confidential State Department Files, Decimal 637*, reel 4.
12. Benjamin R. Young, *Guerilla Internationalism: North Korea's Relations with the Third World, 1957–1989*, A Dissertation submitted to The Faculty of The Columbian College of Arts and Sciences of The George Washington University (2018), 2–3.
13. Young, *Guerilla Internationalism*, 10.
14. Young, *Guerilla Internationalism*, 26, 44.
15. Young, *Guerilla Internationalism*, 43.
16. Young, *Guerilla Internationalism*, 43–4.
17. Young, *Guerilla Internationalism*, 45–8; 'From a 2 June 1967 Memo of the Soviet Embassy in the DPRK (1st Secretary V. NemChinov) About Some New Factors in Korean–Cuban Relations', AVPRF f. 0102, op. 23, p. 112, d. 24, pp. 53–7. Obtained by Sergey Radchenko and translated by Gary Goldberg, available at https://digital-archive.wilsoncenter.org/document/116706.

18. Young, *Guerilla Internationalism*, 53–4.
19. Young, *Guerilla Internationalism*, 43.
20. Max Frankel, 'Castro Remains Out of Spotlight', *NYT*, 25 September 1960, 36; Henry Machirella, 'Castro's Hotel Thins Out the Ladies' Auxiliary', New York *Daily News*, 25 September 1960, 3.
21. Harrison E. Salisbury, 'Premier Is Firm', *NYT*, 25 September 1960, 1, 37; Edward Kirkman, 'K Takes Another Crack at Dag and a Backhand Slap at Nasser', New York *Daily News*, 25 September 1960, 26; 'Gatsby's Gold Coast' at https://www.discoverlongisland.com/things-to-do/famous-long-island/gatsbys-gold-coast/.
22. 'Glen Cove and the Russians' at http://northshorehistoricalmuseum.org/glen%20cove%20history/Russians.htm; https://en.wikipedia.org/wiki/Killenworth; 'Russians Buying Glen Cove Estate as a Recreation Center for Aides', *NYT*, 5 April 1946, 26.
23. PRI's The World, 'This Is the Long Island House the US Is Letting the Russians Keep', 30 December 2016 at https://www.pri.org/stories/2016-12-30/long-island-house-us-letting-russians-keep.
24. Telegram from the Department of State to the Mission at the United Nations, 18 September 1960, *FRUS, 1958–1960, United Nations and General International Matters, Volume II*, document 173.
25. Salisbury, 'Premier Is Firm', *NYT*, 25 September 1960, 1, 37; Kirkman, 'K Takes Another Crack at Dag and a Backhand Slap at Nasser', New York *Daily News*, 25 September 1960, 26; 'Glen Cove and the Russians' at http://northshorehistoricalmuseum.org/glen%20cove%20history/Russians.htm.
26. Cairo to Secretary of State, 22 September 1960, telegram #681, 320/9-2260, College Park; 'Memorandum for the President, 25 September 1960, Subject: Your appointment in New York on September 26 at 4:00 p.m. with President Nasser of the United Arab Republic', 1, DDE Diaries, Reel 27, Box 53, Staff Notes (2) September 1960, RIAS.
27. Robert Stephens, 'Conciliation Efforts in New York', *Observer*, 25 September 1960; Foster Hailey, 'Nasser Kept Busy in Round of Talks', *NYT*, 25 September 1960, 36.
28. Salisbury, 'Premier Is Firm', *NYT*, 25 September 1960, 1.
29. 'News Conference at Glen Cove', 24 September 1960, in *Khrushchev in New York*, 97–8; Mohamed Heikal, *The Cairo Documents: The Inside History of Nasser and His Relationship with World Leaders, Rebels, and Statesmen* (New York: Doubleday & Company, 1973), 151.
30. 'News Conference at Glen Cove', 24 September 1960, in *Khrushchev in New York*, 97–103.
31. Hailey, 'Nasser Kept Busy in Round of Talks', *NYT*, 25 September 1960, 36.

## 9. SUNDAY 25 SEPTEMBER

1. Piers Brendon, *The Decline and Fall of the British Empire, 1781–1997* (New York: Alfred A. Knopf, 2008), 484–6.
2. 'Nasser Caravan Visits Harlem Oasis', *New York Citizen-Call*, 1 October 1960, 3; Sara Slack, 'Nasser, Nehru, Visit Harlem', New York *Amsterdam News*, 1 October 1960, 1.
3. Hall, *1956*, 209–21; 317–35; 392 (for collusion see 257–69).
4. On the wider role of Nasser, and Egypt, in the anticolonial struggle see, for example, Reem Abou-El-Fadl, 'Building Egypt's Afro-Asian Hub: Infrastructures of Solidarity and the 1957 Cairo Conference', *Journal of World History*, vol. 30, no. 1–2 (June 2019), 157–92, esp. 164–5, 170–3.
5. 'Biographic Sketch', DDE Diaries, Reel 27, Box 53, Staff Notes (2) September 1960, RIAS.

6. Frederico Vélez, *Latin American Revolutionaries and the Arab World: From the Suez Canal to the Arab Spring* (Farnham: Ashgate, 2016), 23; Ray Bush, 'Coalitions for Dispossession and Networks of Resistance? Land, Politics and Agrarian Reform in Egypt', *British Journal of Middle Eastern Studies*, vol. 38, no. 3 (2011), 395.

7. Jorge Castañeda, *Compañero: The Life and Death of Che Guevara* (London: Bloomsbury, 1997), 159, 160–5.

8. Heikal, *The Cairo Documents*, 343; Castañeda, *Compañero*, 161.

9. Heikal, *The Cairo Documents*, 344; Vélez, *Latin American Revolutionaries and the Arab World*, 29–30.

10. 'Memorandum of Discussion at the 411th Meeting of the National Security Council, Washington, June 25, 1959', *FRUS, 1958–1960, Volume VI, Cuba*, 542 (document 325).

11. Vélez, *Latin American Revolutionaries and the Arab World*, 31–2; 'Memorandum from the Deputy Director of Intelligence and Research (Arneson) to the Secretary of State', 19 August 1959, Subject: '"Che" Guevara's Mission to Afro-Asian Countries', *FRUS, 1958–1960, Volume VI, Cuba*, 589–90 (document 355); 'Memorandum of Discussion at the 429th Meeting of the National Security Council, Washington, December 16, 1959', *FRUS, 1958–1960, Volume VI, Cuba*, 703 (document 410).

12. 'The UAR Backs Cuba', Boletin (Prensa), Public Relations Department, Ministry of Foreign Relations, 20 March 1960, 1, WHCF – General File, Box 805, Cuba (5), DDE.

13. Vélez, *Latin American Revolutionaries and the Arab World*, 37.

14. Max Frankel, 'Nasser Asks Cuba to Join Neutrals', *NYT*, 26 September 1960, 1, 16; Heikal, *The Cairo Documents*, 346–7; Vélez, *Latin American Revolutionaries and the Arab World*, 39.

15. Sara Slack, 'Nasser, Nehru, Visit Harlem', New York *Amsterdam News*, 1 October 1960, 1; Frankel, 'Nasser Asks Cuba to Join Neutrals', *NYT*, 26 September 1960, 16; 'Nasser Caravan Visits Harlem Oasis', *New York Citizen-Call*, 1 October 1960, 28.

16. 'Fidel and Nasser' ('Fidel y Nasser'), *Bohemia*, 2 October 1960, 54.

17. 'Castro Elated at Chance to Meet Nasir', Cairo, Egyptian Home Service, 27 September 1960, *Foreign Broadcast Information Service, Daily Report, Foreign Radio Broadcasts, No. 189* (28 September 1960), B19–20.

18. 'Fidel and Nasser' ('Fidel y Nasser'), *Bohemia*, 2 October 1960, 54.

19. Frankel, 'Nasser Asks Cuba to Join Neutrals', *NYT*, 26 September 1960, 16.

20. Geyer, *Guerrilla Prince*, 264; Heikal, *The Cairo Documents*, 346–7; The Secretary's Staff Meeting, 26 September 1960, Minutes & Notes of the Secretary's Staff Meetings, 1952–1961, Box 10, College Park; 'UAR/United Nations – Comments of UAR Officials in NY on Proceedings in UNGA', 24 September 1960, 2 in White House Office, Office of the Staff Secretary: Records, 1952–61, International Series, Box 16, 'United Nations General Assembly – September 1960 (2)', DDE.

21. See, for example, Remi Benoit Piet, 'What Was Behind Fidel Castro's Strong Ties with the Middle East', Al Arabiya English, 27 November 2016, at http://english.alarabiya.net/en/perspective/features/2016/11/27/What-was-behind-Fidel-Castro-s-strong-ties-with-the-Middle-East-.html; Heikal, *The Cairo Documents*, 349, 352–3.

22. Slack, 'Nasser, Nehru, Visit Harlem', New York *Amsterdam News*, 1 October 1960.

23. Slack, 'Nasser, Nehru, Visit Harlem', New York *Amsterdam News*, 1 October 1960.

24. Frankel, 'Nasser Asks Cuba to Join Neutrals', *NYT*, 26 September 1960, 16; 'The Talk of the Town', *The New Yorker*, 8 October 1960, 36; Henry Machirella and Henry Lee, 'Cops Seize 15 in Rioting at Castro Hotel', New York *Daily News*, 26 September 1960, 2, 26.

10. MONDAY 26 SEPTEMBER

1. Franqui, *Family Portrait*, 85. On the significance and purpose of Fidel's speeches see Guerra, *Visions of Power in Cuba*, 44–5.
2. 'Khrushchev Follows Madison Avenue Line', *NYT*, 26 September 1960, 14; 'News Conference at Glen Cove', 25 September 1960, in *Khrushchev in New York*, 103.
3. Excerpts from John Diefenbaker's speech to the UN General Assembly, *NYT*, 27 September 1960, 18.
4. https://pugwash.org/history/ and https://www.thinkerslodgehistories.com/anne-eaton.html.
5. 'Address of Cyrus Eaton, American Industrialist, at Luncheon Honoring Nikita S. Khrushchev, Chairman of the Council of Ministers of the USSR and Attended by Representative Americans and Canadians, New York City, Monday, September 26, 1960, 1, 5, 320/10-360, College Park.
6. 'Speech at Cyrus Eaton Luncheon', 26 September 1960, in *Khrushchev in New York*, 107–13; Harrison E. Salisbury, 'Khrushchev Places Disarmament First, With Control Later', *NYT*, 27 September 1960, 1.
7. Marcus Gleisser, *The World of Cyrus Eaton* (Kent, Ohio: The Kent State University Press, 2005), 256–8.
8. 'Favourites of Washington – the Governments of Force' ('Favoritos de Washington – los Gobiernos de Fuerza'), *Revolución*, 27 September 1960, 3, 13.
9. Max Frankel, 'Cuban Puts Case', *NYT*, 27 September 1960, 21.
10. 'Favourites of Washington – the Governments of Force' ('Favoritos de Washington – los Gobiernos de Fuerza'), *Revolución*, 27 September 1960, 13.
11. Frankel, 'Cuban Puts Case', *NYT*, 27 September 1960, 1, 21; Waldo Frank, *Cuba: Prophetic Island* (New York: Marzani & Munsell, Inc., 1961), 12.
12. Frank, *Cuba*, 11, 12, 15; Rafael Rojas, *Fighting over Fidel: The New York Intellectuals and the Cuban Revolution* (Princeton: Princeton University Press, 2016), 71.
13. Sam Pope Brewer, 'Cuban's Address Fails to Stir New African Nations at U.N.', *NYT*, 27 September 1960, 20.
14. Fidel Castro, 'At the United Nations General Assembly', 26 September 1960, in David Deutschmann and Deborah Shnookal (eds), *Fidel Castro Reader* (Melbourne: Ocean Press, 2007), 138–40, 142, 151, 153–6.
15. Castro, 'At the United Nations General Assembly', 160–7.
16. Castro, 'At the United Nations General Assembly', 169.
17. Castro, 'At the United Nations General Assembly', 171–2.
18. Castro, 'At the United Nations General Assembly', 176–8.
19. For a good overview of this see Mark Philip Bradley, 'Decolonization, the Global South, and the Cold War, 1919–1962' and David S. Painter, 'Oil, resources, and the Cold War, 1945–1962', in Leffler and Westad, eds, *Cambridge History of the Cold War: Volume I*, 464–85; 486–507.
20. Castro, 'At the United Nations General Assembly', 184–6.
21. Castro, 'At the United Nations General Assembly', 187.
22. 'Fidel at the UN – He Broke the Barrier of the Dollar' ('Fidel en la ONU – Rompió la Barrera del Dólar'), *Bohemia*, 2 October 1960, 74.
23. Geyer, *Guerrilla Prince*, 263; Quirk, *Fidel Castro*, 342; Franqui, *Family Portrait*, 86; 'Castro Backs Nkrumah', *Ghanaian Times*, 28 September 1960, 1; Stout, *One Day in December*, 367; 'Castro Vowed Brevity And Spoke 4½ Hours', *NYT*, 27 September 1960, 21.
24. 737.00, Joint WEEKA no. 39, 3 October 1960, Psychological – 4. 'Fidel in the United Nations', *Confidential State Department Files, Decimal 737*, reel 23; various photo captions in *Revolución*, 27 September 1960, 9.

25. *Revolución*, front page, 27 September 1960; caption in *Bohemia*, 2 October 1960, 50; 'Favourites of Washington – the Governments of Force' ('Favoritos de Washington – los Gobiernos de Fuerza'), *Revolución*, 27 September 1960, 2.

26. J. M. Vázquez Mora, 'What They Could Not Prevent' ('Lo Que No Pudieron Impedir'), *Revolución*, 3 October 1960, 12.

27. José Antonio Cabrera, 'The Historic Role of Cuba at the UN' ('El Papel Histórico de Cuba ante la ONU'), *Revolución*, 3 October 1960, 18.

28. Havana, Radio Mambi, 27 September 1960 – Armando Nuñez Commentary, *Foreign Broadcast Information Service, Daily Report, Foreign Radio Broadcasts, No. 189* (28 September 1960), g4.

29. Editorial in *La Nación*, San José to State Department, 27 September 1960, 737.00/9-2760 and article by Guido Fernandez S. in *Diario de Costa Rica*, San José to State Department, 28 September 1960, 737.00/9-2860 in *Confidential State Department Files, Decimal 737*, reel 6.

30. 'United Nations – The Bad Loser', *Time*, 10 October 1960; 'Farewell, Fidel', *New York Herald Tribune*, 28 September 1960.

31. Meeting with Prince Sihanouk, 27 September 1960, 10.45 a.m. (Waldorf-Astoria), 3, in Whitman, DDE Diary Series, Box 53, Folder, 'Staff Notes – September 1960' (1), DDE.

32. Cyril Dunn, 'Picking the Stars on the World's Stage', *Observer*, 2 October 1960, 5.

33. 'It's Part of their History' ('Es Parte de la Historia de Ellos'), *Bohemia*, 2 October 1960, 50. See also Thomas J. Hamilton, 'Leaders at the UN: Unique Galaxy Has Added Interest But Has Slowed the Heavy Schedule', *NYT*, 2 October 1960, E11.

34. FO371/153638 – UN22912/153 – 12 November 1960.

35. FO371/148345 – AK2291/4 (8 October 1960) Patrick Dean (UK UN Mission) to H. N. 'Norman' Brain (FO).

36. Richard F. Pederson to Ambassador Wadsworth, Memo for Cabinet Meeting, 6 October 1960, in Records and Document of the Cabinet Meetings of President Eisenhower, Reel 10, RIAS.

37. Quirk, *Fidel Castro*, 342; Moore, *Castro, the Blacks, and Africa*, 77.

38. *Fair Play*, 7 October 1960, 3; D. D. Guttenplan, *American Radical: The Life and Times of I. F. Stone* (New York: Farrar, Straus and Giroux, 2009), 351.

39. William Appleman Williams, *The Tragedy of American Diplomacy* (New York: World Publishing Company, 1959); J. A. Thompson, 'William Appleman Williams and the "American Empire"', *Journal of American Studies*, vol. 7, no. 1 (April 1973), 91–105 (esp. 92); Gosse, *Where the Boys Are*, 158; Van Gosse, *Rethinking the New Left: An Interpretative History* (New York: Palgrave Macmillan, 2005), 66; Paul Buhle, *History and the New Left: Madison, Wisconsin, 1950–1970* (Philadelphia: Temple University Press, 1990).

40. See, for example, Paul Potter, 'Naming the System', 17 April 1965 at https://www.sds-1960s.org/sds_wuo/sds_documents/paul_potter.html; Carl Oglesby, 'Let Us Shape the Future', 27 November 1965 at https://www.sds-1960s.org/sds_wuo/sds_documents/oglesby_future.html; and Christian G. Appy, 'What Was the Vietnam War About?', *NYT*, 26 March 2018 at https://www.nytimes.com/2018/03/26/opinion/what-was-the-vietnam-war-about.html.

## 11. TUESDAY 27 SEPTEMBER

1. 'Support for UN Secretary?', *Guardian*, 26 September 1960, 1; Peter Kihss, 'Nehru Flies Here; Arranges Talks', *NYT*, 26 September 1960, 1; 'Memorandum of Conference with the President, September 27, 1960', DDE Papers as President of the United States, 1953–61 [Ann Whitman File], DDE Diary Series, Box 53, , Staff Notes – September 1960 (1), DDE.

2. 'Memorandum of Conference with the President, September 27, 1960'; Secretary's Delegation to the Fifteenth Session of the United Nations General Assembly, New York, 19–24 September 1960, Memorandum of Conversation, 20 September 1960, 3.00 p.m., Suite 2707, Waldorf Towers, 320/9-2060, College Park.

3. For the NAACP's response see, for example, letter, Roy Wilkins to Dag Hammarskjöld, 7 October 1960, in NAACP Records, Group III, A326, 'United Nations – General, 1959–63', and 'Radio-Television News from the NAACP', 19 October 1960, in NAACP Records, Group III, A326, 'NAACP Press Releases, 1960–61', Library of Congress.

4. New York (Wadsworth) to Secretary of State (Herter), 30 September 1960, telegram #859, 'Discrimination Against New African Dels', 320/9-3060 and New York (Wadsworth) to Secretary of State (Herter), 13 October 1960, telegram #973, 'Incident Involving Oyono Cameroon Delegate', 320/10-1360, College Park.

5. 'President Nasser Suggests New Disarmament Approach', *The Times*, 28 September 1960, 12; A. Adzhubei, 'New York Roars and Howls', *Izvestia*, 23 September in *The Current Digest of the Soviet Press*, vol. XII, no. 38, 6.

6. Foster Hailey, 'Macmillan and Nasser Trade Smiles and Handshakes at U.N.', *NYT*, 27 September 1960, 19.

7. Foster Hailey, 'Nasser Wins Hearty Applause in First Address Before U.N.', *NYT*, 28 September 1960, 16.

8. President Nasser's speech before the Fifteenth Session of the UN General Assembly, 27 September 1960, A/PV.873, 145–53.

9. Hailey, 'Nasser Wins Hearty Applause in First Address Before U.N.', *NYT*, 28 September 1960, 16.

10. James Morris, 'Day of Back-stairs diplomacy', *Guardian*, 28 September 1960, 1.

11. Cable from Havana to State (E. A. Gilmore, Acting Deputy Chief of Mission', 4 October 1960, *Confidential State Department Files, Decimal 737*, reel 6; 'Nasser's Speech to the UN' ('Discurso de Nasser en la ONU'), *Revolución*, 28 September 1960, 6.

12. Max Frankel, 'Winds Up His Stay Visiting Leaders', *NYT*, 28 September 1960, 19. On Nkrumah see, for instance, Hall, *1956*, 114–16, 118–19, 388–9; David Birmingham, *Kwame Nkrumah: The Father of African Nationalism* (Athens: Ohio University Press, 1998). On Ghana's appeal to African Americans during the long 1960s see Gaines, *American Africans in Ghana*.

13. 'Now – Off to a Big Welcome', *Daily Graphic*, 22 September 1960, 1; 'Countless Thousands See Osagyefo Off to U.N.', *The Ghanaian Times*, 22 September 1960, 1.

14. 'Memorandum of Conversation, 22 September 1960, Subject: President Nkrumah's Call on the President', in Executive Secretariat Conference Files, 1949–1963, CF1767-1773, College Park.

15. 'Kwame Makes His Big Speech', *Daily Graphic*, 26 September 1960, 1; 'Osagyefo arrives at General Assembly in Grand Style', *The Ghanaian Times*, 24 September 1960, 1.

16. Kwame Nkrumah speech before the UN General Assembly, 23 September 1960, A/PV.869.

17. 'The big applause', *Daily Graphic*, 24 September 1960, 1; Dana Adams Schmidt, 'Nkrumah Speaks', *NYT*, 24 September 1960, 1.

18. David Anderson, 'American Angry', *NYT*, 24 September 1960, 1, 10.

19. Memorandum of Conversation, 28 September 1960 [Herter–Meir], Executive Conference Files, 1949–1963, CF1767-1773, College Park.

20. 'Herter & Co. Blunder', *Ghanaian Times*, 27 September 1960, 2; 'Herter and the African', *Daily Graphic*, 26 September 1960, 1.

21. 'Nkrumah: I'm Surprised', *Ghanaian Times*, 26 September 1960, 1.

22. 'The Neutralists', *NYT*, 27 September 1960, 36. For other examples of criticism see C. L. Sulzberger, 'Our Case Is Better Than Our Argument', *NYT*, 1 October 1960, 18, and Letter, St Clair Drake, Professor of Sociology, Roosevelt University (Chicago) and University College, Ghana, 'The "Black Presence" at UN', *Guardian*, 1 October 1960, 6.

23. UN22912/141 – 14 October 1960, Delhi to Commonwealth Relations Office, FO371/153638; 'Mr. MacDonald Ends His Term in India', *The Times*, 18 October 1960, 10.

24. 'Memorandum of a Conversation, Waldorf Towers, New York, September 27, 1960, 2:45 p.m.', *FRUS, 1958–1960, Volume II, United Nations and General International Matters*, 363.

25. Philip E. Muehlenbeck, *Betting on the Africans: John F. Kennedy's Courting of African Nationalist Leaders* (Oxford: Oxford University Press, 2012), 24. See also W. Scott Thompson, *Ghana's Foreign Policy, 1957–1966: Diplomacy, Ideology, and the New State* (Princeton: Princeton University Press, 1969), 165–6.

26. Muehlenbeck, *Betting on the Africans*, 3–4, 8–9, 12; *Al Sabah* editorial, 24 September 1960, in US Embassy, Tunis, to Secretary of State, 26 September 1960, 320/9-2660, College Park. See also Cary Fraser, 'An American Dilemma: Race and Realpolitik in the American Response to the Bandung Conference, 1955' in Plummer, ed., *Window on Freedom*, 115–40 and James H. Meriwether, '"Worth a Lot of Negro Votes": Black Voters, Africa, and the 1960 Presidential Campaign', *Journal of American History*, vol. 95, no. 3 (December 2008), 752–3.

27. 'Memorandum of Conference with the President, October 7, 1960', 3, Box 53 Staff Notes (2) October 1960, DDE Diaries, Reel 27, RIAS.

28. Alessandro Iandolo, 'Beyond the Shoe: Rethinking Khrushchev at the Fifteenth Session of the United Nations General Assembly', *Diplomatic History*, vol. 41, no. 1 (2017), 137.

29. 'Minutes of the Cabinet Meeting, White House, Washington, October 7, 1960', *FRUS, 1958–1960, Volume II, United Nations and General International Matters*, 404.

30. Drew Pearson, 'American Sold Castro on Overture to U.S. Negroes', *Easton Express*, 26 September 1960, in 'Newspaper and Periodical Articles on Robert F. Williams, 1 Jan 1959 – 31 Dec 1960', Robert F. Williams Papers; Department of State, outgoing telegram, 320/9-860, College Park.

31. Muehlenbeck, *Betting on the Africans*, 5; Eisenhower, *Waging Peace*, 581–2; 'Memorandum of Conference with President Eisenhower, 23 September 1960', *Foreign Relations of the United States, 1958–1960, Africa, Volume XIV*, document 74.

32. Iandolo, 'Beyond the Shoe', 146; Harold Macmillan to Dwight Eisenhower, 9 December 1960 and 12 December 1960, in Presidential and Secretary of State Correspondence with Foreign Heads of State, 1953–1964, College Park; telephone calls, Ike and Herter, 8 December 1960, 4.10 p.m. and 9 December, 10.50 a.m. and 5.25 p.m. in Christian A. Herter Papers, Box 10, 'Presidential Telephone Calls, 7/1960–1/20/61', DDE.

33. William Federici and Henry Lee, 'Castro Is Leaving Us Today', *Daily News*, 28 September 1960, 2; Thomas Buckley, 'Hussein Finally Gets His Chance at a Rolls-Royce Nkrumah Used', *NYT*, 6 October 1960, 17.

34. Moore, *Castro, the Blacks, and Africa*, 83.

35. Antonio Núñez Jiménez, *En Marcha con Fidel 1960* (Havana: Editorial de Ciencas Sociales, 2003), 287.

36. Gaines, *American Africans in Ghana*, 42–3; Meriwether, *Proudly We Can Be Africans*, 172–6; Peter Kihss, 'Harlem Hails Ghanaian Leader as Returning Hero', *NYT*, 28 July 1958, 1, 4.

37. 'Nkrumah Makes Visit to Harlem', *New York Amsterdam News*, 8 October 1960, 1, 11.

38. Moore, *Castro, the Blacks, and Africa*, 83.
39. 'Need to Check Current Trends Stressed', *The Times of India*, 29 September 1960, 8; 'Land Reform Topic and Castro-Nehru Talks', FIEL network, 28 September 1960, *Foreign Broadcast Information Service, Daily Report, Foreign Radio Broadcasts, No. 189* (28 September 1960), g5.
40. Delhi to Commonwealth Relations Office, 14 October 1960, FO371/153638, UN22912/141.
41. H. R. Vohra, 'Dinner Diplomacy Proves a Success', *The Times of India*, 29 September 1960, 1; Kennett Love, 'Foes Meet Foes at Nehru's Party', *NYT*, 28 September 1960, 18. For Khrushchev's diet see, for instance, Dmitry Sukhodolsky, 'The Kremlin Diet: From Lenin to Gorbachev', 28 May 2014, *Russia Beyond* – at https://www.rbth.com/arts/2014/05/28/the_kremlin_diet_from_lenin_to_gorbachev_37005.html.
42. Harold Macmillan, address before the UN General Assembly, 29 September 1960, A/PV.877; D. R. Thorpe, *Supermac: The Life of Harold Macmillan* (London: Chatto & Windus, 2010), 480.
43. Taubman, *Khrushchev*, 475–6. There is some debate on whether Khrushchev actually banged his shoe on the desk: see William Taubman, 'Did He Bang It? Nikita Khrushchev and the Shoe', *NYT*, 26 July 2003.

12. WEDNESDAY 28 SEPTEMBER

1. Federici and Lee, 'Castro Is Leaving Us Today', New York *Daily News*, 28 September 1960, 2.
2. 'Castro, Go Home!', *New York Citizen-Call*, 1 October 1960, 14, 19; Julian Mayfield, 'Chapter Ten: To Monroe and Back', 207, in Julian Mayfield Papers, Box 15, Folder 9, Schomburg.
3. William Federich, '"Castro Was Here" – Theresa Ain't The Same', New York *Daily News*, 29 September 1960, 6; 'Theresa Hotel Owner Doesn't Want Castro Back', Associated Negro Press, 10 October 1960, Claude Barnett Papers.
4. 'Harlem Hotel Doesn't Want Fidel Castro Back', Chicago *Daily Defender*, 29 September 1960, 2; Gerald Kessler and Henry Lee, 'Cuban Plane Seized, Reds Fly Fidel Home', New York *Daily News*, 29 September 1960, 3, 6; Max Frankel, 'Castro Flies Home With Praise for Khrushchev and U.S. People', *NYT*, 29 September 1960, 15.
5. 'Harlem Hotel Doesn't Want Fidel Castro Back', Chicago *Daily Defender*, 29 September 1960, 2.
6. James Booker, 'Castro Leaves an Unruffled Harlem', *New York Amsterdam News*, 1 October 1960, 1, 35.
7. Mayfield, 'Chapter Ten: To Monroe and Back', 207.
8. Kessler and Lee, 'Cuban Plane Seized, Reds Fly Fidel Home', New York *Daily News*, 29 September 1960, 3, 6; Frankel, 'Castro Flies Home With Praise for Khrushchev and U.S. People', *NYT*, 29 September 1960, 15.
9. 'Cold Comfort for Castro Strandee', New York *Daily News*, 29 September 1960, 1; Kessler and Lee, 'Cuban Plane Seized, Reds Fly Fidel Home', New York *Daily News*, 29 September 1960, 3; Frankel, 'Castro Flies Home With Praise for Khrushchev and U.S. People', *NYT*, 29 September 1960, 15; Thomas C. Mann to George Cochran Doub (Assistant Attorney General, Department of Justice), 28 September 1960, Bureau of Inter-American Affairs, Office of the Coordinator of Cuban Affairs, Subject Files, 1960–1963, Box 4, College Park; 'Cubana Plane Released', *NYT*, 30 September 1960, 8.
10. 'The US Whimsically Interprets Diplomatic Immunity' ('Caprichosamente Interpreta E.U. la Inmunidad Diplomática') and cartoon, *Revolución*, 29 September

1960, 3; Kessler and Lee, 'Cuban Plane Seized, Reds Fly Fidel Home', New York *Daily News*, 29 September 1960, 3; 'Cubana Plane Released', *NYT*, 30 September 1960, 8.

11. Frankel, 'Castro Flies Home With Praise for Khrushchev and U.S. People', *NYT*, 29 September 1960, 15; 'Theresa Hotel Owner Doesn't Want Castro Back', Associated Negro Press, 10 October 1960, Claude Barnett Papers; Quirk, *Fidel Castro*, 343.

12. Frankel, 'Castro Flies Home With Praise for Khrushchev and U.S. People', *NYT*, 29 September 1960, 15; Quirk, *Fidel Castro*, 343.

13. 'Record of Conversation Between the Prime Minister and Mr. Khrushchev on September 29, 1960, in the Building of the Soviet Mission to the United Nations', in Executive Secretariat Conference Files, 1949–1963, CF1767-1773, College Park.

14. Macmillan, *Pointing the Way*, 280.

15. https://www.state.gov/t/isn/5191.htm.

16. Sir Patrick Dean, 'Reflections on Mr. Khrushchev's attendance at 15th General Assembly', UN22912/153, 12 November 1960, FO371/153638; Iandolo, 'Beyond the Shoe', 128–54 (Nehru quoted on p. 140). See also 'Memorandum of a Conversation, Waldorf Towers, New York, September 26, 1960, 3 PM', *FRUS, 1958–1960, Volume II*, 359.

17. 'Declaration on the Granting of Independence to Colonial Countries and Peoples', Adopted by General Assembly resolution 1514 (XV) of 14 December 1960, https://www.un.org/ga/search/view_doc.asp?symbol=A/RES/1514(XV). On Resolution 1514 see also Getachew, *Worldmaking after Empire*, 90–2, 100–6.

18. Mazower quoted in Iandolo, 'Beyond the Shoe', 148.

19. 'Speech on Return to Moscow', 20 October 1960, in *Khrushchev in New York*, 244.

20. 'Fidel, Glorious Guide of Cuba' ('Fidel, Glorioso Guía de Cuba') and photo caption (top right), *Revolución*, 29 September 1960, 4; 'Thousands Welcome Fidel' ('Millares Dieron la Bienvenida a Fidel'), *Revolución*, 3 October, 14.

21. 'Fidel's Delirious Reception – Each Cuban is Worth More Than a Thousand Imperialists' ('Delirante Recibimiento a Fidel – Cada Cubano Vale Mas Que Mil Imperialistas'), *Revolución*, 29 September 1960, 4; 'Speech of Fidel Castro on his return to Cuba', 29 September 1960, FO371/148183, AK1015/73; 737.00(W)/10-360 – despatch 3 October 1960 – Joint WEEKA No. 39, *Confidential State Department Files, Decimal 737*, reel 23; Bonsal to State, 28 September (telegram 1518), *Confidential State Department Files, Decimal 737*, reel 23; Interview with G. Harvey Summ, *Frontline Diplomacy*, RIAS. On Bonsal's confinement see *Revolución*, 17 September 1960. For a discussion of the importance of mass rallies in establishing, sustaining and displaying the popularity, and the authority, of the revolutionary government – as well as their highly organized qualities, see Guerra, *Visions of Power in Cuba*, 37–8 and 75–6.

22. Bonsal to State, 28 September (telegram 1518), *Confidential State Department Files, Decimal 737*, reel 23; Dorticós speech in *Revolución*, 29 September 1960, 4.

23. 'Speech of Fidel Castro on his return to Cuba', 29 September 1960, FO371/148183, AK1015/73; Bonsal to State, 28 September (telegrams 1518 and 1519), *Confidential State Department Files, Decimal 737*, reel 23; '150,000 Greet Castro', *NYT*, 29 September 1960, 15.

24. 'Castro Again Warns U.S. on Guantánamo', Havana, FIEL Network, in Spanish to Cuba, 29 September 1960, *Foreign Broadcast Information Service, Daily Report, Foreign Radio Broadcasts*, No. 190 (29 September 1960), g2–g3; '150,000 Greet Castro', *NYT*, 29 September 1960, 15.

25. Bonsal to State, 28 September 1960, Telegram 1521, 737/13/9-2860, *Confidential State Department Files, Decimal 737*, reel 23; 'Castro Again Warns U.S. on Guantánamo', g5; Quirk, *Fidel Castro*, 344–5.

26. 'Castro Again Warns U.S. on Guantánamo', g6–g7.

27. 'Castro Again Warns U.S. on Guantánamo', g11.

28. 'Castro Speaks on "Meet the Press" Program', Havana, CMP Television Network, 30 September 1960, *Foreign Broadcast Information Service, Daily Report, Foreign Radio Broadcasts, No. 191* (30 September 1960), g1.

29. 737.00(W)/10-360 – despatch 3 October 1960 – Joint WEEKA No. 39, *Confidential State Department Files, Decimal 737*, reel 23.

30. 'Speech of Fidel Castro on his return to Cuba', 29 September 1960, FO371/148183, AK1015/73.


13. 'iVIVA LA REVOLUCIÓN!'

1. 'Excerpts of Remarks of Senator John F. Kennedy, Public Rally, Hotel Theresa, New York, NY', 12 October 1960, *Public Papers of the Presidents of the United States*, at https://www.presidency.ucsb.edu/documents/excerpts-remarks-senator-john-f-kennedy-public-rally-hotel-theresa-new-york-ny; Peter Kihss, 'Kennedy Charges Nixon Risks War', *NYT*, 13 October 1960, 1, 25; 'Kennedy Vows Action for Rights', *Baltimore Afro-American*, 22 October 1960, 6.

2. Meriwether, '"Worth a Lot of Negro Votes"', 743–4; 'Remarks of Senator John F. Kennedy in the Senate, Washington, D.C., July 2, 1957' at https://www.jfklibrary.org/archives/other-resources/john-f-kennedy-speeches/united-states-senate-imperialism-19570702.

3. Muehlenbeck, *Betting on the Africans*, 34–7.

4. Freedman, *Kennedy's Wars*, 32.

5. Freedman, *Kennedy's Wars*, 123.

6. Thomas G. Paterson, 'Fixation with Cuba: The Bay of Pigs, Missile Crisis, and Covert War Against Castro' in Paterson, ed., *Kennedy's Quest for Victory: American Foreign Policy, 1961–1963* (New York: Oxford University Press, 1989), 125.

7. 'Remarks of Senator John F. Kennedy, Paterson, NJ, City Hall', 15 September 1960, *PPUS* at https://www.presidency.ucsb.edu/documents/remarks-senator-john-f-kennedy-paterson-nj-city-hall.

8. Harold Jinks to Robert Kennedy, 'Comment on Cuba', Democratic National Committee Inter-Office Memorandum, 16 October 1960, Robert F. Kennedy Pre-Administration Papers, Political Files, Box 34, Folder 14, 'Cuba as a Campaign Issue, October 6–27, 1960', JFK Library.

9. 'Statement on Cuba by Senator John F. Kennedy', 20 October 1960, *PPUS* at https://www.presidency.ucsb.edu/documents/statement-cuba-senator-john-f-kennedy.

10. AK10345/174, AK10345/165 – 21 October 1960, FO371/148220; Herbert Parmet, *JFK: The Presidency of John F. Kennedy* (Harmondsworth: Penguin Books, 1984), 46–9.

11. Nixon, *Six Crises*, 354–5.

12. For the importance of Africa to Kennedy's 1960 campaign see Meriwether, '"Worth a Lot of Negro Votes"', 737–63; G. Scott Thomas, *A New World To Be Won: John Kennedy, Richard Nixon, and the Tumultuous Year of 1960* (Santa Barbara: Praeger, 2011), 227–30, 256; Edmund F. Kallina, Jr, *Kennedy v. Nixon: The Presidential Election of 1960* (Gainesville: University Press of Florida, 2010), 155.

13. See, for example, Theodore H. White, 'For President Kennedy: An Epilogue', *Life*, 6 December 1963, 158–9 and Arthur M. Schlesinger, *A Thousand Days: John F. Kennedy in the White House* (Boston: Houghton Mifflin, 1965).

14. 'Excerpts of Remarks of Senator John F. Kennedy, Public Rally, Hotel Theresa, New York, NY', 12 October 1960, https://www.presidency.ucsb.edu/documents/excerpts-remarks-senator-john-f-kennedy-public-rally-hotel-theresa-new-york-ny.

15. Bissell, *Reflections of a Cold Warrior*, 153–62; Rabe, *Eisenhower and Latin America*, 168–72.
16. Rasenberger, *The Brilliant Disaster*, 104–5, 108–9.
17. Freedman, *Kennedy's Wars*, 139–46; Szulc, *Fidel*, 607–21; Rasenberger, *The Brilliant Disaster*, 189–313; Paterson, 'Fixation with Cuba', 131–2. See also Kornbluh, ed., *Bay of Pigs Declassified* and Howard Jones, *The Bay of Pigs*.
18. Paterson, 'Fixation with Cuba', 137.
19. Paterson, 'Fixation with Cuba', 136–40.
20. Taubman, *Khrushchev*, 535, 541–7; James G. Hershberg, 'The Cuban Missile Crisis' in Leffler and Westad, eds, *Cambridge History of the Cold War, Volume II*, 67–70.
21. Paterson, 'Fixation with Cuba', 136–42. On the Kennedy administration's use of covert operations against Cuba see Bohning, *The Castro Obsession*; on the Soviet decision to deploy the missiles to Cuba see Taubman, *Khrushchev*, 541–53.
22. Paterson, 'Fixation with Cuba', 147–8; Taubman, *Khrushchev*, 572–3. For a history of the Cuban Missile Crisis see Freedman, *Kennedy's Wars*, 161–224; Aleksandr Fursenko and Timothy Naftali, *'One Hell of a Gamble': Khrushchev, Castro, and Kennedy, 1958–1964* (New York: W. W. Norton, 1997) and Hershberg, 'The Cuban Missile Crisis', 65–87.
23. Taubman, *Khrushchev*, 579–81; Szulc, *Fidel*, 652.
24. Szulc, *Fidel*, 649.
25. Brown, *Cuba's Revolutionary World*, 90–1; Taubman, *Khrushchev*, 597–8; Quirk, *Fidel Castro*, 456–69; Szulc, *Fidel*, 653–5.
26. Gorsuch, '"Cuba, My Love"', 520–3; Piero Gleijeses, *The Cuban Drumbeat: Castro's Worldview: Cuban Foreign Policy in a Hostile World* (London: Seagull Books, 2009), 13–15; Jorge I. Domínguez, *To Make a World Safe for Revolution: Cuba's Foreign Policy* (Cambridge, MA: Harvard University Press, 1989), 63–76.
27. Gleijeses, 'Cuba and the Cold War', 329, 334–5; Gleijeses, *The Cuban Drumbeat*, 12.
28. Bonsal to State Department, 29 September 1960, 737.13/9-2960, *Confidential State Department Files, Decimal 737*, reel 25.
29. Besenia Rodriguez, '"De la Esclavitud Yanqui a la Libertad Cubana"', 62.
30. John A. Gronbeck-Tedesco, 'The Left in Transition: The Cuban Revolution in US Third World Politics', *Journal of Latin American Studies*, vol. 40, no. 4 (November 2008), 659–60; Manuel Barcia, 'Locking Horns with the Northern Empire: Anti-American Imperialism at the Conference of 1966 in Havana', *The Journal of Transatlantic Studies* 7, no. 3 (2009), 208–17; Brown, *Cuba's Revolutionary World*, 97–8; Robert Buzzanco, 'Fidel Castro (1926–2016) and Global Solidarity', *The Sixties: A Journal of History, Politics and Culture*, vol. 10, no. 2, 275; 'Resolutions Adopted by the Conference' at http://www.latinamericanstudies.org/tricon/tricon5.htm. See also Ali Raza, 'Despatches from Havana: The Cold War, Afro-Asian Solidarities, and Culture Wars in Pakistan', *Journal of World History*, vol. 30, no. 1–2 (June 2019), 223–46.
31. Gleijeses, 'Cuba and the Cold War', 330–3, 340–1; Gleijeses, *Conflicting Missions*, 21; Domínguez, *To Make a World Safe for Revolution*, 119–26; Chomsky, *A History of the Cuban Revolution*, 100–5. For a detailed history of Cuba's promotion and support of liberation movements, and socialist revolution, overseas, see Gleijeses, *Conflicting Missions* and Brown, *Cuba's Revolutionary World*. On Havana's attempts to fashion a global anti-imperialist movement see, for example, Barcia, 'Locking Horns with the Northern Empire', 208–17.
32. Gleijeses, 'Cuba and the Cold War', 335.
33. Gleijeses, 'Cuba and the Cold War', 335; Domínguez, *To Make a World Safe for Revolution*, 76; Chomsky, *A History of the Cuban Revolution*, 55–8.
34. Teishan A. Latner, *Cuban Revolution in America: Havana and the Making of a*

*United States Left, 1968–1992* (Chapel Hill: The University of North Carolina Press, 2018), 5.

35. Gosse, *Where the Boys Are*, 162–3.

36. Quoted in Latner, *Cuban Revolution in America*, 17.

37. Latner, *Cuban Revolution in America*, 12.

38. Tyson, *Radio Free Dixie*, 285, 292–4; letter, Robert F. Williams to Fidel Castro, 28 August 1966, Richard T. Gibson Papers, Box 13, Folder 5, GWU.

39. Kepa Artaraz and Karen Luyckx, 'The French New Left and the Cuban Revolution 1959–1971: Parallel Histories?', *Modern and Contemporary France*, vol. 17, no. 1 (2009), 71.

40. Deutschmann and Shnookal, eds, *Fidel Castro Reader*, 12, 285.

41. Mark Kurlansky, *1968: The Year that Rocked the World* (London: Jonathan Cape, 2004), 149; Timothy Scott Brown, *West Germany and the Global Sixties: The Anti-Authoritarian Revolt, 1962-1978* (Cambridge: Cambridge University Press, 2013), 234.

42. See Sarah Seidman, 'Tricontinental Routes of Solidarity: Stokely Carmichael in Cuba', *Journal of Transnational American Studies*, vol. 4, no. 2 (2012).

43. Gronbeck-Tedesco, 'The Left in Transition', 665.

44. Latner, *Cuban Revolution in America*, 47-48.

45. 'Solidarity with Latin America' in Stokely Carmichael, *Stokely Speaks* (Chicago: Chicago Review Press, 2007), 101, 104–5.

46. Seidman, 'Tricontinental Routes of Solidarity'.

47. Stokely Carmichael with Ekwueme Michael Thelwell, *Ready for Revolution: The Life and Struggles of Stokely Carmichael (Kwame Ture)* (New York: Scribner, 2003), 587–8.

48. Angela Davis, *Angela Davis: An Autobiography* (London: Arrow Books, 1976), 202–10.

49. Davis, *Autobiography*, 216.

50. Latner, *Cuban Revolution in America*, 4–9. See also Gronbeck-Tedesco, 'The Left in Transition', 651–73; Ann Garland Mahler, 'The Global South in the Belly of the Beast: Viewing African American Civil Rights through a Tricontinental Lens', *Latin American Research Review*, vol. 50, no. 1 (2015), 95–116; and Young, *Soul Power*, passim.

51. For a discussion of *Topaz* and the cultural history of Fidel's stay in Harlem see Quiroga, *Cuban Palimpsests*, 33–47. See also Gosse, *Where the Boys Are*, 150.

52. Vincent Canby, 'Alfred Hitchcock at His Best', *NYT*, 20 December 1969, 36; Vincent Canby, 'The Ten Best of 1969', *NYT*, 28 December 1969, D1, 13.

53. Pauline Kael, 'The Current Cinema', *The New Yorker*, 27 December 1969, 49; Penelope Mortimer, 'Hitch in a Heavy Mood', *Observer*, 9 November 1969, 32.

54. Mortimer, 'Hitch in a Heavy Mood', *Observer*, 9 November 1969, 32; Andrew Sarris, 'Films in Focus', *Village Voice*, 25 December 1969, 26; Kevin Thomas, '"Topaz": A Spy Adventure by Hitchcock', *LA Times*, 19 December 1969, section IV, 1, 15.

55. Quiroga, *Cuban Palimpsests*, 43.

56. *Topaz* (Alfred Hitchcock, Universal Pictures, 1969).

57. 'The Talk of the Town', *The New Yorker*, 8 October 1960, 33.

58. Mealy, *Fidel and Malcolm X*, 61.

59. Brenda Gayle Plummer, 'Castro in Harlem: A Cold War Watershed', in Allen Hunter, ed., *Rethinking the Cold War* (Philadelphia: Temple University Press, 1998), 133.

60. 'Red All the Way', *Time*, 10 October 1960.

# INDEX

Numbers in *italics* show pages with illustrations.